BRITAIN AND THE POLITICS OF RHODESIAN INDEPENDENCE

Britain and the Politics of Rhodesian Independence

ELAINE WINDRICH

AFRICANA PUBLISHING COMPANY

New York

A division of Holmes & Meier Publishers, Inc.

First published in the United States of America 1978 by
AFRICANA PUBLISHING COMPANY
A division of Holmes & Meier Publishers, Inc.
30 Irving Place, New York, N.Y. 10003

Library of Congress Cataloging in Publication Data

Windrich, Elaine, 1921-
    Britain and the politics of Rhodesian independence.

    Bibliography p.
    Includes index.
    1.   Great Britain–Foreign relations–Rhodesia,
Southern. 2.   Rhodesia, Southern–Foreign relations–
Great Britain. 3.   Great Britain–Politics and government-- 1964
4.   Rhodesia, Southern–Politics and
government–1966--   I. Title.
DA47.9.R5W56 1978   327.41'0689'1   78-4070
ISBN 0-8419-0366-2

Printed and bound in Great Britain

CONTENTS

To Nik, who will inherit the consequences

PREFACE

This book was begun (under the title *Mr Wilson's Cuba*) as a critique of the Labour party's failure to implement its policy commitments on Rhodesia. In the course of writing it, however, it soon became obvious that the Conservative party's record was a comparable one, at least in terms of previous commitments and subsequent actions. The scope of the book was therefore extended to become a study of British policy regarding Rhodesian independence and of the party political differences that arose over the issue.

The account of that failure, which was a notable exception to an otherwise reasonable pattern of decolonisation, is a necessarily repetitive one, in which the lessons of the past had virtually no effect on the efforts of the present or the aspirations of the future. For over a decade successive British governments attempted to resolve the Rhodesian independence conflict, but the only effective means of doing so were ruled out as a policy option. The dilemma, as they defined it, was that in Rhodesia they had 'responsibility without power'. They had either to accept the situation prevailing in their 'self-governing colony', which meant condoning a racially segregated society as a basis for independence, or intervene to alter it. Unable, or unwilling, to do either, they opted instead for a compromise, one that would paper over the more apparent differences between the two sides but still leave the fundamental ones unchanged. The quest for such a solution was evident from the various settlement schemes put forward by the British – the pre-UDI offers, the *Tiger* and *Fearless* proposals, the Home-Smith terms – all of which conceded independence on the basis of white minority rule but provided a facade of respectability by allowing for token African political participation. Reliance on economic sanctions to bring about the downfall of the Rhodesian regime, or at least make them more amenable to agreement, was also a part of that compromise. But just as Britain would not use force to impose a constitutional settlement, so it would not challenge the main sources of support for the rebels. Consequently, the solution which it sought was never within the realm of the possible: first, because South Africa and Portugal refused to implement the sanctions programme; and secondly, because the Rhodesian Front, assured of external support to sustain the rebellion, rejected any independence terms that would inhibit progression towards their stated goal of 'separate development'.

The alternative for Britain, having failed to negotiate an independence agreement acceptable to both sides in Rhodesia, was to stand aside while the Rhodesians settled their own differences or while others with more power in the area intervened to ensure that they did. The possibility that a settlement would emerge from within Rhodesia was, however, even more remote. While the British had been unable to effect any change in their own colony, the Africans had to pursue the same objective while subject to the jurisdiction of a police State. A deadlock between the two sides was in any case inevitable, since the Rhodesian Front refused to envisage the possibility of majority rule and the Africans would consent to nothing less. In these circumstances, which coincided with the collapse of Portuguese rule in Africa, the threat that the guerrilla war in Rhodesia would escalate to a general conflagration in southern Africa prompted the neighbouring countries to intervene. Thus the bilateral negotiations begun by Britain and carried on within Rhodesia gave way to the diplomacy of détente, involving South Africa, which had military forces in Rhodesia, and the 'front-line' African States, which were supporting the guerrillas.

Although Britain had stood aside from the abortive détente efforts, with the intervention of the USA, seeking to redress Soviet influence in the aftermath of the Angolan civil war, it was once more obliged to play a direct role in resolving the conflict. However, the limitations set by previous British governments in their negotiations with the Rhodesians were equally applicable to the new initiative. Unless the rebel regime would agree to the proposed settlement, and there was never any evidence that they would, Britain had no intention of imposing such a solution. Whether others would be prepared to assist in doing so remained to be seen. But the alternative would continue to be an intensification of the armed conflict, and by that means Britain's last colonial responsibility in Africa would be discharged by the Africans themselves.

In declaring my 'interests' in the subject, it is of some significance to mention my research and advisory work with Labour party spokesmen on colonial affairs in the Parliamentary Labour Party and the National Executive Committee during the early 1960s, when the commitment to Rhodesian independence on the basis of majority rule was adopted as official party policy. In spite of this previous involvement, I have sought to observe the detachment essential for a credible analysis of the subject. Although I have had access to confidential party and government documents, I have not made use of any information that is not already available for publication. The book was partly written at Stanford University, where research facilities were generously provided. I am also grateful to my colleagues at the University of California Los Angeles, where I was a Visiting Scholar, and particularly to Professors John Galbraith and Leo Kuper, who kindly took the time from their own research to read the manuscript.

Stanford University, February 1978.

1 THE INDEPENDENCE ISSUE

'The most complicated issue which any government of this country has ever had to face in this century.'

Harold Wilson, 8 December 1966.

The issue of Rhodesian independence was a major preoccupation of successive British governments, from Harold Macmillan's in 1959 to Harold Wilson's in 1964 and Edward Heath's in 1970. The British case was that the principle of decolonisation governing their withdrawal from other colonial territories — a transition to majority rule by the indigenous population — should apply also to Southern Rhodesia.[1] The Rhodesians, however, in rejecting the application of this principle to their territory, maintained that they had been a self-governing colony since 1923, exercising most of the attributes of independence. They had never experienced British rule and even the reserve powers which Britain retained to intervene in their internal affairs on behalf of African interests had never been exercised in more than an occasional advisory manner during the four decades of their application. The independence which they sought was legal recognition of the *status quo* and the surrender of the sovereignty of the Westminster Parliament.

In view of these seemingly incompatible positions, there would have been no basis for negotiations had the British not conceded that Southern Rhodesia's unique status as a self-governing colony was a sufficient justification for making an exception to the usual pattern of decolonisation. Nevertheless, they continued to maintain that the colony's prevailing constitutional system, unamended, could not be considered as a basis for independence. With all other British territories advancing to independence under majority rule, it was not possible for them to confer legal recognition on a white minority regime unless the right of the black majority to advance towards a similar status, albeit in the far distant future, were established.

What suddenly precipitated the crisis over independence was the British decision to dissolve the Central African Federation, of which Southern Rhodesia had been the dominant member for a decade, and to concede to the other member territories independence under African majority rule. In the process of decolonisation in the 1960s, Britain's responsibility for the Northern Territories (then Northern Rhodesia and

11

Nyasaland) could only be enforced by detaching them from a federation controlled by a white minority in Salisbury. The Europeans in Southern Rhodesia had used every means at their disposal, including the threat of force, to oppose this trend, since their main purpose in establishing the Federation had been to gain access to the wealth of the Copperbelt in Northern Rhodesia. For them, the ultimate objective had been the achievement of an independent white-ruled dominion in central Africa — a hope that was shared by many of the Conservative party architects of the Federation in Britain. By 1960, however, that hope that been dashed by Britain's recognition of the 'wind of change' in Africa.

During the concluding years of the Federation, while the British were gradually introducing measures of political advance for the Africans in the Northern Territories, the Southern Rhodesians began to press for their own independence. Although they would have preferred to retain control at both the federal and territorial level, it was the latter that was to take priority as it became increasingly evident that the dissolution of the Federation was inevitable. In preparation for this eventuality the United Federal party, which, under various labels, had ruled the colony for most of its history, appealed to the British Government for a new constitution which would remove Britain's remaining power to intervene in internal affairs and thus prepare the way for independent status. The constitutional negotiations were begun by the UFP Prime Minister, Sir Edgar Whitehead, towards the end of 1959, while the Monckton Commission was gathering evidence in the central African territories in preparation for the review of the future status of the Federation. These preliminary negotiations were followed by a full-scale constitutional conference in 1961, which produced a new Constitution, replacing the Letters Patent of 1923. While the Southern Rhodesian Government had succeeded in eliminating Britain's reserve powers, in exchange for the inclusion in the new Constitution of alternative (but inadequate) safeguards for the protection of African rights, they were one step short of independence. Sovereignty still resided in the British Parliament, which retained the power to revoke the Constitution it had conferred.

Except for their attendance at the constitutional conference in January 1961, the African nationalists were excluded from all of the independence negotiations between the British and Southern Rhodesian Governments. Their representations at the conference was a result of British pressure on the Whitehead Government, an endeavour aimed at obtaining African support for the constitutional settlement. But the concessions which the European minority were prepared to endorse — a mere 15 seats in a parliament of 65, elected on a highly restrictive franchise — were insufficient to convince the Africans that they would be able to improve their political position in the immediate future or achieve the majority rule that the British were willing to concede to their counterparts in the Northern Territories. There was sufficient evidence for African mistrust of the intentions of a white minority regime, unfettered by even the potential threat of British intervention. The years immediately preceding the conference had been marked by political tension and violent confrontation between the two races, arising from the Government's plans for constitutional change in the territory itself and in its relationship with the Federation. The Africans, denied any voice in these preliminary negotiations, turned to public protest and demonstration as the only means available to them of expressing their political grievances; and this action met with severe repression by the Whitehead Government. The state of emergency declared in February 1959 led to the banning of the main African nationalist organisation, the African National Congress (ANC), and the arrest of its leadership. A series of drastic security measures were enacted — including the Unlawful Organisations Act, the Preventive Detention Act, the Law and Order (Maintenance) Act — for the purpose of restricting the activities and harassing the membership of the successor African organisations, the National Democratic party (banned in 1961) and the Zimbabwe African People's Union (banned in 1962).

The dilemma for the Whitehead Government was that they were obliged to convince the Europeans of their determination to suppress the African opposition and to assure the British Government of their intention of implementing a policy of 'partnership' with the Africans as a basis for an independent Southern Rhodesia. The two objectives were clearly incompatible, since the repressive measures enacted between the years 1959 and 1962 had the effect of offending a large section of British opinion, as well as most of the world community, as reflected in United Nations condemnation. At the same time, the profession of partnership, particularly the declared intention of repealing the Land Apportionment Act, which enshrined an unequal distribution of the country's land resources, and the prediction (however unlikely) of African majority rule in fifteen years' time, resulted in alienating the white electorate. The beneficiary of the UFP's loss of European support was the newly formed coalition of right-wing forces, the Rhodesian Front, which made no pretence of partnership

in advocating a policy of racial 'separate development' and independence for Southern Rhodesia under permanent white rule. The result
was that in the first general election held under the new Constitution,
in December 1962, the Rhodesian Front, led by Mr Winston Field,
inflicted an unexpected, but nevertheless decisive, defeat on the ruling
UFP.

With the victory of a 'go it alone' party in Southern Rhodesia
and with African majority rule asssured in the Northern Territories,
the Federation was to all intents and purposes finished. To preside
over its liquidation, the British Government had appointed the First
Secretary, Mr R.A. Butler, as Minister in charge of the Central Africa
Office established for the purpose. In that role, Mr Butler had to
confront not only the defenders of the doomed Federation – the
Prime Minister, Sir Roy Welensky, and his Tory supporters in Britain –
alleging broken pledges on the part of the British Government, but
also a new government in Southern Rhodesia demanding immediate
independence as a condition for their co-operation in dismantling the
Federation. Although he succeeded in bringing about an orderly dissolution of the Federation, mainly because it no longer had the support
of any of the parties in power in the three constituent territories, a
solution of the problem of Southern Rhodesia's independence eluded
him, as it did all successive British Ministers.

The Art of the Possible

While preparations were being made for convening the conference
on the dissolution of the Federation, at Victoria Falls in June 1963, the
new Rhodesian Front Prime Minister opened his Government's campaign to obtain independence. In a series of exchanges which took
place between March and June 1963, Mr Field's claim for independence
on the basis of the 1961 Constitution was considered and in turn
rejected by Mr Butler. Instead, Mr Butler conceded that a constitutional
conference would not be necessary to implement that independence
and that Britain would enter into negotiations with Southern Rhodesia
not later than the date on which negotiations for the independence of
the other two territories were begun.[2] On the essential conditions for
Southern Rhodesian independence, however, Mr Butler claimed that he
had stood firm: 'The same facts stared me in the face then as confronted the Labour Government later: to give independence to an
administration unprepared to open multi-racial paths to government
is contrary both to British tradition and to Commonwealth unity.'
He made it clear to Mr Field that until there was an end to discrimina-

tion, including a repeal of the Land Apportionment Act, a blocking third of Africans in the Legislative Assembly to deal with attempts to alter the Constitution, and a broadening of the franchise there would be no independence, because there would be no prospect of a future African government. As for Mr Field's claim that he had been offered independence before the opening of the Victoria Falls conference,[3] Mr Butler was equally insistent: 'I know perfectly well that I did not give the Southern Rhodesians an assurance of independence; on the contrary, I *asked* for assurances in terms which the Southern Rhodesian Prime Minister was unable to accept.'[4] Consequently, since the Rhodesian Front refused to meet Mr Butler's conditions, an independence date for Southern Rhodesia could not be agreed, as Mr Field had demanded, either at the same time as the dissolution of the Federation or the initiation of independence for the other central African territories.

Although the Southern Rhodesians had failed to emerge from the Victoria Falls conference with their independence assured, they did rather better on the controversial matter of the disposition of the Federal military forces, which, like their independence, was also discussed outside the formal conference. The record of the conference merely noted that when the Federal Government ceased to exercise responsibility for defence, the position in regard to the operation and control of the forces should revert to that which obtained before 1953, when Southern Rhodesia was responsible for its own forces and Britain had operational control of the forces in the Northern Territories.[5] However, as a result of the subsequent recommendations of a 'defence committee' of European officials meeting in Salisbury, which were endorsed by their respective Governments,[6] most of the Federal forces, in fact, went to Southern Rhodesia.

The preliminary defence arrangements announced by Mr Butler in Parliament on 11 July 1963 and the full agreement which emerged in Salisbury in October were subjected to severe criticism by the Opposition in Britain and by the overwhelming majority of the United Nations membership. The main concern of the Labour party, according to the National Executive Committee statement, was that the allocation of powerful and well-equipped forces to a government determined to resist the process of racial integration and democratic evolution would inflame an already dangerous situation in central Africa.[7] Furthermore, although the decision was alleged to have been taken by the British and Southern Rhodesian Governments, with the associated agreement of the other territories, the African leadership in the Northern Territories had not participated in the negotiations nor been a party to the final agreement.[8] On the extent of the armed forces, the Labour party was concerned that Southern Rhodesia would gain a great deal more than it had originally put into the Federal defence pool. It would have one of the most advanced air forces in Africa, with Canberra bombers, Hunter fighters and Alouette helicopters, the latter being effective instruments for internal repression. As a result of this arrangement, a self-governing colony, whose external relations and defence were Britain's responsibility, would be in possession of an air force suitable for an independent State and under the direct control of the Government in Salisbury.[9]

As the Labour party had also pointed out, the decision on the allocation of Federal forces placed Britain in the position of being in violation of a request by the United Nations not to do precisely that.[10] The widespread concern, particularly among the African States, that these forces would be used against the African opposition was expressed in a Security Council resolution of 13 September 1963 calling upon Britain 'not to transfer to its colony of Southern Rhodesia the armed forces and aircraft as envisaged by the Central Africa conference of 1963'. The result was that for the first time since the Suez crisis of 1956, Britain resorted to the veto, thereby also rejecting the appeal not to transfer to Southern Rhodesia 'any powers or attributes of sovereignty until the establishment of a government fully representative of all the inhabitants of the colony'.[11]

In defence of the British position, the permanent representative, Sir Patrick Dean, denied that the situation in Southern Rhodesia constituted 'a threat to international peace and security', requiring Security Council action under Chapter VII of the Charter, and dismissed allegations about the use of the Royal Rhodesian Air Force to terrorise the African population as 'irrelevant, untrue and wildest flights of the imagination'. He also assured the Council that the forces transferred to Southern Rhodesia would no more be available for external adventures than they were at present, and that the British Government would retain control of their use outside the frontiers of Southern Rhodesia as long as their responsibility in relation to that territory remained unchanged. As for the Council's concern that Britain would concede independence to Mr Field's Government, Sir Patrick reaffirmed Mr Butler's statements to Parliament (on 18 June and 16 July 1963) that Southern Rhodesia must first make proposals for amendments to its Constitution which would result in broadening the basis of representation in the legislature.[12]

After the controversy over the defence provisions of the Victoria Falls agreement, no other major issue arose to impede the dissolution of the Federation. It was formally brought to an end with the consent of Parliament on 17 December 1963. Although the Conservative Government were attacked by their backbench supporters for their failure to assume responsibility for the debts of the Federation (as they had been for consenting to secession by the Northern Territories in December 1962),[13] no attempt was made to force a vote on the issue, in spite of the protests of such architects of the Federation as Lords Salisbury, Colyton and Boyd. To the Government's contention of the inevitability of dissolution, they could only reply with a lament for the shabby treatment of stockholders. A more significant and valid objection to the provisions for dissolution, however, was the division between the three territories of the Federal public debt. While federation had provided Southern Rhodesia with the opportunity of unloading a heavy public debt, Northern Rhodesia, which had made a large net contribution to Federal revenues, came out of the Federation with a debt more than five times the amount it had when it went in. For the Europeans in Southern Rhodesia the foreign exchange reserves from Northern Rhodesian copper had complemented their own deficit economy. For them, a white-ruled dominion in central Africa had also been an attractive economic proposition.[14]

Field's Final Effort

The Rhodesian Front had not abandoned their efforts to achieve independence on the basis of the 1961 Constitution, in spite of Mr Butler's refusal to concede it during the negotiations concerning the dissolution of the Federation. Nor had they been willing to meet the conditions laid down by him as essential for the granting of independence. Consequently, negotiations between the two Governments were to continue for another two years, following the same pattern of disagreement, with only the participants changing.

Towards the end of 1963, there were growing signs of dissatisfaction within the Rhodesian Front. After nearly a year in office they had failed to achieve the objective for which they had been elected. There were also indications that Mr Field, who was bearing the blame for this failure, might be replaced by a new leader, although in this so-called 'cowboy regime' the choice of a successor was necessarily limited by the scarcity of talent and experience.[15] Mr Field's final effort, before he was removed from office, came with the change of leadership in the Conservative Government in Britain in October 1963.

With Sir Alec Douglas-Home (formerly Lord Home) replacing Mr Macmillan as Prime Minister and Mr Duncan Sandys resuming the responsibility for Southern Rhodesia which Mr Butler had carried at the former Central Africa Office, the Rhodesian Front Government formally renewed their demand for immediate independence.

According to Mr Harold Wilson's interpretation of the changes (he had also succeeded to his party's leadership that year), Home's selection as Prime Minister had raised the hopes of 'embattled opponents of democracy in the dying Federation' and prompted the Southern Rhodesian Government, in less than a week, to renew a demand which for months had been stalled and evaded by Mr Butler. He therefore urged the new Prime Minister, as he had urged Mr Butler during his negotiations with Mr Field the previous April, to give a clear assurance that the Government would not concede independence until a new constitution was in force which accepted the principle of democratic government. The Labour party, Mr Wilson recalled, had fought a bitter fight against the Constitution of 1961 and still regarded it as fundamentally undemocratic because it denied the vote to 99 per cent of the Africans.[16]

There was no doubt about the Rhodesian reception of the appointment of Sir Alec Douglas-Home as Prime Minister. His tenure at the Commonwealth Office[17] had been identified with the championship of European interests, particularly his support for the preservation of the Federation, an issue raised by Mr Macmillan's 'wind of change' speeches in Africa in 1960.[18] But the Rhodesians were in for a disappointment if they expected to obtain from the Home Government the unconditional independence denied them by the preceding Macmillan administration. No progress in this direction emerged from the first talks which the Rhodesian deputy Prime Minister, Mr Ian Smith, had with the new Government in November 1963. The only sign of encouragement for the Rhodesians was perhaps Sir Alec's statement to Parliament that, while their franchise was 'in accordance with the principle of majority rule', the issue was one of 'pace'.[19] The Rhodesians, however, refused to give any assurance of their willingness to alter that pace, as the renewed correspondence between Mr Field and Mr Sandys on the independence issue revealed. In what was to be the last important exchange between the two Governments in which Mr Field was a participant, Mr Sandys made it clear that his Government were concerned with the likely reaction of other Commonwealth Governments to a decision by the British to grant independence to Southern Rhodesia at a point in time when the franchise was 'incomparably more restricted than that of any territory which has acquired independence in the last fifty years'.[20] Within less than two months of this communication, in April 1964, Mr Field had been replaced by Mr Smith as the leader of the Rhodesian Front Government.

The Sayings of Mr Smith

Although there had been no indication that Mr Smith's talks with the Home administration in November 1963 had been any more successful than Mr Field's earlier efforts, his elevation to the leadership was an indication of the changing mood within the Rhodesian Front, which was reflected more accurately in the public utterances of Mr Smith than in those of the more restrained Mr Field. Mr Smith's replacement of Mr Field was not so much a swing to the right in Rhodesian politics as the shifts from Mr Garfield Todd to Whitehead and from Whitehead to Field had been. Whereas the earlier leaders had been replaced because of their intention to reform some of the worst excesses of discriminatory legislation (in Mr Todd's case the franchise and in Whitehead's the land apportionment), no such accusation could be levelled against Mr Field. The difference between the two Rhodesian Front leaders was more a matter of tactics and style or, as Sir Alec Douglas-Home had said of the Southern Rhodesian franchise, the issue was one of 'pace'.

Even before assuming the leadership, Mr Smith had already begun to talk about the after-effects of a Rhodesian seizure of independence. Early in January 1964, he told the right-wing journal *Newsfront* that he did not believe that there would be any 'belt-tightening' once Rhodesia got its independence, because the days of belt-tightening would be over. As far as the City of London was concerned, he thought that the event would be 'a three-day wonder'. For that reason, he expected that a Friday afternoon would be the best time for the declaration: ' ... by Monday morning all the excitement, if any, would be over'.

Although this 'airy optimism', as the *Rhodesia Herald* called it,[21] might have heartened the Rhodesian Front rank and file to expect more results from Mr Smith's leadership, it caused considerable dismay in most of the local Press, which was controlled by the Argus interests[22] and tended to support the Rhodesian Establishment. In fact, the warnings sounded by the *Sunday Mail*[23] were to anticipate those later issued by the Wilson Government. Mr Smith was told that if Southern Rhodesia declared its independence, it would become embroiled in a first-class wrangle with Britain; it would not be allowed to remain in the Commonwealth; and, in the councils of the world, it would find itself isolated from any friendly governments, except perhaps the South African and the Portuguese. As for the City of London, it would not want to have anything to do with Rhodesians under such circumstances: it would not risk lending them a farthing.

In order to retain the support of his Rhodesian Front followers, Mr Smith had to be seen to be taking a tougher line on the independence issue than had his predecessors. Between the time he took office in April 1964 and his declaration of independence in November 1965, his statements for home consumption consisted of assurances of the retention of government in 'civilised' hands and the achievement of independence without incurring retaliatory hardships or inconveniences; and his communications with Britain comprised a mixture of threat, cajolery and an interpretation of previous commitments that had no basis in reality. Perhaps his favourite theme, and certainly the most quoted one, was that there would never be African majority rule in his lifetime. He said this at a press conference a few days after his succession to the leadership[24] and repeated it on innumerable occasions thereafter.

On the methods by which he hoped to obtain independence, Mr Smith vacillated between optimistic predictions of successful negotiations and despairing references to the necessity of resorting to other means. In May 1964, he told an audience at Inyanga that, while his Government would try desperately to gain independence by negotiations, they would reserve the right 'in the event of other parties reneging on their promises, obligations and contracts', to take matters into their own hands.[25] Within a month, he was telling a meeting at Bulawayo that anyone who still believed that there was much hope of negotiating independence on the lines they wanted it was indulging in wishful thinking.[26] Nevertheless, he would not relinquish the pursuit of independence, because as long as there was 'even a thread of an apron string' attaching Rhodesia to the British Government, then some Rhodesians would continue to look to Britain to exert its influence on their affairs, instead of realising that their problems had to be solved within their own country. However, he added the assurance that, without the substantial support of the electorate (in effect, the Europeans), his Government would not resort to a unilateral declaration of independence.[27]

But Mr Smith's statements for internal consumption did not go entirely unchallenged, especially after he began to claim overwhelming support for a unilateral declaration of independence. One of his outspoken opponents, the former Chief Justice, Sir Robert Tredgold, went so far as to advocate that if the Government resorted to such illegal action, 'it would be the plain duty of every soldier, policeman or civilian to do everything in his power to defeat these actions, even by the use of force'.[28] While conceding that a large majority of the Europeans supported the aims of the Rhodesian Front, Sir Robert insisted that there was still a substantial minority, 'qualitatively worthy of consideration', that was utterly opposed to them and all that they stood for. As for their claim of a large measure of support among the Africans, he found this to be 'utterly and demonstrably untrue'.[29] Also of concern to the European opposition was the Rhodesian Front's tendency to make a fetish of independence, to regard it as an end in itself. As the former Prime Minister, Sir Edgar Whitehead, put it, while the Rhodesian Front believed that the very limited remaining powers which Rhodesia lacked were of absolutely vital importance, his party felt that it was not worth sacrificing the country's real interests in order to acquire such powers. Nor could he accept the Rhodesian Front's case for the grant of unconditional independence. Despite Mr Smith's (and also Mr Field's) claims to the contrary, he maintained that no promise of independence under the 1961 Constitution had been made to Southern Rhodesia.[30]

Sir Edgar's assertion confirmed what the British Prime Minister had already stated to Mr Smith on 20 May 1964 (and was to repeat on 7 and 16 September), namely that there had been no pledge to give Southern Rhodesia independence in return for the territory's acceptance of the 1961 Constitution and that the grant of that Constitution carried with it 'no undertaking, explicit or implicit, that on the dissolution of the Federation, which was at that time not contemplated by the British Government, Southern Rhodesia would automatically be granted independence'.[31] Nevertheless, Mr Smith was to persist in his charge that such a pledge had been made, and he was still claiming it a year later, when Sir Alec had been replaced by Mr Wilson in the exchanges. If there was one feature that most characterised Mr Smith's art of negotiation, it was surely repetition. Even when it was pointed out to him that a particular charge that he was making had already been disproved on a previous occasion, he was not to be deterred from making it again, and again.

Mr Smith was also to repeat his conviction that the majority of the population, including the Africans, supported his request for independence on the basis of the existing Constitution and franchise. In his final meeting with the Conservative Government in September 1964, he proposed to prove this contention by holding an *indaba* (council meeting) of Chiefs and Headmen, at which he intended to offer the single option of independence under the 1961 Constitution. He would make it clear to them that the alternative was an African nationalist government; and he believed that the great majority of them would be so appalled by this prospect that they would vote in favour of his proposal.[32]

The British Government were certainly not assured that an *indaba* of chiefs, paid servants of the Rhodesia regime, would be sufficient to convince world opinion that the African population supported Mr Smith's proposal for independence on the basis of the 1961 Constitution. In reply to Mr Smith's suggestion, Sir Alec Douglas-Home insisted that the proposed *indaba* would not suffice by itself; it had either to be replaced or at least supplemented by a referendum or 'something equivalent to a referendum'. In addition to specifying sufficiently representative institutions as a condition of the grant of independence, Sir Alec made the unprecedented statement that his Government had also publicly indicated that 'independence could only be conceded on the basis of majority rule'.[33] Possibly he was referring to his assurance to the United Nations General Assembly and to Mr Wilson in the House of Commons that they believed in the general principle that majorities should rule and minorities should be protected;[34] but in this case he had made a leap from the general to the specific, in a statement that was not to be repeated again. His reference to 'sufficiently representative institutions' was undoubtedly a gesture in the direction of the Commonwealth Prime Ministers, whose meeting in July 1964 had laid down such a condition. But no effort was made to meet their demand for a constitutional conference to work out an independence agreement on the basis of majority rule,[35] since Mr Smith, like Mr Field before him, had already ruled out such a conference.

The Conservative Government had also to take into account the possibility that the Rhodesian Front, having rejected all of the principles laid down by the British side, would resort to an illegal seizure of independence. They therefore repeated the warning that, quite apart from the dire economic consequences of such a declaration, serious constitutional results would follow: the declaration would have no legal validity and Southern Rhodesia would be in revolt against the Crown.[36] Before the end of the negotiations in September 1964, Sir Alec Douglas-Home challenged Mr Smith to convince the British Government that they were wrong in their assessment of Rhodesian opinion. He said that while they continued to regard an increase in African representation as a precondition of the grant of independence, if the Southern Rhodesian Government could produce — and they very much doubted that they could — evidence clearly showing that the people of that territory considered that they already had sufficiently representative institutions, then a new situation would arise which would have to be considered on its merits. The joint communiqué issued on 11 September showed how wide the gap was between the two sides in the negotiations.[37] The British Government could only reserve their position on Mr Smith's claim that the majority of the population supported his request. They, in turn, would need to be satisfied that the basis on which independence would be granted was 'acceptable to the people of the country as a whole' — the first statement of what was to become the Fifth Principle.

Uniting for Independence

In spite of the Conservative Government's persistent refusal — from Mr Butler to Sir Alec Douglas-Home and Mr Sandys — to agree to unconditional independence for Southern Rhodesia, as a result of either the break-up of the Federation or the concession of independence to the other two territories, the Rhodesian Front proceeded with their independence campaign on the home front while simultaneously pursuing the abortive negotiations with successive Tory Ministers. The first step in their strategy was to ensure that no internal opposition, either African or European, would remain to impede their plans. Once this was achieved, the way would be paved for the second stage, namely, convincing the British of the desire of the Rhodesian people for independence on the basis of the existing constitutional system.

The task of liquidating the African opposition was made easier by the fact that the nationalist movement, unlike its counterparts in other territories in Africa, had failed to maintain the unity essential for the achievement of its ultimate goal of African majority rule. Instead of consolidating its forces against white minority rule, it allowed them to be dissipated in a factional power struggle for control of the movement. By the time the Rhodesian Front came to power in December 1962, the African nationalist movement had already been weakened by the prohibitive legislation of the Whitehead Government and by its internal dissensions, mainly over the tactics to be adopted in response to the repeated bannings, but also over the type of leadership necessary to operate under such restricted conditions. Although Mr Joshua Nkomo had one of the longest periods of service in the African nationalist cause — going back to his trade union activities of the 1940s and his participation in the foundation of the African National Congress — and had the largest following among the mass supporters of the movement, the quality of his leadership was increasingly criticised by an influential section of the movement, particularly the intellectual wing, many of whom resented his international junketing and his preference for maintaining his leadership in exile while others were in detention. But whatever may have been Mr Nkomo's shortcomings, his hold over the mass of the Rhodesian Africans was then indisputable, and it was for this reason that the Smith regime and their supporters both at home and abroad did their best to discredit him.

These differences within the African nationalist movement were accentuated during the difficult year following the banning of the third of their parties – the Zimbabwe African People's Union (ZAPU) – in September 1962. The split finally came in August 1963, when a new party – the Zimbabwe African National Union (ZANU) – was formed by a breakaway group from ZAPU, led by Rev. Ndabaningi Sithole and including in its executive council Mr Leopold Takawira, Mr Robert Mugabe, Mr Enos Nkala, Mr Washington Malianga and Mr Herbert Chitepo. Explaining why ZANU had been formed, Rev. Sithole told a press conference on 8 August that the result of not having a political party for the previous year had been confusion among the rank and file and a political crisis within the leadership of the nationalist movement. From the policy statement issued by the new party, it was evident that it differed from ZAPU not so much on policy issues, although it was more militant, but on tactics and leadership: both were committed to African majority rule on the basis of one man, one vote; and to the principles of African socialism and pan-African unity.[38]

In response to the establishment of the breakaway ZANU group, supporters of the Nkomo faction held a 'people's conference' at Cold Comfort Farm, two days later, to reaffirm their allegiance to their leader, to support his decision not to form a new party and to confirm the suspension of former ZAPU members now in ZANU for 'conspiring and plotting to side-step the people by forming a party and dividing the people'. Mr Nkomo was elected life president, with power to appoint and replace any member of his executive; and a People's Caretaker Council (PCC) was formed for the purpose of establishing 'caretaker committees' throughout the country.[39]

With the Unlawful Organisations Act at the disposal of the Rhodesian Front Government, it was unlikely that either ZANU or the PCC would be able to avoid the fate of their banned predecessors, irrespective of the claim of the latter that it was not a political party. The two factions were not only hampered by the harassment of the security authorities; they were also weakened by the incessant political warfare in which their respective supporters were engaged. Within a year of the split, in August 1964, both organisations were banned and their leadership detained. The Rhodesian Front Government's extension of the Unlawful Organisations Act for a further five years provided the 'legal' basis for deterring any further opposition from the African nationalist movement.

After crushing the African opposition, the Rhodesian Front turned against the Europeans of the former ruling Establishment. The decisive defeats inflicted on their white rivals resulted in destroying any credible alternative to the Smith regime and any effective opposition to their inexorable drive towards an illegal seizure of independence. The first evidence of this trend came with the failure of the new Rhodesia party, formed in August 1964 as a successor to the United Federal party, to hold what were regarded as safe seats. In two key by-elections held on 1 October, the Rhodesian Front succeeded in capturing both of the former UFP seats in a campaign in which jingoist propaganda was employed to discredit as treason any opposition to an illegal seizure of independence. The defeat of the Rhodesia party's candidate for the Arundel seat, the former Prime Minister of the Federation, Sir Roy Welensky, was considered as so essential by the regime that they had arranged for their deputy Prime Minister, Mr Clifford Dupont, to resign from office in order to contest the seat. The result was that, for a seat which the UFP held with a majority of 300 over the Rhodesian Front candidate in the previous general election, Sir Roy polled only 633 votes to Mr Dupont's 1,079. In the other contest, at Avondale, the Rhodesian Front candidate polled more than twice as many votes as his Rhodesia party opponent.

Bolstered by their increasing electoral popularity and determined to convince the British Government that they had a mandate for independence, the Rhodesian Front proceeded with their plans to produce evidence of African support by staging an *indaba* and of European support by holding a referendum. In spite of the previous British warning that the effect of a verdict by the chiefs would be negligible, they sent an ultimatum to the British High Commissioner in Salisbury on 14 October, stating that the proposed *indaba* would take place as planned. Both the Conservative Government, in a message to Mr Smith on 15 October, and the Labour Government, which took office the following day, made it clear that they could not regard the secret *indaba* of Chiefs as evidence that independence was 'acceptable to the people of the country as a whole'. Nevertheless, the *indaba* was held, the Chiefs said 'yes' (secretly and unanimously, after being entertained by a display of the prowess of the RRAF) and, in return, received an assurance of Government support for enlarging their authority.[40]

European endorsement of independence was ensured by the staging of a virtually all-white referendum on 5 November 1964, on the question 'do you want independence under the present Constitution?' Although the Government obtained an overwhelming majority, the question was phrased in such a way that the affirmative vote merely meant that independence was desired under the existing Constitution, but not necessarily by an illegal declaration. Nevertheless, only some 62 per cent of the electorate voted and only 56 per cent (about 58,000) voted 'yes'. The boycott among African, Asian and Coloured voters, of whom only about 12,000 were registered, was almost unanimously observed. Much of the uncertainty among the European abstainers was perhaps caused by the reluctance of the Rhodesia party to do more than advise its supporters to 'think before you vote'. Since virtually no Europeans were against independence under the 1961 Constitution, the referendum was, in the opinion of the opposition party, a waste of time and money. But the Rhodesian Front considered that they had produced sufficient evidence to convince the British of the support of the Rhodesian people for unconditional independence.

Thus the situation in Southern Rhodesia had reached a critical point at a time when Britain was engaged in a general election and the resulting take-over of power by a new government. Although the *indaba* and the independence referendum did not take place until after polling day in Britain, the Rhodesian Front were determined to proceed with their independence plans, irrespective of the outcome of the British contest. They had also made contingency arrangements on the military front, reorganising the command of the armed forces, with the result that the General Officer Commanding Rhodesia, Major-General John Anderson, known to be hostile to any treasonable action against the Crown, was retired on grounds of age (at 51) and replaced by a presumably more pliable successor, Major-General Rodney Putterill.[41] The stage was thus set for an illegal seizure of independence and whichever part was returned to power in Britain would be obliged to deal with the situation.[42]

Notes

1. Southern Rhodesia is the official name of the colony, but the Southern was dropped from common usage after Northern Rhodesia became independent as Zambia in 1964. 'Zimbabwe' is the name used by the African nationalists and their supporters.

2. *United Kingdom-Southern Rhodesian Exchanges, April-June 1963*, Cmnd. 2073, 1963; Cmnd. 2000, 29 March 1963.

3. The allegation, repeated by the deputy leader, Mr Ian Smith, appears in a number of sources supporting the claims of the Rhodesian Front. See Kenneth Young, *Rhodesia and Independence*, 1969, for this interpretation.

4. R. Butler, *The Art of the Possible*, 1971, pp. 225-6. Mr Butler's terms for independence were far more favourable to African interests than those later proposed by his successors.

5. Central Africa Office, *Report of the Central African Conference*, Cmnd. 2093, July 1963.

6. According to the Federal Defence Minister, Sir Malcolm Barrow, *Federal Assembly Debates*, vol. 20, 16 October 1963, cols. 1494-5.

7. *Report of the 63rd Annual Conference of the Labour Party*, London, 1964.

8. The leader of the African majority in Northern Rhodesia, Dr Kenneth Kaunda, at a press conference on 17 October 1963, dissociated his party from the agreement.

9. See 684 *HC Deb.*, 12 November 1963, cols. 570-1; vol. 686, 17 December 1963, cols. 1083-4, for statements of Mr Arthur Bottomley and Mr George Thomson.

10. See General Assembly resolution 1883 (XVIII), adopted 14 October 1963 by 90-2, with 13 abstentions.

11. Security Council, *Official Records*, 18th Year, 1069th Meeting, 13 September 1963. The vote on the draft resolution was 8-1 (UK).

12. Ibid., 1066th Meeting, 10 September 1963.

13. See 245 *HL Deb.*, 19 December 1962; 669 *HC Deb.*, 19 December 1962.

14. See Shirley Williams, *Central Africa: The Economics of Inequality*, 1960. The division of the Federal debt, according to the Conservative Minister, Mr John Boyd-Carpenter, was 52 per cent to Southern Rhodesia, 37 per cent to Northern Rhodesia, 11 per cent to Nyasaland. 686 *HC Deb.*, 17 December 1963, col. 1172.

15. According to Lord Malvern (formerly Sir Godfrey Huggins and UFP leader), the Rhodesian Front were 'not much of a show' and would be 'lucky to last two years'. 245 *HL Deb.*, 19 December 1962, cols. 1173-4.

16. 684 *HC Deb.*, 12 November 1963, cols. 30-1; see also vol. 675, 11 April 1963, col. 1455.

17. The name Commonwealth Office is used until its merger with the Foreign Office in 1968, although it was not established as such until 1966, when the Commonwealth Relations Office and Colonial Office were joined.

18. Home told a press conference in Salisbury on 26 February 1960 that Britain had no intention of permitting secession from the Federation, after Mr Macmillan had conceded (in Lagos on 13 January and Salisbury on 19 January) that Federation could only be preserved with the consent of its member territories.

19. 685 *HC Deb.*, 28 November 1963, col. 468.

20. *Southern Rhodesia: Documents Relating to the Negotiations between the United Kingdom and Southern Rhodesian Governments, November 1963-November 1965*, Cmnd. 2807, 1965.

21. 11 January 1964.

22. The Rhodesian Printing and Publishing Company, established in 1927 as a subsidiary which acquired the Rhodesian interests of the Argus company, based in South Africa.

23. Salisbury, 12 January 1964.

24. *Rhodesia Herald*, 17 April 1964.

25. *Sunday Mail* (Salisbury), 3 May 1964.

26. *Rhodesia Herald*, 6 June 1964.

27. Broadcast on 25 June 1964.

28. Address to the Rhodesia National Affairs Association, *The Times*, 2 July 1964.

29. *The Rhodesia That Was My Life*, 1968, p. 244.

30. *Southern Rhodesia Legislative Assembly*, vol, 57, 29 July 1964, cols. 105-10; 25 August 1964, col. 1212.

31. Cmnd. 2807, 2965.

32. Ibid.

33. 9 September 1964, ibid., p. 35.

34. See 685 *HC Deb.*, 28 November 1963, col. 468.

35. *Commonwealth Prime Ministers' Meeting, 1964, Final Communiqué*, London, 15 July 1964, Cmnd. 2441.

36. The Commonwealth Prime Ministers had also stated that they would not recognise a unilateral declaration of independence. (Ibid.) In addition, the Organisation of African Unity, meeting in Cairo, 17-21 July 1964, had pledged 'vigorous and appropriate measures' against any illegal action.

37. Cmnd. 2464, 1964.

38. See Ndabaningi Sithole, *African Nationalism*, 1968.

39. Zimbabwe African People's Union, *Zimbabwe: History of a Struggle*, 1972.

40. *The Domboshawa Indaba*, Salisbury, October 1964.

41. General Anderson claimed that he had the support of some members of the other services and security forces for his opposition to unconstitutional action. (*Rhodesia Herald*, 24 October 1964.) Even General Putterill, when he retired, joined the multi-racial Centre party in protest against the Rhodesian Front's racial 'Constitution' of 1969.

42. For an account of the political developments between 1960 and 1965, see James Barber, *Rhodesia, The Road to Rebellion*, 1967.

2 THE LABOUR GOVERNMENT'S INHERITANCE

'The Labour party is totally opposed to granting independence to Southern Rhodesia so long as the government of that country remains under the control of a white minority'.

Harold Wilson, 2 October 1964.

Although Southern Rhodesia did not become an issue in the general election campaign of October 1964, mainly because of domestic preoccupations but also because the immediate crisis had been temporarily postponed as a result of the inconclusive talks in London the previous month,[1] over the years preceding the election there had been a basic difference of approach between the two parties. The Labour party had been opposed to the establishment of the Central African Federation, on the ground that it would be dominated by a European minority in Southern Rhodesia and imposed on an unwilling African majority, particularly in the Northern Territories, who would be subject to the racial policies prevailing in the south.[2] However, having failed to prevent the imposition of federation by a Conservative Government, it had pressed for an increase in African political participation and a recognition of their basic rights as members of a multi-racial society. When it became evident that no progress in this direction was possible, because the European minority was prepared to resort to repressive measures to retain control of political power, it had turned its efforts to supporting the African nationalist demand for dissolution of the Federation and the transfer of power to African majorities in the constituent territories.

In pursuance of that policy, the Labour party had also opposed the Conservative Government's new Constitution for Southern Rhodesia, regarding it as a concession to the retention of white minority rule and an inadequate means of safeguarding African interests in exchange for the surrender of Britain's reserve powers to intervene on their behalf. The party spokesmen in Parliament — Mr James Callaghan, Mr Denis Healey, Mr Arthur Bottomley, Mr George Thomson, the late Arthur Creech Jones, John Strachey, Hilary Marquand and James Griffiths — had led a continuing struggle against the adoption of that Constitution. During the year 1961 alone there were three major debates on the issue, and in two of them the Labour Opposition had voted against the measures as a means of recording their protest.[3] In a remarkably prophetic speech, Mr Callaghan had warned that Britain was running a great risk

29

in passing its reserve powers to a territory which might well elect to power the Dominion party (precursor of the Rhodesian Front). That party would not be inhibited by a Declaration of Rights in the Constitution, he said: the ideology of many of its members was the ideology of the Government of South Africa. And he recalled Keir Hardie's speech against the South Africa Bill of 1909, by which Britain had surrendered its power to intervene in the affairs of that country, as evidence of what could happen in Southern Rhodesia after Britain had relinquished its reserve powers.[4]

The NIBMAR Pledge

By October 1964, many of the Labour party's objectives regarding Southern Rhodesia's future status had already been accepted by previous Conservative Ministers. Mr Butler had rejected Mr Field's requests for unconditional independence to coincide with the dissolution of the Federation or the grant of independence to the other central African territories; and the Home Government had refused to concede independence to either Mr Field or Mr Smith without an assurance that the existing Constitution would be amended to provide for 'sufficiently representative institutions'. Although the Labour party had never accepted the 1961 Constitution, the relevant question was what a Labour Government would do about its existence. On the basis of the party's commitments, it was pledged either to alter or abolish it, for the purpose of securing greater African representation. Mr Wilson had said, in one of his first public pronouncements on the subject after assuming the leadership, that if Labour returned to power, the Southern Rhodesian Constitution would be amended to allow the people of that territory to control their own destinies.[5] The Labour party conference had similarly called for constitutional reform, recommending in particular a more equitable and realistic African franchise, the election of a representative legislature and the restoration of civil and political rights.[6]

It was evident from these statements, as well as those of front bench spokesmen in Parliament, that the Labour party was clearly committed to the establishment of majority rule in Rhodesia, because this could be the only meaning of 'allowing people to control their own destinies' and the only result of 'the election of a representative legislature'. The party's position on the issue of 'one man, one vote' was, however, less precise. The NEC spokesman at the 1962 conference, Miss Jennie Lee, had described it as 'the next step' and 'the end of the journey' and advised that the Africans should accept nothing less. This was partly due to the fact that even without one man, one vote, a liberal broadening of the franchise would ensure a rapid transition to African majority rule. But it was also because this was an issue that aroused strong emotions in Rhodesia: for the Africans it was a recognition of their dignity and equality; for the Europeans it spelled the end of their political domination. A Labour government would be obliged to negotiate a settlement acceptable to both sides, and it was perhaps for this reason that the party took a more cautious line on this divisive issue.

The Labour party was also committed to withholding independence from a Rhodesia under white minority rule. This had been the party's line throughout the Conservative Government's exchanges with the Whitehead, the Field and the Smith Governments and during the negotiations on the dissolution of the Federation. The NIBMAR pledge (no independence before majority African rule) had been established party policy since the question of Southern Rhodesian independence was first raised in the last years of the Federation. Mr Wilson was to confirm this commitment in a letter written during the 1964 election campaign, in which he told Dr E. Mutasa, an African political leader, that:

> The Labour party is totally opposed to granting independence to Southern Rhodesia so long as the government of that country remains under the control of a white minority. We have repeatedly urged the British Government to negotiate a new constitution, with all of the African and European parties represented, in order to achieve a peaceful transition to African majority rule.[7]

In view of these commitments, it was not surprising that the victory of the Labour party in the general election was welcomed by the Africans in Southern Rhodesia but regarded with a feeling akin to horror by most of the Europeans. For the Africans, the Labour party had been the main force in British politics to champion their interests. Its commitment to decolonisation and its record in creating the multi-racial Commonwealth were recalled, with the hope that the policies introduced by the Labour Government after 1945 would be resumed by their successors in 1964. A close relationship with the African nationalist movement had been established by the Fabian Commonwealth Bureau, founded in 1940 (as the Colonial Bureau) by a number of the party's colonial experts, such as the late Arthur Creech Jones and Rita Hinden, to work as a pressure group within the party to further the development of self-determination as well as socialist movements in the colonial territories. It had been particularly active in opposing the Central African Federation and had supported the African case for its dissolution.[8] Most of the members of the Wilson Government were also members of the Fabian Society and several of the Ministers responsible for relations with the Smith regime (Mr Bottomley, Mr Thomson, Mr Maurice Foley) had been active in the work of the Fabian Commonwealth Bureau. Many of the African nationalists who had been on missions to London had received moral support and material assistance, in such matters as petitions to the Commonwealth or Colonial Office or statements to the Press, from the Fabian Society, the Commonwealth Department of the Labour party and other sympathetic groups (such as the Africa Bureau, Anti-Apartheid, the Movement for Colonial Freedom), whose membership was largely drawn from the Labour movement.

The Europeans in Southern Rhodesia had also taken seriously the Labour party's commitments on African majority rule, and they continued to do so long after the Africans had experienced disillusionment. Convinced as they were that the Labour party was pledged to withholding independence from a white minority regime, they could foresee no possibility of obtaining from the new Government the unconditional independence they had hoped to achieve from a Conservative administration. The Smith regime had reflected this suspicion and distrust by refusing to meet the Commonwealth Secretary while he was in Lusaka for the Zambian independence celebrations, and by rejecting Mr Wilson's invitation of 23 October to come to London for talks, the latter on the ground of preoccupation with their referendum campaign.

In view of the hostile reaction of the Europeans, the Labour Government could not rule out the possibility of their taking precipitate action to seize independence. With the purpose of deterring this threat, they issued a strongly worded statement on 27 October, setting out the consequences of illegal action. The statement warned that a mere declaration of independence would have no constitutional validity: it would be an open act of defiance and rebellion and it would be treasonable to give effect to it. The British Government would be bound to sever relations with those responsible for such a declaration; it would not be possible for Southern Rhodesia to establish a new and special relationship with the Crown; and Southern Rhodesians would cease to be British subjects. The economic consequences would be equally disastrous: all financial and trade relations with Britain would be jeopardised, any further aid or access to the London money market would be ruled out, and trade with the rest of the world would be seriously disrupted. As for Southern Rhodesia's external relations, since no Commonwealth Government would be able to recognise a unilateral declaration, there

would be no possibility of Southern Rhodesia becoming a member of
the Commonwealth. The reaction of foreign governments would also be
sharp and immediate. Not only were they (with one or two exceptions)
unlikely to recognise Southern Rhodesia's independence or enter into
diplomatic relations, many of them might even recognise a government-
in-exile if one were established. In essence, the warning meant that an
illegal seizure of independence would bring to an end Southern Rhodesia's relationship with Britain; would cut it off from the rest of the
Commonwealth, from most foreign governments and from international
organisations; would inflict disastrous damage upon its economy and
would leave it isolated and virtually friendless in a largely hostile continent.

One effect of the Labour Government's warning was to postpone
any immediate action by the Rhodesian Front regime. The British
statement was reinforced by the former Rhodesian Prime Minister, Sir
Edgar Whitehead, who added his own warning that the British Government might use force if there were an illegal declaration of independence. He told the Rhodesian Legislative Assembly, on the day the
British statement was issued, that a Government didn't talk about
'rebellion' and 'treason' unless they reserved the right to use force as a
last resort. And if independence were seized, he predicted that it would
end in an African nationalist government within six months.[9] While
there was no indication that Mr Smith shared Whitehead's dire forecasts,
he had to admit, in a broadcast two days later, that he had abandoned
his hope of independence by Christmas, because the British Government's move had 'upset everything'.

The statement at least heartened the African nationalists in Rhodesia,
who regarded it as a portent of better things to come so far as they
were concerned. One of their spokesmen wrote that 'the strong, defiant
tone' of Mr Wilson's warning gave Africans hope that at last Britain
would show Mr Smith who was boss. They certainly expected that warning to be followed up by immediate steps to call the constitutional
conference that Mr Wilson had recommended in his letter to Dr Mutasa
during the general election.[10] But on this expectation they were to meet
with the first of their many disappointments. When the subject was
again raised by the United Nations Special Committee on Decolonisation
on 28 October, the British delegate presented to the Committee the
Government's statement of warning. This at least fulfilled the Committee's previous demand (on 23 March 1964) that Britain 'warn the
minority settler government against the consequences of a unilateral
declaration of independence', although by this time it had been partially

met by the Conservative Government's warning to Mr Smith on 7 September. On the prospects of a constitutional conference, however, which had been repeatedly called for in previous United Nations resolutions, no commitments were forthcoming from the new Labour Government. Their delegation could only offer an assurance that their policy was to negotiate a new constitution that would ensure a peaceful transition to African majority rule.[11]

In spite of the Labour Government's severe warning concerning the dire consequences of illegal action, it soon became evident (to all but the Europeans in Rhodesia) that they had no intention of imposing a constitutional settlement on Rhodesia. Instead, their policy was to seek a negotiated agreement, an objective which could only be achieved with the consent and co-operation of the ruling white minority. The main obstacle, however, was that the Europeans were not prepared to enter into negotiations with a Government committed to African majority rule. Mr Smith reflected this view when he began the long series of correspondence and meetings which he was to have with Mr Wilson in the course of the year preceding the illegal declaration of independence. His main concern, at the outset, was the pledge contained in the Mutasa letter. First, in his dispatch of 25 November 1964, and again in those of 15 December 1964 and 25 January 1965, he was to insist that there could be no basis for any agreement with the Labour Government, because Mr Wilson, in his letter to Dr Mutasa, had made it clear that they were determined to withhold independence so long as Southern Rhodesia remained under white minority rule.[12]

Although Mr Smith failed to elicit a satisfactory reply from Mr Wilson concerning the Mutasa letter, the subject was temporarily abandoned (only to be revived later as a justification for the UDI), because he was beginning to obtain from the Labour Government instead assurances that amounted to a repudiation of the contents of the letter. By the end of January he had met with Mr Wilson in London, on the occasion of Winston Churchill's funeral, and had agreed to a visit to Rhodesia of the Commonwealth Secretary and the Lord Chancellor. The agreement included the concession from Mr Smith, which he had denied to the Commonwealth Secretary the previous October, that the British Ministers would be allowed to meet a cross-section of European and African opinion, although not persons detained on 'criminal' charges. In return, Mr Bottomley conceded that the Labour Government would abide by the convention whereby Britain undertook not to intervene in the internal affairs of Rhodesia except with the agreement of the Rhodesian Government.[13] The Commonwealth Secretary's assurance was reinforced by Mr Wilson's message to Mr Smith on 29 March, which repeated the promise that they did not contemplate either the immediate imposition of majority rule or the advent to power of 'persons who have not served a political apprenticeship'. Instead, they wished to see a peaceful transition to majority rule, a principle which they now maintained was enshrined in the Constitution they had so vigorously opposed while in Opposition.[14]

Electoral Considerations

Mr Wilson's conciliatory message did not result in the renewal of negotiations, since Mr Smith had already turned his attention to electoral considerations at home. Although the Rhodesian Front had a commanding majority in the Legislative Assembly, which had been reinforced by the by-election victories of October 1964, they did not yet have the two-thirds majority necessary for amendments to the Constitution. In calling a general election, they also aimed to impress the British Government with the extent of European support for independence, although the means of achieving it were no more clarified by the 1965 election than they had been by the 1964 referendum. In addition, they hoped to gain electoral advantage from the growing popularity of Mr Smith (nominated 'man of the year' by the Lions Club) and to dispose of the remaining European opposition, already weakened by the by-election defeats and the loss of such Establishment figures as Sir Roy Welensky and Sir Edgar Whitehead, who had retired from the political scene. No opposition from the Africans was to be expected, since their leadership had been detained, their parties and Press outlawed and their electoral participation restricted by a highly qualified franchise.[15] The few thousand Africans registered on the 'B' roll could only elect a maximum of 15 of the 65 seats; and there weren't enough of them to have any significant effect on the 'cross-voting' provided by the 1961 Constitution to enable the two races to have some influence on the selection of each other's candidates.

For the Rhodesian Front, the main consideration in the electoral campaign was to dispel any doubts in the minds of the European electorate about the consequences of a unilateral declaration of independence, especially since it was known that a large section of the business community was opposed to any action which might disrupt trade and commercial relations with Britain and with Rhodesia's other trading partners. Accordingly, during the week preceding the election, the Rhodesian Government issued a White Paper on the economic aspects of a declaration of independence, purporting to establish the benefits that would accrue to an independent State. In particular, it claimed that a great proportion of Rhodesia's exports, including tobacco, the greatest export earner, could be marketed in countries other than Britain, then the largest single customer. The Paper also sought to reassure Rhodesians that after independence was declared money would be forthcoming for investment in Rhodesia from what it termed 'countries not unfriendly' towards it.[16]

However the presumptions in the White Paper might have been received by the Rhodesian electorate, there was no doubt about the reaction of the British Government. In a statement to the House of Commons on 29 April 1965, Mr Wilson reaffirmed the Government's adherence to their declaration of 27 October 1964, pointing out that nothing that had happened in the preceding six months had afforded any reasons for modifying their position in any way. Consequently, the only means by which Rhodesia could achieve independence without grave consequences to itself was by the process of constitutional negotiation. A resort to illegal action, he warned, would have disastrous effects upon the Rhodesian economy, particularly in its external trade and its relationship with the Commonwealth.[17]

Equally pessimistic forecasts, contained in the reports of the Rhodesian industrial, commercial and agricultural associations, were also released to the Press before the election.[18] The timing was obviously not coincidental, particularly in the case of the Institute of Directors, whose memorandum warning of the economic and financial consequences of a unilateral declaration of independence had been prepared the previous November, immediately after the Labour Government's statement of 27 October 1964. Since then, a poll taken among its membership showed that nearly 95 per cent were opposed to an illegal declaration of independence. The dire warnings contained in the reports of the Association of Rhodesian Industries and the Associated Chambers of Commerce of Rhodesia were, in fact, almost identical with those in the Labour Government's statement. The industrialists were concerned with the possible loss of raw material supplies, which amounted to 30 per cent of imports; the withdrawal of Commonwealth preferences; exclusion from the Sterling Area and Commonwealth commodity agreements; the severance of sources of investment and the disruption of financial and credit machinery between Rhodesia and the outside world. The Chambers of Commerce also expected that there would be import and exchange controls and, ultimately, devaluation. The Rhodesian National Farmers' Union predicted a loss to the tobacco and sugar industries of at least £14 million and a cut in the tobacco crop to 170 million lbs, a reduction of some 80 million from the current crop.

But the logic of economics failed to prevail over the emotional wave of white nationalism. On 7 May 1965 the European electorate accordingly returned all 50 Rhodesian Front candidates to the 'A' roll seats, only 28 of which were even contested. The opposition Rhodesia party, under the leadership of Mr David Butler, who lost his own seat, managed to win only 10 seats, on the 'B' roll, and those were won by African candidates elected by a few hundred voters. The remaining 5 seats went to Independents, one of whom, Mr Ahrn Palley, was a European elected by 'B' roll voters. Mr Palley was to be the lone spokesman for the conscience of the European opposition, a role then comparable to that of Mrs Helen Suzman in the South African Parliament. For the first time in the history of the Rhodesian Parliament, the official leader of the Opposition was an African. With the virtual annihilation of the multi-racial Rhodesia party, the pretence of 'partnership' in Rhodesian politics came to an end. The rump group of 14 African MPs, who really represented no significant sector of Rhodesian society, were to form a new party, the United People's party, under the leadership of a Mr Josiah Gondo. This was an Opposition that the Rhodesian Front could safely ignore.

The British Government maintained a discreet silence during the Rhodesian election campaign, including the Commonwealth Secretary, who had been reprimanded by the leader of the Conservative party for his hostile remarks about the Rhodesian Front on the occasion of the independence referendum the previous November. No criticism was officially made of the unrepresentative nature of the electorate nor of the imbalance of racial representation. But the silence was not maintained so far as the outside world was concerned, and Britain, as the 'administering Power', was held responsible for the situation in Rhodesia by both the United Nations and the Commonwealth.

Colonial Status

Ever since the question of Southern Rhodesia's status as a 'non-self-governing territory' was first raised in 1961, the British position had been to deny United Nations intervention, pleading domestic jurisdiction under Article 2 (paragraph 7). In spite of continuing British opposition, the General Assembly's Special Committee of Decolonisation had placed the subject on its agenda and had decided that Southern Rhodesia had not attained a full measure of self-government. On the basis of this conclusion, it had recommended that the Constitution of 1961 should be abrogated and new constitutional arrangements agreed, and that a sub-committee should consult with the British Government on measures to implement United Nations resolutions on the subject. Although the British Government had agreed to meet with the sub-committee, in London in April 1962, they did not alter their position on the status of Southern Rhodesia as a self-governing colony. This was evident from their refusal to accept a series of General Assembly resolutions calling for a constitutional conference of all parties in Southern Rhodesia, for the purpose of establishing majority rule on the basis of one man, one vote. In addition, the British case for non-intervention had not been improved by the inclusion in their delegation at the Fourth (Trust and Non-Self-Governing Territories) Committee in October 1962 of Sir Edgar Whitehead, whose Government had rejected further constitutional negotiations with the African nationalists and introduced a state of emergency outlawing their political activities. One of the final acts of the Conservative Government's delegation at the United Nations had been to oppose the Security Council's competence to deal with the question of Southern Rhodesia, denying that the situation in that territory called for action under Chapter VII, as 'a threat to international peace and security'. Failing to prevent the Council from considering a draft resolution sponsored by the African States, they had cast the first of the nine vetoes on the subject that were to be recorded by British delegations.[19]

If the African States and their allies at the United Nations expected that a Labour Government would reverse the policies of their Conservative predecessors, particularly when their permanent representative was Lord Caradon (formerly Sir Hugh Foot), who had resigned from the Conservative Government's delegation in October 1962 because of his disagreement with their stand on Rhodesia, they were in for a disappointment. In May 1965, as in October 1962, a general election was to take place in Rhodesia. On the earlier occasion, the Conservative delegation had refused to support a General Assembly resolution calling for the cancellation of those elections and the suspension of the Constitution under which they were to be held.[20] With a Labour Government in office in 1965, the British delegation, once again led by Lord Caradon, could not accept a Security Council resolution noting the serious implications of holding elections under a Constitution which had been rejected by the majority of the Rhodesian people. As in 1962, the British delegation maintained that, since Southern Rhodesia had been a self-governing colony for decades, they could only reserve their position on the elections and on the other assumptions regarding the internal affairs of the colony. While the Labour Government, like their Conservative predecessors, had issued clear warnings about the consequences of any illegal action, they also favoured consultations, and the decision of how those were to proceed would remain within their competence.[21]

Although the Rhodesian elections were over when the Commonwealth Prime Ministers assembled in London in June 1965, the Labour Government had still to justify the basis of their negotiations with the Rhodesian Government, which had been resumed at the beginning of that month. The main concern expressed by the Commonwealth leaders was that the settlement of the Rhodesian issue should be approached not by the prevailing bilateral talks but by a constitutional conference representing all the main political groups in the colony. Such a conference, they recommended, should be convened within a period of three months, in order to establish the means by which Rhodesia might proceed to independence on the basis of majority rule. If, however, the Rhodesian Front refused to participate in the conference, then the British Government should suspend the Constitution and appoint an interim government to prepare for free elections.

It was evident from the British Government's evasive reply that they had no intention of accepting such a proposal, particularly while they were engaged in discussions with the Rhodesian Government. The most that they would concede was that a constitutional conference, 'at the appropriate time', would be a natural step in the process of seeking to reach agreement on Rhodesia's advance to independence. But it was they who would decide: if the negotiations did not develop satisfactorily 'in a reasonably speedy time', they would be prepared to consider promoting such a conference. The responsibility for leading Rhodesia to independence, they insisted, must continue to rest with Britain.[22]

The Principles

Although the negotiations failed to proceed satisfactorily, nothing more was said about promoting a constitutional conference. Instead, the Government sent the Commonwealth Minister of State, Mr Cledwyn Hughes, to Salisbury in July to continue the talks begun by Mr Bottomley and Lord Gardiner the previous February. It was not surprising that the meeting failed to produce any agreement, since the terms put forward by the Rhodesians were virtually the same as those already put to the two British Ministers. Mr Smith acknowledged this position when he told his Parliament that, while the Rhodesians were prepared to examine any proposals from Britain, they were firmly convinced that they had made all the concessions they could morally be called upon to make when they had been 'bribed' into accepting the existing Constitution as 'a stepping-stone to independence'.[23] He himself had not improved the atmosphere of the negotiations by announcing to the *Rhodesia Herald*, while Mr Hughes was still in Salisbury, that he would 'put his shirt' on the possibility that there would not be a black prime minister in Rhodesia in at least thirty, possibly forty, years.[24] In addition, even if any movement in the Rhodesian negotiating position had been intended, it was forestalled by the intervention, in the middle of the talks, of the Rhodesian Front chairman, Colonel William Knox, who warned Mr Smith of the party's attitude towards making any concessions. According to his statement to the *Sunday Mail*, it had been necessary for him to call on the Prime Minister in view of certain articles which had appeared in the local Press (*The Citizen*, a supporter of the Rhodesian Front, had said that Mr Smith was prepared to compromise with party principles to get independence). The Colonel claimed that as a result of his interview he had received the Prime Minister's assurance that the Government were not contemplating any action which could be construed as contravening the principles of the Rhodesian Front, and that independence, however it came about, would be 'without strings'.[25]

Since the Labour Government had also made a statement that no deviation from their principles had taken place during the talks,[26] it was evident that the two sides were as far apart as they had been after the Ministerial visit the previous February. The Commonwealth Secretary confirmed this division when he wrote to Mr Smith on 21 September that the Rhodesian Front's proposals amounted to a flat rejection of all of the 'Five Principles' on which the negotiations were supposed to be based. Those principles, which had originated with the previous Conservative Government, were formulated in the following terms:[27]

(1) the principle and intention of unimpeded progress to majority rule already enshrined in the 1961 Constitution would have to be maintained and guaranteed;
(2) there would also have to be guarantees against retrogressive amendment of the Constitution;
(3) there would have to be immediate improvement in the political status of the African population;
(4) there would have to be progress towards ending racial discrimination;
(5) the British Government would need to be satisfied that any basis proposed for independence was acceptable to the people of Rhode-

sia as a whole.[28]

Even at this stage of the negotiations, Mr Smith was already apprehensive about the outcome of any test of acceptability, because in
his reply to the Commonwealth Secretary's message he warned that if
their two Governments ever did manage to reach agreement on a basis
for independence, it could be invidious and embarrassing to them both
if this were subsequently rejected, simply because the Fifth Principle
required the approval of the Rhodesian people as a whole[29] — a prophetic
warning that was to materialise in 1972, to the embarrassment of both
Mr Smith and Sir Alec Douglas-Home.

Another factor contributing to the division had been the Rhodesian
Government's announcement on 27 July,[30] at the conclusion of the
Hughes visit, of the appointment of their own diplomatic representative to the Portuguese Government, Mr Harry Reedman, an act in
defiance of the constitutional provision that Britain had the responsibility for Rhodesia's external affairs. Although both the Commonwealth and the Foreign Secretary (Mr Michael Stewart) insisted that
Britain retained this responsibility, no measures were proposed to
enforce it. Instead, Mr Stewart maintained that, while Mr Reedman was
officially received by the Portuguese authorities as a representative
of Rhodesia, his appointment was not in the capacity of an 'accredited
diplomatic representative'.[31] With a diplomatic representative already
in South Africa, the Smith Government were consolidating their links
with the white-dominated regimes of southern Africa.

In spite of the Rhodesian Front's growing impatience with the
course of the independence negotiations, no ministerial visit to
Rhodesia could be arranged while the Labour party was preparing for
its annual conference in October 1965 and a meeting with Mr Smith in
London could not be held until the conference was concluded. Although the Rhodesian question was not down for debate at the conference, there was considerable concern among party members about
the possible outcome of the forthcoming meeting between Mr Wilson
and Mr Smith. While the Government's warning of the consequences
of an illegal seizure of independence the previous October had been
welcomed as an indication that a strong line would be taken on the
terms of independence, it was felt that in the negotiations with the
Smith regime since that time there had been a steady erosion of the
party's commitments on Rhodesia. The policy of withholding independence from a white minority regime — to which the party had been
pledged in Opposition — had been given a new and less precise inter-

pretation. In its place was the principle of unimpeded progress to majority rule, but the pace of that progress was to be left to a white minority government. Mr Wilson's assurances that there would be no immediate imposition of majority rule may have been welcomed by the Europeans in Salisbury, but it was regarded with suspicion by a large section of his party, concerned that the pledges previously made to the African nationalists might be sacrificed to the expediency of reaching an agreement with the Europeans.

Expressing this concern, a group of some forty Labour MPs at the party conference signed a statement warning that the grant of independence to a government elected on narrow racial lines would create the prospect of another apartheid State in southern Africa. Instead, it was proposed that all Rhodesian parties should come together to prepare a new constitution based on equal rights and democratic principles. If, however, the Rhodesian Government carried out their threat to seize independence, then economic sanctions should be applied and, if these did not prove effective, the use of force should be invoked, not by Britain alone but through the United Nations. No arguments of 'kith and kin', the statement concluded, could absolve Britain of its solemn obligations to all the people of Rhodesia.[32]

'Kith and kin' was also the concern of a group of Conservative MPs and Peers, who attempted to stage a revolt on the Rhodesian issue at their party's annual conference in October 1965. On this occasion, the right-wing Rhodesia Lobby, headed by Lord Salisbury and Mr Patrick Wall, MP, put down an amendment to the official party motion, declaring their total opposition to the imposition of 'penal' sanctions, economic or military, on the ground that they would have the effect of impairing the prosperity of Rhodesia. But the leadership's case (put by Sir Alec Douglas-Home and Mr Selwyn Lloyd) was sufficiently convincing to obtain approval for the official motion, expressing the hope that there would not be a unilateral declaration of independence and that a solution would be found by negotiation on the basis of the Five Principles and a guarantee of the 1961 Constitution.[33] The Conservatives were still convinced that progress could be made if the Africans showed a willingness to co-operate in working the 1961 Constitution and if the Rhodesian Government accepted British assistance for a programme of African educational advance.

Within a few days of the warning issued by the group of Labour MPs at the party conference, Mr Wilson had begun his talks with the Rhodesian leaders in London. Recognising the dilemma raised by the MPs' statement, he admitted that while the whole record of British decolonisation confirmed his Government's insistence on majority rule as a condition of independence, in interpreting this condition as reasonably speedy progress towards majority rule in the case of Rhodesia, they had already made a major concession. He thought that it would be difficult enough to justify this compromise before world opinion; and unless the Rhodesians showed some indication of willingness to meet even these modified requirements, it was most unlikely that any agreement at all could be achieved.[34]

No agreement did in fact emerge from the four days of talks and a joint communiqué was issued confirming this.[35] In his television broadcast on 12 October, Mr Wilson admitted that he had felt that the two sides were living in different worlds, almost different centuries: on every one of the Five Principles the disagreement was almost total and absolute (as Mr Bottomley had already recognised in his despatch to Mr Smith on 21 September). Mr Wilson had been particularly concerned throughout the negotiations that guaranteed and unimpeded progress to majority rule should not be frustrated by the freedom of an independent Rhodesia to amend the 1961 Constitution in a retrogressive manner. This would indeed be possible, because while certain constitutional safeguards were entrenched, other provisions — including the number of MPs to be elected on the 'A' and 'B' rolls — were not and, on a two-thirds Parliamentary majority, could be altered to obstruct progress to majority rule. In addition, the British had failed to get the Rhodesians to agree to an interim period under the existing Constitution during which Africans would be taken into a multi-racial government, trained as junior Ministers and Parliamentary Secretaries, while a massive programme of African education and training was introduced with British financial assistance. To such a suggestion Mr Smith had replied that his Government would think it wrong to accelerate the educational advance of the Africans in order to improve their political status. Nor would they consider a broadening of the franchise, on the ground that when this had been considered some years earlier (presumably by the Todd Government) Europeans had begun to leave the country in large numbers.

Despite the breakdown, Mr Wilson was prepared to continue the discussions, apparently convinced that there were a number of points deserving further consideration, such as the British proposal for a constitutional conference, the Rhodesian scheme for a senate to vote on constitutional safeguards, and a treaty between the two Governments to provide the necessary guarantees. The latter proposal had been raised, according to Mr Wilson's version,[36] at the final meeting on 11

October, after Mr Smith had suggested it during his talks with the Conservative party leaders. However, the function of such a treaty would be only to safeguard a settlement, and this had yet to be agreed. As for the other points supposedly worthy of further consideration, the constitutional conference was unacceptable to the Smith regime; and their proposal for a senate composed of Chiefs was unacceptable to the British as a guarantee against constitutional changes impeding the advance of African majority rule.

In the exchange following the London meeting, Mr Wilson's additional proposal, for a Commonwealth mission headed by the Australian elder statesman, Sir Robert Menzies, also met with a flat rejection. Instead, Mr Smith send an urgent letter on 20 October, demanding the immediate grant of independence on the basis of the 1961 Constitution, combined with a treaty of guarantee: 'Grant us our independence', he said, 'and trust us to abide by the principles of that Constitution.' To this, Mr. Wilson was obliged to explain yet again what his predecessors in office had made clear in September 1964, namely, that there was never any undertaking, explicit or implicit, that Rhodesia would be granted independence on the basis of the 1961 Constitution without further change; and that this position had been acknowledged by the Rhodesian Prime Minister responsible for that Constitution.[37] As for Mr Smith's complaint that Rhodesia was being condemned not for what it had done but for what it might do in the future, Mr Wilson pointed out that the detention or restriction over a long period of time of the African nationalist leaders, the current restriction of a former Prime Minister (Mr Todd) and the banning of a prominent newspaper (the African *Daily News*) had already suggested the pattern of the future. Nevertheless, Mr Wilson must have been convinced that a unilateral declaration of independence would have followed if his Government had rejected the Smith ultimatum, since he responded by announcing his willingness to go to Salisbury with a team of his Ministers to continue the consultations and to meet with representative groups of opinion in Rhodesia.

'Besides the pressures within his own party, Mr Wilson was also subjected to strong criticism of the British position from the international community before his departure for Salisbury. After the breakdown of the London talks, and on the day of his television broadcast, the UN General Assembly adopted a resolution on the Rhodesian situation by the overwhelming majority of 107-2, a vote in which the British delegation refused to participate. Although the resolution contained a number of the same proposals as the British declaration of

27 October 1964, the Government could not accept the request that they take 'all possible measures' to prevent a unilateral declaration of independence or to put an end to the rebellion if it nevertheless occurred.[38] Nor were they prepared to accept the advice of the African Heads of State, meeting in Accra on the eve of Mr Wilson's visit to Salisbury. Their main concern was that the British Government had responded to the threat of rebellion by a mere warning of economic sanctions and non-recognition. Britain, as the administering Power, was urged to suspend the 1961 Constitution; take over the administration of the territory, if necessary by armed force; secure the release of the detained nationalist leaders; and convene a representative conference to adopt a new constitution ensuring majority rule. If Britain failed to carry out these measures, the African States would consider severing their diplomatic relations and would themselves use all possible means, including force, to oppose a unilateral declaration of independence.[39]

Such demands were to be made repeatedly by the African States, not only at the Organisation of African Unity meetings but also at the United Nations and, for the Commonwealth members, at the Ministers' conferences. Mr Wilson was undoubtedly aware of such pressures limiting his freedom of action in seeking an independence settlement, because of his frequent reference to the problem of how he could justify a particular British policy so far as world opinion was concerned. By the time he departed for Salisbury, for what he thought would be a final settlement of the independence issue, he was already obliged to take into account how far he could go in disregarding the views of a large section of his party and of most of the membership of the Commonwealth and the United Nations. To have met their requirements would have ruled out the possibility of any settlement with the Smith Government.

Notes

1. See David Butler and Anthony King, *The British General Election of 1964,* 1965, p. 121.

2. At the Victoria Falls conference in 1951, the Labour Government had refused to implement a scheme for federation without the consent of the African population in the territories. See Cmnd. 8411, 21 September 1951.

3. The debate on 23 March was on the Report of the Southern Rhodesia Constitutional Conference. See Cmnd. 1291. The debate on 22 June was on the proposals for revising the Southern Rhodesian Constitution. See Cmnd. 1399, 1400. The debate on 8 November was on the second reading of the Southern Rhodesia Bill. The vote against the Labour Motion of 22 June was 313-219; and the second reading was carried by 221-156.

4. 642 *HC Deb.,* 22 June 1961, col. 1808.

5. Statement on BBC Africa Forum, March 1963.

6. *Report of the 61st Annual Conference of the Labour Party,* Brighton, 1962.

7. The letter was written by the author and signed by Mr Wilson, on 2 October 1964. It was published in the *Rhodesia Herald,* 19 October 1964.

8. See Arthur Creech Jones, *African Challenge: The Fallacy of Federation,* 1952; Rita Hinden, *No Cheer for Central Africa,* 1958; Shirley Williams, *Central Africa: The Economics of Inequality,* 1960.

9. *Southern Rhodesia Legislative Assembly,* vol. 59, 27 October 1964, col. 436.

10. Nathan Shamuyarira, *Crisis in Southern Rhodesia,* 1965, p. 231.

11. The debate on Southern Rhodesia took place on 26-28 October 1964. The resolution of 23 March 1964 had been adopted by 18-0, with five abstentions. The UK did not participate in the vote.

12. *Southern Rhodesia: Documents relating to the Negotiations between the United Kingdom and Southern Rhodesian Governments, November 1963 – November 1965,* Cmnd. 2807, 1965.

13. 708 *HC Deb.,* 8 March 1965, cols. 37-9, 15 March 1965, col. 197. Mr Bottomley had said during the Rhodesian referendum campaign that the British Government's warning of 27 October would be appreciated by such Rhodesian leaders as Welensky, Whitehead and Todd – a claim that had prompted Sir Alec Douglas-Home to protest about intervention in Rhodesian internal politics to swing the electors away from Mr Smith. See ibid., vol. 701, 3 November 1964, col. 59.

14. Cmnd. 2807, 1965. The requirements of 'political apprenticeship' would have ruled out the Rhodesian Front Cabinet, whose members had not previously held ministerial posts.

15. The 'A' roll qualifications to elect 50 of the 65 seats, as revised (upward) in September 1964, required an income of £792 or immovable property worth £1,650; or Standard 6 education, an income of £528 or immovable property of £1,100; or secondary (Form 4) education, an income of £330 or immovable property of £500. Africans were not allowed to own property in European urban areas and in the Reserves (Tribal Trust Lands) property was owned communally. The average annual income of Africans in employment in 1964 was £122.

16. CSR 15-1965.

17. 711 *HC Deb.,* 29 April 1965, cols. 638-9.

18. For the institute of Directors' report, see *Rhodesia Herald,* 28 April 1965; for the ACCOR and ARNI reports, see *Sunday Mail* (Salisbury), 2 May 1965.

19. See p. 16.

20. General Assembly resolution 1760 (XXVII), adopted 31 October 1962 by 81-2, with 19 abstentions. The UK did not participate in the vote.

21. Security Council resolution 202 (1965), adopted 6 May 1965 by 7-0, with four abstentions (including the UK).

22. *Commonwealth Prime Ministers' Meeting 1965, Final Communiqué,* London, 25 June 1965, Cmnd. 2712.

23. *Southern Rhodesia Legislative Assembly,* vol. 61, 20 July 1965, cols. 1196-7.

24. 21 July 1965. His remarks were the subject of criticism in the Assembly. Ibid., 21 July 1965, cols. 1289-92.

25. Salisbury, 25 July 1965.

26. Commonwealth Secretary, 717, *HC Deb.,* 30 July 1965, col. 909.

27. Mr Wilson claimed the Five Principles were first formally stated during

the Bottomley-Gardiner visit in February 1965. (*The Labour Government, 1964-1970*, 1971, p. 143.)

28. Cmnd. 2807, 1965.

29. Message of 27 September 1965, ibid.

30. *Southern Rhodesia Legislative Assembly*, vol. 61, 27 July 1965, cols. 1469-70.

31. 717 *HC Deb.*, 28 July 1965, col. 469; vol. 718, 1 November 1965, col. 116.

32. *East Africa and Rhodesia*, 7 October 1965.

33. *Report of the 83rd Annual Conservative Party Conference*, Brighton, 1965.

34. 7 October 1965, quoted in Cmnd. 2807.

35. For the British Government's position see 718 *HC Deb.*, 1 November 1965, cols. 646-8.

36. Ibid., cols. 631-2.

37. See Sir Edgar Whitehead, *Southern Rhodesia Legislative Assembly*, vol. 57, 25 August 1964, col. 1212.

38. General Assembly resolution 2012 (XX), 12 October 1965. The votes against such resolutions on Rhodesia were invariably those of South Africa and Portugal.

39. Organisation of African Unity, Secretariat, Addis Ababa, 1965.

3 THE FAILURE OF A MISSION

'I thought they really were willing to negotiate and get a solution . . . I went there, and I think I put a lot of energy into it, but it was wasted.'

Harold Wilson, 7 November 1975.

This was the dilemma confronting Mr Wilson when he arrived in Rhodesia: he had either to disappoint the Africans, and their supporters in the outside world, by refusing to implement majority rule, or the Europeans by insisting on imposing it. The latter were allegedly prepared to resort to force to prevent such an eventuality and the former were rendered powerless by the repressions of a police State. The issue had already been resolved before the Salisbury talks had even begun by the Labour Government's pledge not to use force to impose a constitutional settlement. There was, in fact, no real basis on which the Labour Government could begin to negotiate with the Rhodesian Front until the Africans had been disabused of any illusions they might still retain regarding the Labour party's commitments on majority rule.

Mr Wilson himself had not been personally involved in the making of these commitments, although on the basis of collective party decisions he was equally bound by them. Most of his political career had been devoted to dealing with Britain's economic problems. In the postwar Labour Government he had served at the Ministry of Works and Board of Trade and during the years of Opposition after 1951 he had been the party's front bench spokesman on economic and financial matters. For only a brief period before Hugh Gaitskell's death, he had served as spokesman on foreign (but not Commonwealth or colonial) affairs. It was only after assuming the leadership at the beginning of 1963 that he was obliged to take responsibility in a field in which he had not hitherto ventured. As Leader of the Opposition, his pronouncements on Rhodesia − in the House of Commons, on the BBC, at party meetings and in overseas correspondence − had been strictly in accordance with party policy, and until the electoral victory of 1964, there had been no deviation from that line.[1] Once in Government, however, his main source of advice on Rhodesia was the Commonwealth Office, policy-making having shifted from its previous sources − Transport House, the Commonwealth and Colonies Group of Labour

MPs, the Fabian Commonwealth Bureau – to the Whitehall Establishment. While Mr Wilson (as were his senior Ministers) was well equipped
with party political advisers on other subjects, none were then provided
for Commonwealth or African affairs. Although two of his Commonwealth Ministers (Mr Bottomley and Mr Thomson) had previously been
front bench spokesmen on African affairs, the third (Mr Herbert
Bowden) had served in the domestic political arena and the others
involved in the Rhodesian negotiations, Lord Gardiner and Lord
Goodman, admitted to having had no previous knowledge or
experience of the African political scene.

In Rhodesia Mr Wilson had three long sessions with each of the two
African nationalist leaders – Mr Nkomo of the Zimbabwe African
People's Union and Rev. Sithole of the Zimbabwe African National
Union – and one meeting with Mr Nkomo and Rev. Sithole together.
In a sense, his meetings with the African nationalists were an essential
preparation for negotations with the Europeans. If he could be seen to
be taking a tough line with them, his chances of getting an agreement
with the Europeans would be immeasuably improved. Their division
into two irreconcilable camps meant that neither could lay claim to the
undisputed leadership of the majority of the African people.

With the African nationalists Mr Wilson was brutally frank: his
message amounted to an unequivocal denial of any obligation whatever
on the part of the Labour Government so far as the imposition of
majority rule was concerned. In a memorable statement, repeated at
his final press conference in Salisbury on 30 October 1965 and again in
the House of Commons on 1 November, he disposed once and for all of
any remaining hopes that the Africans still might retain of British
military intervention on their behalf:

> If there are those who are thinking in terms of a thunderbolt hurt-
> ling from the sky and destroying their enemies, a thunderbolt in the
> shape of the RAF, let me say that thunderbolt will not be coming,
> and to continue in this delusion wastes valuable time, and misdirects
> valuable energies.

Although conceding that successive British Governments were irrevocably committed to guaranteed and unimpeded progress towards majority rule, he did not believe that, in the prevailing tragic and divided
condition of Rhodesia, majority rule could or should come 'today or
tomorrow'. A period of time was needed – to remove racial fears and
suspicions and to show that the Constitution could be made to work –

and the time required could not be measured 'by clock or calendar, but only by achievement'. In the meantime, the Africans were advised to unite their bitterly divided forces and to operate under the existing Constitution by persuading their followers to register, to vote and to stand for the Assembly, thus making a reality of a multi-racial parliament, with a multi-racial system of government.

The fear and apprehension and the extraordinary degree of self-deception which Mr Wilson observed in his dealings with the Rhodesians were not limited to the Africans. If anything, the Europeans should have been reassured by his forthright denial of any British intention to use force or to impose African majority rule. The most that they had to endure were warnings of the economic implications of an illegal seizure of independence, and these they had already heard from their own business community. Nevertheless, in the ensuing negotiations, every British proposal was viewed with a suspicion bordering on paranoia, and the suggestions put forward by the Rhodesians were so far removed from the Five Principles upon which the negotiations were supposed to be based as to be beyond serious consideration.

Any hope that the negotiations might succeed, where those in London the previous fortnight had failed, on the basis of a solemn treaty of guarantee was soon dissipated by the failure of the two sides to agree on any contents. Much had been made of the treaty proposal, both by Mr Smith in his letter containing the proposal and by the Conservative party, which took credit for originating the idea. The new party leader, Mr Heath, told his constituents in Bexley on 22 October that he, together with Sir Alec Douglas-Home and Mr Selwyn Lloyd, had first mentioned the treaty proposal to Mr Smith on 10 October, and that the Rhodesians had passed it on to Mr Wilson the following day. Mr Heath seemed to attach great importance to the idea, urging the two Governments to consider extending it to cover more than just the principle of unimpeded progress towards majority rule. Mr Wilson also indicated some interest in the subject when he announced at a press conference the day he left for Salisbury that the British team were planning to examine the treaty proposals very thoroughly. But by the time the negotiations were under way, and the Attorney-General (Sir Elwyn Jones) had flown out from London especially to advise on the subject, Mr Wilson discovered that the proposal for a treaty of guarantee was 'not a runner' and that it played 'no real part in Rhodesian thinking'. Although the Rhodesian motive in raising the issue (irrespective of whether it originated with the Tories) was never established, Mr Smith was apparently convinced that a treaty to guarantee that

Rhodesia would abide by the 1961 Constitution was all that was required for the grant of independence, for this is what he told a Salisbury audience on 22 October. The treaty idea was therefore dropped (for the moment, at any rate, until it was revived in the post-UDI negotiations) and the decision to abandon it was accepted by both sides.

But moving from a scheme for treaty guarantees to one for constitutional safeguards was equally unproductive. No agreement followed on the contents of the settlement to be safeguarded, irrespective of the means. Much of the discussion was taken up by such matters as the number of Africans who would qualify to register on the 'B' roll, which then elected fifteen of the sixty-five Parliamentary seats. On this point, the alleged concession by the Rhodesians of virtually universal suffrage on the 'B' roll was rendered meaningless by the stringent literacy test which would deter the registration of even the 60,000 Africans estimated by the Smith Government to be immediately eligible. And again, educational assistance, financed by the British Government for the purpose of advancing the pace of African enfranchisement, was firmly rejected.

A Royal Commission

By the final day of the talks, with no progress recorded and with signs not only of a breakdown of the negotiations but of imminent illegal action, Mr Wilson put to the Rhodesian Ministers two final proposals. One was for a referendum to test Mr Smith's assertion that the majority of Rhodesian people wanted independence on the basis of the 1961 Constitution. But this referendum, unlike that of November 1964, would be held under a franchise which would include the majority of Africans on the single test of tax-paying, and it would be subject to safeguards to ensure freedom of political organisation and canvassing. The second proposal was to set up a Royal Commission, under the chairmanship of the Rhodesian Chief Justice (Sir Hugh Beadle)[2] to recommend amendments to the 1961 Constitution implementing the principles enunciated by the British Government and to determine their acceptability to the Rhodesian people as a basis for independence. What Mr Wilson envisaged was that the Commission, in addition to taking formal evidence, would be free to hold 'a running and informal constitutional conference'.

However, the Smith Government would not accept either a broadly based referendum or amendments to their Constitution which incorporated the principles they had rejected in the London talks on 8

October. Instead, they offered their own interpretation of a Royal Commission, apparently attracted by the prospect of Beadle as chairman. They wanted it to include an additional Rhodesian member and one nominated by the British Government, and for it to operate on the basis of a unanimous report. The Commission would receive from the two Governments an agreed independence document based on the 1961 Constitution and then proceed to ascertain whether such a document were acceptable to the Rhodesian people. In effect, the Rhodesians would have a double veto on the proceedings.

The British Government's initial response was to reserve their position on the Commission's narrower terms of reference, since it would no longer be able to recommend amendments to the 1961 Constitution. They also raised the possibility of the Commission first producing an interim report on the methods recommended for consulting Rhodesian opinion. But the real obstacle was that the two Governments had yet to agree on the contents of the document which the Commission would put to the Rhodesian people. There were still important differences left unresolved. These included the vital issues of ensuring a blocking third or a blocking quarter of elected African MPs to control amendments to the Constitution of clauses which were not entrenched and also of providing effective safeguards for the specially entrenched clauses. The Rhodesian proposal to augment the elected African members by a number of Chiefs remained unacceptable, because the British Government could not consent to an arrangement which would enable an independent Rhodesian Parliament to reduce the 'B' roll seats or increase the 'A' roll seats for the purpose of postponing the achievement of majority rule. This was not a hypothetical situation, since Mr Smith had stated in the discussion on 26 October that his Government had to retain the power to delay an African majority prevailing on the 'A' roll, which he estimated occurring within fifteen and fifty years; and he made no secret of the fact that after independence they would feel free to reduce the number of 'B' roll seats in order to delay an African majority.[3]

The formal meetings adjourned, with only an agreement that the proposal for a Royal Commission should be further examined. The Commonwealth Secretary and the Attorney-General were to stay on in Salisbury to work out the terms of reference. Mr Wilson, before his departure on 30 October 1965, told a press conference that the choice was not between illegal independence today or an African majority tomorrow. Both sides had been warned: the Africans not to expect Britain to impose majority rule and the Europeans not to resort to illegal measures that could only result in their economic destruction. While

Mr Wilson saw the Royal Commission proposal as one more effort to find a basis for a settlement, Mr Smith predicted that if the idea failed, it would be 'the end of the road', the last chance for a negotiated independence.[4]

After his departure Mr Wilson went on to Zambia, Nigeria and Ghana, to consult with the African Commonwealth leaders on the results of his Rhodesian visit. The Commonwealth Secretary was to follow on, to Tanzania and Kenya, for a similar purpose after completing the detailed arrangements in Salisbury.

No further progress emerged from the extended negotiations carried on by the Commonwealth Secretary and the Attorney-General. On the contrary, it was now clear that there was no prospect of agreement on the changes which should be made to the 1961 Constitution. In addition, Mr Smith had once more reverted to his claim that he had an agreement with the previous British Government that Rhodesia could have independence on the basis of the 1961 Constitution if it could be proved that it were acceptable to the Rhodesian people — a claim that Mr Wilson promptly refuted by citing the disagreement in the Home-Smith exchanges of September 1964 on the means by which the proof would be established. At the same time, however, Mr Wilson, having already retreated from his original conception of the role of the Royal Commission, was now prepared to agree that the Rhodesian Government's proposals should be put to the test of acceptability. The main condition attached to the new offer was that it had to be made clear that the British Government disagreed with those proposals. In addition, the Royal Commission, before canvassing the views of the population, would be required to submit a unanimous interim report on how they proposed to determine acceptability. When the Commission had completed the process of ascertaining opinion, they would submit a final report which, as agreed, had to be unanimous. But the British Government could not commit themselves in advance to accept that report, particularly since the final decision rested with the Parliament at Westminster. The British Government also reserved their freedom of action, should the Royal Commission's findings show a negative response, to pursue other means of dealing with the problem, such as their original suggestion for a Royal Commission with the substantive task of devising a new constitution or their proposal for a constitutional conference.

The Smith Government did in fact reject all of Mr Wilson's alternatives, refusing to allow the Royal Commission to make any recommendations for a new constitution and rejecting a referendum as quite outside

the scope of their proposals. They also objected that the British Government were not prepared to accept in advance the decisions of the Royal
Commission, to agree that the Commission should be able to submit a
majority report or to commit themselves to advocating its acceptance to
Parliament.

State of Emergency

While stating these objections for the record, the Rhodesian Front had
already declared a state of emergency (on 5 November), thereby pre-
cluding the possibility of a Royal Commission operating under such
conditions. Nor were they prepared to take up Mr Wilson's suggestion
for a further meeting of the two Prime Ministers, possibly in Malta,
although no objection was raised to the invitation to the Rhodesian
Chief Justice to come to London for the purpose of preparing such a
meeting, possibly because he could be regarded for their purposes as
a useful Trojan horse. In extending this invitation, Mr Wilson was still
labouring under the delusion that Sir Hugh Beadle would be welcome
'not only for his sagacity, judgement and humanity, but also as a man
with the courage of a lion'.[5] However, there was no indication that the
Rhodesian Chief Justice had any authorisation from the Smith Government to enter into any commitments on their behalf. On the contrary,
he was acting in his capacity as chairman-designate of the proposed
Royal Commission, while his colleagues in Salisbury were making
the final preparations for the seizure of independence. His contribution
to the negotiations on 9 November was therefore limited to that of a
messenger between the two sides. He was to return to Salisbury at the
conclusion of the talks, authorised to inform his colleagues of the
precise position of the British Government on every aspect of the working of the Commission which could affect the issues still in dispute.
Nevertheless, Mr Wilson still thought it necessary to send a detailed
message to Mr Smith on 10 November, again explaining his Government's position on the outstanding items, adding that Sir Hugh Beadle
would be able to give further clarification on every point.

In spite of Mr Wilson's conviction that what he proposed in his
message met every requirement raised by the Rhodesian Government,
he was nevertheless aware that they were, in his words, 'hell-bent on
illegal and self-destroying action'. With the hope of averting this action,
he arranged for an eleventh-hour telephone conversation with Mr Smith,
on the day the declaration occurred, repeating the offer contained in
his message of the previous day. In this, he went to the very limits of
concession to meet all of the Rhodesian objections to his original

conception of the role of the Royal Commission. He conceded that it would be merely 'seized' of the British objections to the Rhodesian proposals; there would be no British canvassing against those proposals in Rhodesia; the Commission itself would decide whether to make an interim report as to the method of consultation, and whether in their view there was free expression of opinion by the Rhodesian people. Also abandoning their earlier reservations, the British Government would agree to commend to Parliament acceptance of a unanimous report of the Commission which said that the Rhodesian people wanted independence on the basis of the 1961 Constitution. All that was required of the Rhodesian Government in return was an undertaking that they would drop their claim to independence on the basis of that Constitution if the Commission submitted a unanimous report to the effect that it was not acceptable. In the latter circumstances, the British Government would then propose that the Commission be reconstituted with wider terms of reference.

Whether it was Mr Wilson's intention or not, Mr Smith was not required to agree, as he had been the day before, that in the event of an adverse report against the Rhodesian proposals, the Commission should then proceed to devise a new Constitution, giving effect to the principles enunciated by the British Government. This particular point was singled out by Mr Smith as the issue that was causing his Cabinet the most concern. They were apprehensive that if the Commission did not report favourably on their proposals, the British would then be in a position to put their own proposals to the Rhodesian people. Mr Smith claimed that they had always believed that if the Commission did not find in their favour, the alternative would be to continue as they were under the existing Constitution.

While Mr Wilson denied his Government's intention of making any proposals about altering the 1961 Constitution unless the two Governments agreed to set up a Royal Commission to do so, he allowed that there was nothing against the Rhodesians continuing as they were, so long as they understood that there would then be no basis for agreed independence under that Constitution in the absence of a unanimous report by the Commission. In the event of a majority report (which the Rhodesians were obviously prepared to accept because they constituted a majority of the Commission's membership), the British proposal was that both Governments would reserve their position and would have to resume talks again, particularly about reconstituting the Royal Commission.

After a confused confession that his Cabinet members were worried

about 'that thing which has now been brought in' (apparently a reference to their concern about what would follow from the British side if
the Commission were to reject their proposals), Mr Smith concluded by
saying that they were further apart than ever before and that 'this thing
has gone too far'.[6] Within a few hours of this telephone conversation,
the unilateral declaration of independence was announced by Mr Smith.

Notes

1. Mr Nkomo claimed that Mr Wilson had told him in April 1963 that a Labour
Government would change the 1961 Constitution to provide independence under
universal suffrage. See E. Mlambo, *Rhodesia: The Struggle for a Birthright*, 1972,
p. 251.

2. Sir Hugh Beadle was later to be recognised by Mr Wilson as a devious
'go-between' in the post-UDI negotiations. See Marcia Williams, Mr Wilson's
political secretary, *Inside No. 10*, 1972, pp. 158, 165, 246.

3. See Cmnd. 2807, 1965.

4. *Rhodesia Herald*, 31 October 1965.

5. 720 *HC Deb.*, 9 November 1965, col. 29 See Williams, *Inside No. 10*, p. 158.

6. See Cmnd. 2807, 1965, for a record of the negotiations leading up to the
declaration of independence.

4 THE ILLEGAL DECLARATION OF INDEPENDENCE

> 'From the Rhodesian side, it was nothing more than a confirmation of something already existing. For Britain suddenly to take moral stands on issues that she had ignored totally for decades was unreal, absurd.'
>
> Doris Lessing, *Going Home,* 1968.

It was the timing rather than the occurrence of the UDI that had been in doubt. Such a declaration had been threatened for years, but its implementation became increasingly likely as the centre of political power shifted to a new party and a new leader determined to produce the results, whatever the costs or the risks involved. To all intents and purposes, Rhodesia already possessed most of the attributes of independence. But what the Rhodesian Front needed independence for – and this point was not lost on Sir Robert Tredgold, although it was on successive British negotiators – was to control the pace of African advance.[1] It was arguable that they already posssessed such powers in the 1961 Constitution – under which the more realistic estimates for African majority rule were about forty years[2] – and that had they been willing to operate under the *status quo* they would have achieved the same objective for which they were claiming independence. But they were convinced that the retention of the British connection provided the Africans with a last remaining hope of intervention on their behalf. Once they had made the final break with Britain, they would be able to render ineffective the safeguards for the Africans which had been included in the 1961 Constitution in exchange for the withdrawal of Britain's reserve powers. That this was their objective was evident from the changes they introduced in their independence 'Constitution', in particular, the abolition of the requirement of a referendum of the four races voting separately on amendments to the entrenched clauses, and the replacement of the Judicial Committee of the Privy Council by the High Court in Salisbury as the final court of appeal. Retrogressive amendments to the 'Constitution' prohibited by the Five Principles, could thus be enacted by 'legal' means. Any possibility of intervention by the Governor, representing the Crown, was precluded by his replacement by an 'Officer Administering the Government' in the person of Mr Clifford Dupont.

The Soft Option

On the British side, the UDI was received with a sense of shock and outrage. Mr Wilson had remained convinced, up to the last moment, that the tragedy could be averted. After it occurred, his main concern was to prove that he had done everything in his power to prevent it. In one sense, this was indeed true, since he had gone to the very limits of concession, even at the cost of devaluing the Five Principles to which his Government were pledged. But while continuing to hope that something would come out of the prolonged negotiations, he was making no real preparations for the eventuality of their failure, thus sacrificing his only credible option to prevent the threat of a rebellion from becoming a reality.[3] His repeated assertion that the British Government would never use force either to prevent or to reverse an illegal seizure of independence was undoubtedly the greatest single inducement to the Smith regime to try to pull off such a *coup* with the minimum possibility of retaliation.

Why Mr Wilson, a highly skilled negotiator, should have renounced in advance his only effective deterrent has yet to be established. His Tory predecessors, who had to face the threat for a much longer period, had apparently not thought it necessary to declare that they would never resort to force to deter a rebellion in what was still, in law, a British colony. Whether they would have responded differently remains a matter of conjecture. But, ironically, one of the European opponents of the Smith regime, and a fierce critic of the Tory settlement in 1971, maintained that had the Conservatives been in power at the time of the UDI, they would probably have reacted more strongly against a treasonable act and, with the support of the Labour party, might well have resorted to the use of force.[4]

The interpretation advanced by Mr Wilson himself (and later confirmed by Mr Butler) was that his options were limited by the fact that the Conservative Government had already 'sold the pass' by their agreement in 1963 to transfer to Southern Rhodesia the military forces of the former Federation.[5] However, in terms of military power, Rhodesia, although armed with modern and effective equipment, would have been no real deterrent to a British force committed to suppress a rebellion. It was even questionable whether the Smith regime, which had already sacked one chief of the armed forces, could command the military power exercised by men who owed loyalty only to the Queen, men trained in the British tradition that politics are not for soldiers. The same tradition applied to Britain's forces, and to have alleged (as some opponents of the use of force did) that British troops would never consent to fight their own 'kith and kin' was to disregard not only this tradition but all of the instances (including Ireland) in which this very thing had occurred. A suggestion to test the loyalty of the Rhodesian forces by a demand for Mr Smith's arrest had been proposed by Mr Wilson's adviser on security matters, Colonel (later Lord) Wigg, who claimed that his first real difference with Mr Wilson arose over Rhodesia. But even Wigg admitted that he respected the reasons why the question had not been posed, because he shared his colleagues' abhorrence of the use of force, in spite of his own abhorrence of 'capitulation to racially-inspired Fascist force'. Although supporting sanctions, Wigg continued to regard them as a weapon of defence and their choice as the only weapon as 'a soft option'.[6]

It was also possible that Mr Wilson was unduly influenced in his choice of policies by domestic political considerations. The Labour party, coming to power after thirteen years in Opposition, had managed to survive its first year in office with an overall majority of only about four. Some of its backbench members would undoubtedly have been against the use of force: on the basis of pacifist, racial, economic or electoral considerations. There were even a few sympathisers with the Rhodesian cause (such as Reginald Paget and the late Frederick Bellenger), some of whom had been converted by the free public relations tours organised by Voice and Vision on behalf of the Federation Government. It is probably an exaggeration, or even an irrelevance, to suggest that a vote on this issue would have brought the Labour Government defeat,[7] since any decision to take short, sharp military action would have been subject to security considerations and therefore not an issue on which Parliamentary consent would have been sought in advance. Even if Parliamentary approval had become necessary at any stage of the operations, the support of some of the Liberals was assured, since Mr Jeremy Thorpe (party leader after 1967) had advanced the ingenious plan of destroying the road link along which essential supplies to frustrate sanctions would need to flow from South Africa to Rhodesia; and a few sympathetic Tories might well have at least abstained, if not given their outright support, to counterbalance any defections from the Labour majority.

Except for the small but vocal Rhodesia Lobby, whose views were expressed mainly through the medium of the right-wing Monday Club, there was no significant support for the cause of the Smith regime. It is therefore all the more surprising that Mr Wilson seemed to be so pre-occupied with the possibility of Mr Smith's making a favourable impact upon the British public.[8] If anything, they were more likely to be indifferent to a colonial issue which did not directly affect them. This was evident from the rating of the subject of Commonwealth and colonies at the bottom of the poll among the issues of most concern to the voter in recent elections.[9] The racialist policies of the Rhodesian Front might have appealed to the supporters of Mr Enoch Powell and other 'keep Britain white' groups, but these were small and unrepresentative segments of the electorate, in spite of the wide press coverage they received. Nor was the British public likely to regard Mr Smith as a George Washington, an image the Rhodesians had attempted to convey by framing the UDI in the words used by the American colonies in 1776. His treason against the Crown would have been regarded as a serious offence, not likely to arouse a sympathetic hearing from a people with a high respect for tradition and observance of the legal order, and all the more serious for having been unprovoked in any manner by successive British Governments. In any event, the British public would not take kindly to being pushed around by colonials, even white ones, and the illegal seizure of power in a British colony was an affront to British sensibilities on the subject of being a second-rate Power. While the Conservatives might seize upon the issue as a stick with which to beat the Labour Government, not least for their inept handling of the situation, even they had to concede that rebellion against the Crown could never be condoned. So the pressures on Mr Wilson to take the 'soft option' with the rebels were not greatly significant in terms of electoral support. There may have been few votes to gain for the cause of African nationalism, but there were even fewer for the offence of treason against the Crown.

On the other side, Mr Wilson had to take account of pressures from those who believed that Britain's primary responsibility was to fulfil its obligations of trusteeship for the four million Africans. While those who continued to press this view remained in a minority, they constituted a highly articulate and influential group and, as keepers of the party's conscience, a stronghold against the surrender of previous commitments. There were, of course, differences of approach within this camp, and also a shifting membership, which reflected increasing disillusion with the methods pursued by their Government. There were those who took the view from the outset that to negotiate with a racialist regime was in itself an act of betrayal: no agreement acceptable to a white minority could possibly take account of the legitimate aspirations of the African majority. Others, late converts, were only convinced of this fact as Mr Wilson's repeated negotiations proved abortive and as the true nature of the Rhodesian Front's policies — apartheid and police State repression — were revealed to those hitherto unaware of the actual situation in the territory. Within this group there were also differences on tactics: some were uncompromising on the use of force, rejecting any alternative as abject surrender; some were willing to give economic sanctions a chance to bring about the desired result, admittedly more slowly; and others placed their faith in international action — co-operation with the UN, the Commonwealth, the OAU — to achieve diplomatic, economic and, in some cases, military intervention. But the common denominator to which they all subscribed was that Britain should not concede independence until African majority rule had been achieved. The lesson of South Africa in 1909 should be a guide in determining the course for Rhodesia in 1965.

Critics of Mr Wilson's policy on these grounds were not confined to the Labour party. They included a significant portion of the Liberal party, especially the Young Liberals; church groups, such as Christian Action and members of the British and the World Council of Churches; the left and liberal Press, particularly the *New Statesman, Tribune, The Observer* and *The Guardian*; and numerous societies such as the Africa Bureau, Anti-Apartheid, the Anti-Slavery Society, the Movement for Colonial Freedom, and organisations of jurists concerned with the repressive measures of the Rhodesian regime.

An indication of the pressure on Mr Wilson to uphold previous commitments on Rhodesian independence was the message from the Archbishop of Canterbury (Dr Michael Ramsay) on behalf of the British Council of Churches, meeting in Aberdeen on 27 October. While approving the Government's efforts to reach a constitutional settlement in harmony with the Five Principles, the Council assured the Prime Minister that if, notwithstanding all efforts, there should be a breakdown and the Government should judge it necessary to use force to sustain Britain's obligations, then a great body of Christian opinion would support such action.[10] Although Mr Wilson merely conceded that on the question of the use of force the Archbishop must be free to make his own statements,[11] a group of some thirty-five MPs, consisting of a wide cross-section of opinion within the Parliamentary Labour Party[12] and also a few Liberals, sent a message congratulating the Council of Churches on their courageous stand on the Rhodesian conflict. Many of the signatories joined other Labour MPs as supporters of the Movement for Colonial Freedom's statement issued the same week, urging the Government to suspend the Constitution and call a representative conference to establish a democratic system of government in Rhodesia. It warned that if the Government failed to use all necessary force to implement this decision, they would be regarded as conniving in the attempt to impose permanent white minority dictatorship in Rhodesia, and the result would be that the Africans would be left with no alternative but to resort to violence in defence of their own rights.[13]

Mr Wilson confirmed the Government's refusal to consider the use of force when he told the House of Commons, just after the UDI occurred, that they did not contemplate any national, let alone international, action, such as sending what would amount to a major military expedition for the purpose of imposing a constitutional system. Their only commitment was that if the legally constituted Government of Rhodesia (which consisted of the Governor, Sir Humphrey Gibbs) were to seek help in preserving law and order, then they would have to give the fullest consideration to such a request.[14]

What in fact the Labour Government did to meet the situation arising from the UDI was to apply the measures set out in their statement of 27 October 1964. They condemned the declaration as an illegal act, an act of rebellion against the Crown and the Constitution, warning that actions taken to give effect to it would be treasonable. Through the Governor, they informed the Rhodesian 'Prime Minister' and other 'Ministers' that they ceased to hold office and, as private persons, could exercise no legal authority in the colony. All British subjects in Rhodesia were urged to remain loyal to the Queen, and to the law of the land, and to recognise the continuing authority and responsibility for Rhodesia of the British Government. As for the members of the armed forces and the police, on the one hand, and public servants, on the other, they were merely requested, respectively, to refrain from taking up arms in support of the illegal regime or doing any work which would 'help them to pursue their unlawful courses' or 'tend to further the success of the rebellion'. The effect of such vague and confusing instructions was that the civil and military forces would continue to receive their salaries from the illegal regime and to implement policies determined by illegal 'Ministers'. Whether their work constituted 'furthering the success of the rebellion' was never defined and how they would be able to refrain from doing such work, if they were so inclined, was never determined. All that they were told, through the Governor, was that it was their duty to carry on with their jobs and to help maintain law and order, but that they must themselves be the judges of any possible action which they might be asked to take and which would be illegal in itself or illegal in the sense of furthering the rebellion.

Without the co-operation of the civil and military services the Smith regime would have collapsed, but, on the instructions of the British Government, those services would continue to function. It was, of course, impossible to estimate what proportion of the services was prepared to defy the rule of the rebel regime, but those who were had been given no encouragement by the British Government to do so. It would have been possible for the British Government to supply the Governor with the necessary funds for the salaries of the civil servants, as it would have been possible to instruct the armed forces to arrest the rebel 'Government'.[15] But by refusing to contemplate any sort of intervention, they sacrificed the loyalty of those Rhodesians who opposed the illegal action and who were willing and prepared to defy it if they had been given the lead and the means to do so. As it turned out, under the illegal 1965 'Constitution', civil servants and judges could be directed to stay at their posts indefinitely and the Chief Justice and other judges could be required to accept that 'Constitution' on pain of automatic dismissal without compensation.

Some Sanctions

Instead of intervention, the Labour Government proposed a series of measures which would not be 'punitive' in nature nor applied in a spirit of 'recrimination'. As Mr Wilson put it, they were not aiming to inflict pain or hardship; nor were they out to punish or even to deter. Every measure to be taken had been judged by its ability to restore the rule of law and the functioning of a democratic constitution.[16]

The Government's policy was to have no dealings with the rebel regime: the British High Commissioner in Salisbury would be withdrawn, the Rhodesian High Commissioner in London would be asked to leave, and Britain would not recognise passports issued or renewed by the illegal regime. Export of arms, including spares, would be stopped. All British aid would cease, Rhodesia would be removed from the Sterling Area, special exchange control restrictions would be applied, exports of British capital to Rhodesia would not be allowed, Rhodesia would no longer be permitted access to the London capital market and the Export Credits Guarantee Department would give no further cover for exports to Rhodesia. Other economic penalties included the suspension of Rhodesia from the Commonwealth preference area, from the Ottawa Agreement of 1932, governing British trading relations with Rhodesia, and from the Commonwealth Sugar Agreement. There would be a ban on further purchases of Rhodesian tobacco, the chief export product, as well as a ban on the purchase of Rhodesian sugar. The most obvious omission from the list was oil, and on this product, so crucial to the survival of the Rhodesian economy, the Government had no proposals to make. Nor had they made any detailed preparations for such an embargo during all the weeks and months preceding the UDI. Another significant omission was the failure to include the means to undermine the stability of the Rhodesian currency and to produce uncontrolled inflation. While the Exchange Control Act was used to limit the use of balances held in London by official Rhodesian bodies and private residents and also to prohibit entirely British investment in Rhodesia, what it did not do was to limit Rhodesian payments in return for British imports, which could still be paid for from Rhodesian balances (official reserves alone were estimated at £30 million).[17]

While the Labour Government fully intended to seek the support of other countries in the application of these economic measures, Mr Wilson was determined that they should retain control of the situation, get other nations to follow their lead, and avert 'excessive action' by the United Nations. His main concern was that if they were not able to show world opinion, especially those who had it in their power, irrespective of what Britain did, to go in for military action, that they themselves were carrying out effective measures, then they would be inviting the intervention of 'a Red Army in blue berets'.[18] For that reason, their permanent representative at the United Nations, Lord Caradon, was instructed to request a meeting of the Security Council and the Foreign Secretary, Mr Stewart, was to go to New York to present the British case.

The Labour Government's efforts to prevent what they regarded as 'excessive action' by the United Nations were not entirely successful. In proposing their own resolution in the Security Council on 13 November, calling for non-recognition of the UDI and support for their measures of economic retaliation, they found that they could not secure a majority because, in the opinion of most of the other delegations, it did not go far enough. Nor were they prepared to accept an alternative resolution, proposed by the Ivory Coast on behalf of the African States, citing the Rhodesian situation as a threat to peace and calling for comprehensive economic sanctions and the implementation of the objective of one man, one vote. The deadlock was finally broken when a compromise resolution was adopted, but only after the British had entered important reservations and the Foreign Secretary had conceded the extension of their sanctions to include oil.[19] Although consenting to the resolution, the British delegation made it clear that they did not regard the Rhodesian situation as 'a threat to international peace and security' (subject to the enforcement measures of Chapter VII of the Charter) and they could not accept the injunction 'to take immediate measures in order to allow the people of Rhodesia to determine their own future'. As Lord Caradon put the case, while guaranteed and unimpeded progress to majority rule was their confirmed policy, they did not believe that this could, or should, be implemented immediately.[20]

Mock Party Polemics

In British domestic politics, the bipartisan approach to the crisis caused by the UDI was a short-lived one. Although the two main parties were united on condemning the illegal seizure of independence, differences immediately arose over the policies which had brought it about and those which were designed to bring it to an end. Some of these differences were undoubtedly real; others could be attributed to the constitutional practice of the Opposition to oppose, irrespective of the policies upon which the Government chose to embark.

In their attempt to offer an alternative policy, the Conservative Opposition found themselves limited by their previous commitments. They had been strongly opposed to a UDI, they had taken measures to dissuade the Rhodesians from resorting to it and they had condemned it when it occurred. Being responsible for the origin of the Five Principles, upon which both they and their Labour successors had conducted the independence negotiations, they could scarcely renounce their contents. Although they had also been responsible for the establishment of the 1961 Constitution, to which the Labour party had taken strong exception, they had subsequently insisted that it could not be considered (unamended) as a basis for Rhodesian independence.

Once Mr Wilson had denied the Government's intention of resorting to force to impose a constitutional solution, the Conservatives were left with virtually nothing fundamental to oppose. Since they had also warned the Rhodesian Front of the dire economic consequences of a UDI, they were in no position to object to the imposition of sanctions. They could complain that the sort of sanctions they envisaged were not 'punitive', but neither were Mr Wilson's, since they were in the first instance, when it really mattered, neither comprehensive nor mandatory. They could also charge the Labour Government with having failed to negotiate an independence agreement, but they too had failed and over a longer period of time. It was arguable that in the final stage of the negotiations, just before the UDI, Mr Wilson had gone much further in the way of concessions than had his Tory predecessors. Nor could The Conservatives fault the Labour Government on the issue of outside interference, since Mr Wilson had repeatedly made it clear, to the Commonwealth and the United Nations, that the sole responsibility for Rhodesia lay with Britain.

What prompted the Tories to engage in what might be regarded in some instances as mere token opposition was the division of opinion within their own party, a factor that was more in evidence under the leadership of Mr Heath than it had been under his more confident predecessor. On the Rhodesian issue the Tories could be said to be split into three wings, as they showed on the crucial vote on oil sanctions in December 1965. The bulk of the party, the broad centre, was committed to the Five Principles, in varying degrees and interpretations; they were opposed to the use of force by Britain or anyone else; and they were determined that Britain alone should be responsible for the future status of Rhodesia. Their opposition to the Labour Government's policies was on the basis of tactics, timing and party political considerations. Whenever they tended to oppose a policy because they considered it too harsh on the Smith regime, they found their so-called left wing, including some of the Bow Group and PEST (Progressive Economic and Social Toryism) members, refusing to go along, either by abstaining from a vote or actually supporting the Labour Government. Although small in number, this group contained a high proportion of the party's intellectual wing and some of its most experienced members in colonial affairs, such as Lord Alport and Mr Nigel Fisher.

The most vocal and persistent criticism within the Conservative party came from the right — the Rhodesia Lobby, representing the views of the Monday Club and the Anglo-Rhodesian Society. This group, which had economic, financial, ideological or even family ties with the white Rhodesians, consisted of a number of influential peers, such as Salisbury and Colyton, who had served in the Colonial or Commonwealth Office of previous Conservative Governments, and a number of backbench MPs, such as Mr Patrick Wall, Mr Paul Williams, Mr John Biggs-Davison, Mr Julian Amery and Mr Stephen Hastings. Many of them had been active in the 'Katanga Lobby' in the early 1960s, supporting the secessionist Tshombe regime (also backed by the Federation Government) and opposing UN intervention on the side of the Congolese Government. They had also lobbied on behalf of the Europeans in Southern Rhodesia for the establishment of the Federation and for its imposition in the face of opposition from the Africans and from a large section of British opinion, including the Labour and Liberal parties. On this, they were at least in harmony with their party leadership. But on the issue of dissolving the Federation and conceding the right of secession to the Northern Territories, they fiercely attacked their own Ministers, especially Mr Macleod and Mr Butler, and even their Prime Minister, Mr Macmillan, for having allegedly broken their promises to preserve the Federation. Once the Federation was dissolved, they supported the Rhodesian claim to independence, on the basis of the 1961 Constitution, despite the fact that it was never intended as an independence constitution. While they could not, as patriotic, loyal subjects of the Crown, openly support a UDI, they opposed every measure to deter it or to bring it to an end once it had occurred. 'Conciliation, not coercion, peace, not punishment' was their slogan:[21] conciliating the Smith regime at any price, even if the concession of independence violated every one of the Five Principles adhered to by their party leadership. For at least some of the Rhodesia Lobby, a white minority regime in Salisbury was regarded as the saviour of civilisation and Christian values and the main bulwark against the advance of 'communism' from the north. While many of the claims put forward by this group could be dismissed as coming from the lunatic fringe, their membership was sufficiently influential in Tory Establishment circles to make Mr Heath uncomfortably aware of their presence. It was even possible that his tendency to over-react in opposing the Labour Government's policies, often on substance but mainly on tactics, was somehow connected with the pressures from his own right wing. As Mr Wilson said, he himself had only the Rhodesian problem to handle; Mr Heath had to handle his own party.[22]

Zambian Hostage

As a result of the decision of the Victoria Falls conference, the Labour Government had inherited a situation in which they were inhibited from using force against a well-armed Rhodesia but also obliged to assume responsibility for a defenceless Zambia, which had been deprived of the air power that had gone to Southern Rhodesia.[23] Not only was Zambia defenceless in a military sense, it was also economically vulnerable in its dependence on the generating stations of the Kariba dam for the supply of electricity to the Copperbelt. Although Kariba was an international project, the control of the power supply was based on the Rhodesian side of the border and its continuance subject to the decision of the rebel regime. Zambia was also dependent on Rhodesia for coal for its mining enterprises, for the supply routes of Rhodesia Railways and for a variety of manufactured goods not readily obtainable elsewhere. While other routes and other goods could gradually be substituted for the Rhodesian, the essential need was electric power, without which an economy dependent on copper exports would soon be destroyed. Fortunately for Zambia, the British economy would also be seriously disrupted if the copper supply were cut off and for this reason the British Government were obliged to act.

It was not until 1 December 1965 that Mr Wilson was able to announce that the Government had agreed to meet the Zambian President's request for air defences. They were to supply a squadron of Javelin aircraft, complete with radar equipment, and a detachment of the Royal Air Force Regiment to ensure the protection of the aircraft and the installations. In addition, as a precautionary measure, HMS *Eagle* would be cruising off the coast of Tanzania. The simultaneous announcement that the Commonwealth Secretary, Mr Bottomley, was already in Zambia to discuss a further request for a battalion of ground troops was, however, an indication that the Zambians were not by any means satisfied with the extent of the British military commitment.

While the defence negotiations proceeded in Lusaka, Mr Wilson was in the position of having to satisfy the Zambians with assurances of protection, and the British Parliament and public regarding the use of British forces. In a statement to the House of Commons and a television broadcast the same day (1 December), he emphasised that any British units sent to Zambia would go there solely for defensive purposes and would be under unequivocal British command. Although the Government had no evidence of an impending attack from the Rhodesian side, there had been threats from the Smith regime that they could always pull the switch and stop Zambia from getting power. Because of this possibility, they were obliged to take account of Zambia's vulnerability without air cover and of the danger that foreign air forces might be stationed on Zambian soil if Britain's were not made available. While admitting that there had been some difficulties with the Zambians about the provision of British ground forces, Mr Wilson remained convinced that it would have been wrong to provide such forces for the Zambian Government's purpose of 'taking out' the generating stations on the Rhodesian side of the Kariba dam. Nevertheless, the British Government would 'not stand idly by' if Rhodesia cut off supplies to the Copperbelt, because it was in their interest as well as the Zambian that those supplies should continue.

Mr Wilson's warning probably caused more concern to the Conservative party than it did to the Rhodesian Front, since it raised the spectre of British forces engaging their own kith and kin. The Rhodesians tended to regard the RAF as their former war-time comrades (Mr Smith and several of his colleagues had served in the RAF), preferring their presence to that of an unknown and hostile force from the outside world. But the Tories had to weigh up the alternative to a British military presence in Zambia and in doing so concluded that foreign troops stationed there would present an even greater danger. Mr Heath, in a television broadcast replying to Mr Wilson's announcement of the decision, reluctantly agreed that British forces should be sent to Zambia, adding the proviso, which the Government had already made, that those forces should remain under British control and should not violate Rhodesian ground or air space. Although the Conservatives also tried to make an issue of the Government's warning that they would not stand idly by if Rhodesia cut the source of the power supplies to Zambia, Mr Wilson denied that this commitment was in any way inconsistent with their repeated pledge not to use national or international forces in Rhodesia.[24]

More Sanctions

Along with the guarantees to Zambia, Mr Wilson had also announced an extension of the embargoes on tobacco and sugar to include other items, such as asbestos, chromium, iron and steel ores, other metals and a range of foodstuffs, thus bringing the embargoed goods up to 95 per cent of Rhodesia's total exports to Britain. Further financial measures included a halt on all current payments by UK residents to residents in Rhodesia and also on remittances. Contractual obligations, although not repudiated, would not be fulfilled in existing circumstances and money due to residents of Rhodesia would be held back until the restoration of legality. A Reserve Bank of Rhodesia Order would secure control of the assets of Rhodesia's Central Bank held outside Rhodesia, whether in the UK (an estimated £9 million) or elsewhere (an estimated £9.5 million), and a new Board, under the chairmanship of Sir Sydney Caine, would replace the suspended Board. In addition, a Southern Rhodesia (Bank Assets) Order would supplement the exchange control measures introduced on 11 November to bring all Rhodesian accounts under Treasury control by enabling the Treasury also to obtain information about the net balances held by banks in the UK on behalf of Rhodesian banks.

Why it had been necessary to introduce the embargo on Rhodesian exports in two stages and delay the financial controls for three weeks was never explained. Mr Wilson had justified the additional measures by saying that they should be 'quick and sharp rather than a long drawn-out agony in Rhodesia'. But if this were the case, then comprehensive and mandatory sanctions should have been applied immediately and the

Government should have taken measures to ensure that an oil sanction, which was still not included, was made effective. Criticism of the Government's delay ranged from *The Financial Times*,[25] which pointed out that during the interval preceding the controls the Reserve Bank of Rhodesia had been buying up all the gold it could, to the *New Statesman*,[26] which said that if the financial controls had been imposed with the UDI they might have toppled the Smith regime.

The new measures belatedly introduced by the Government left the Tories with the dilemma of either opposing them, thus repudiating their initial approval of economic sanctions, or supporting them, thereby alienating their right-wing members. Mr Heath probably best summed up the majority opinion in the party when he said (in his television broadcast on 1 December) that it was a difficult matter of judgement to decide where the line should be drawn in imposing sanctions. Although his party had not challenged the economic measures taken immediately after the UDI, it had warned the Government that a total economic boycott could have the opposite effect from what was intended: it could harden opinion in Rhodesia against the British Government, not against the Smith regime. To 'go the whole hog', as Mr Heath put it, would only produce a feeling of injustice and leave behind a legacy of bitterness which would make conciliation more difficult in the future. From Mr Heath's statement it was still not clear where the Tories were drawing the line on sanctions, except that they were opposed to their being total, as Butler had confirmed in the Lords, when he said that total economic sanctions had seldom been successful in world history.[27] But if sanctions were not to be 'total', because the effect might be to wreck the Rhodesian economy, they would be an ineffective weapon in bringing about the objective for which they were supposedly designed, namely, the downfall of the illegal regime.

In the interval following the Security Council ban on the supply of oil to the rebel regime (on 20 November), the Labour Government had been preparing contingency plans to ensure the continued supply to Zambia. The Prime Minister, while in America to address the UN General Assembly,[28] had obtained the support of President Johnson both for the enforcement of the embargo and the airlift to assist the Zambians; and support from Commonwealth countries and from NATO allies was also being sought. The Minister of State, Mr Hughes, had the unenviable task of persuading the Zambian Government, still resentful over the British refusal to supply ground troops, that the oil embargo was designed to bring about the downfall of the illegal regime with the minimum possible delay. The Zambians were not likely to be appeased by Mr Hughes' assurances, since it was they who would be obliged to bear the economic hardships resulting from the cut-off of their own supply, as well as the increased charges the Rhodesians were putting on the supply of their coal by Rhodesia Railways, while the sanctions were supposed to be having the effect for which they were designed. Nor would the contingency aid promised by the British compensate for the loss of copper export earnings resulting from the reduction of oil supplies and the restrictions on access routes along which the copper had to be exported.

In an attempt to meet Zambia's immediate needs, the British Government had organised an airlift initially consisting of Britannias of Transport Command to fly oil from Dar es Salaam to Ndola, supported by C130s provided by the Canadian Government and DC7s supplied by the Americans, operating from Elizabethville and Leopoldville to Ndola. The airlift was to be supplemented by an additional supply transported by land routes, but the capacity of these was not yet sufficient to meet Zambia's needs. British assistance in improving the road links was designed to be effective in getting the supplies through within a period of about four months.

While the Zambians criticised the Labour Government for what they regarded as the inadequacy of the British response, the Conservative party was concerned that they might go too far in their commitments to enforce the measures. The embargo, which was finally imposed by Order-in-Council on 17 December, prohibited the import of oil and oil products into the territory of Rhodesia and made it a criminal offence for British nationals to supply or transport oil for Rhodesian use. Official Conservative policy was to give a negative sort of support to the Order, by allowing it to go through unopposed but not committing the party to its continuance, a policy designed to satisfy all sections of the party. The case for that compromise, according to Lord Carrington, was that to do less than impose these sanctions might well create a situation which could get out of control and perhaps entail the mounting of expeditionary forces, the intervention of the United Nations with mandatory sanctions and 'other such catastrophes' which up to then had been avoided. While the Tory leader's persuasions succeeded in limiting the number of rebel Peers voting against the Order to a mere 19, the vote in the Commons entailed a three-way split: some 50 Conservative MPs voted against the Order, a somewhat smaller number (about 30) voted with the Labour Government and the majority abstained.[29]

Although the Government had got their oil measures approved, the means by which they intended to enforce them remained undefined.

In the process of consenting to the oil embargo (at least by abstaining from voting against it), most of the Conservatives had drawn the line at using force to back up the measures. While they were confident that the Government had no intention of striking at the road and rail supply routes from South Africa, they remained concerned about a possible naval blockade of the Portuguese coast, and its escalation to include the sea routes of South Africa. Denials of any such intention were made by the Prime Minister and the Leader of the Labour Peers, Lord Longford, although both left the question open by such qualifications as 'not at this stage' or 'not unilaterally'. While Mr Wilson was confident that the ban could be made effective by a boycott by Middle East oil producing countries, together with the action the Government had taken with oil distributing companies under their own control, if there were any 'seepages or leakages', as he put it, the Government would have to consider such violations in consultation with the other countries involved. They might also have to take action to make it illegal for the pipeline from Beira to be used in so far as it was on Rhodesian soil. But Mr Wilson was convinced that if the embargo failed, it would be because it was not sufficiently co-ordinated on the international level. In that case, he predicted, the matter would then be raised at the United Nations, and if there were a decision under Chapter VII of the Charter proposing that a couple of frigates be placed outside Beira to stop oil tankers going through, that would happen by international decision. The Labour Government did not themselves propose to seek such a resolution and they certainly did not propose to take unilateral action to blockade Beira.[30] Within four months of Mr Wilson's statement, the Labour Government were seeking United Nations endorsement for the blockade of Beira.

Zambia, although most directly concerned, was not the only African or Commonwealth country to doubt that the additional economic measures imposed by the Labour Government would bring about the downfall of the rebel regime. A growing feeling of dissatisfaction with the methods by which Britain was meeting the Rhodesian crisis prompted a number of Commonwealth leaders to initiate a special conference of Prime Ministers for the sole purpose of discussing the situation in Rhodesia. Through the offices of the Commonwealth Secretariat, the meeting was convened in Lagos on 11 January 1966, under the chairmanship of the Nigerian Prime Minister, Sir Abubakar Tafewa Balewa.

The Labour Government could not have welcomed the prospect of being put in the dock for their shortcomings in dealing with the Rhodesian question. Nor could they look forward to another inquest only six months after the last. However, they could not have risked offending most of the Commonwealth leaders by refusing to attend, especially when the co-operation of the African States was essential to the success of the sanctions policy they envisaged. They had already experienced the severance of diplomatic relations with two Commonwealth States — Ghana and Tanzania — observing the OAU resolution to do so by 15 December, and relations with Zambia were strained by the dispute over defence support and contingency aid. Although Mr Wilson had reluctantly agreed to attend, as he explained it, in order to hear the views and understand the tremendous passions of other Commonwealth leaders, his Government had already decided their policy and could never agree with the admittedly large number of Commonwealth countries favouring the use of force to bring down the rebel regime.

With positions declared in advance there was not much hope of an agreed solution coming out of the conference. If Mr Wilson went to Lagos to understand the 'tremendous passions', they were certainly evident in the sharp attacks on Britain's refusal to resort to force, which came most notably from the Sierra Leone Prime Minister, Sir Albert Margai, and the Uganda President, Dr Milton Obote. Zambia, whose President and Foreign Minister did not attend, took a more restrained line, being in no position to implement a sanctions programme that would have wrecked its already strained economy. Even the Nigerian chairman, Sir Abubakar, whose role was essentially that of a mediator, spoke for most of the delegates when he insisted that other measures be considered if economic sanctions proved to be ineffective. Mr Wilson's defence was to play for time, a tactic to which he was to resort at subsequent meetings of the Commonwealth leaders. In a statement which he must have regretted ever making, he insisted that, on the expert advice available to him, the cumulative effects of the economic and financial sanctions might well bring the rebellion to an end 'within a matter of weeks rather than months'. While the other Prime Ministers had misgivings about this optimistic forecast, they agreed to the appointment of a committee to review the effect of the sanctions and recommend measures on enforcement. If, however, the sanctions did not succeed in their objective within a period of six months, then the Commonwealth leaders would reconvene to consider further action.

In exchange for the time gained Mr Wilson had to make a number of concessions on the future status of a Rhodesia presumably reduced to submission by the sanctions programme. The first was that a period of direct rule would be established (a policy that Mr Wilson had severely circumscribed when challenged by the Tories), in preparation for the holding of a constitutional conference. That conference, representing all sections of Rhodesian opinion, would be for the purpose of establishing a new constitution on the basis of majority rule. Other objectives endorsed by the meeting were that those detained for political purposes should be released, political activities should be free from intimidation, and repressive and discriminatory laws should be repealed. The principle that one man, one vote was the very basis of democracy and should be applied to Rhodesia, agreed at the previous conference, was also reiterated without British dissent.[31] However, the implementation of these policies was dependent upon the collapse of the Smith regime as a result of the sanctions measures, because none of them would be acceptable to the Rhodesian Front. And the alternative, to impose them by force, had already been ruled out by the British Prime Minister in his retort to the Sierra Leone Prime Minister on the difficulties of mounting an invasion against a well-armed and landlocked country.

Notes

1. Sir Robert Tredgold, *The Rhodesia that Was My Life,* 1968, p. 243.
2. See Claire Palley, *The Constitutional History and Law of Southern Rhodesia*, 1966, pp. 416-24.
3. See R.H.S. Crossman, *Diaries of a Cabinet Minister, 1964-66*, vol 1, 1975, pp. 356, 377-9.
3. See Judith Todd, daughter of the former Prime Minister, in *The Right To Say No*, 1972, p. 39.
5. 270 *HL Deb.*, 15 November 1965, cols. 262-3.
6. Lord Wigg, *George Wigg*, 1972, p. 326.
7. As Richard Hall, *The High Price of Principles*, 1969, p. 122, suggested. Mr Wilson claimed that if the Government had decided to intervene by force of arms, Mr Heath would have 'led a united party, and almost certain won majority support in the country'. (*The Labour Government, 1964-1970*, 1971, p. 181.)
8. See Marcia Williams, *Inside No. 10*, 1972, p. 372.
9. See the Nuffield College election studies, 1959 to 1964.
10. British Council of Churches, *Rhodesia and Ourselves*, November 1965.
11. 718 *HC Deb.*, 4 November 1965, cols. 1232-3.
12. Signatories ranged from Mr Eric Heffer on the left to Mrs Shirley Williams on the right.
13. *East Africa and Rhodesia*, 4 November 1965. The same week the British Government were urged by the United Nations to take all necessary measures, including military force, to meet the threat to international peace and security arising from the situation in Rhodesia. See General Assembly resolution 2022 (XX), adopted 5 November 1965 by 82-9, with 18 abstentions, and the UK not participating in the vote.
14. 720 *HC Deb.*, 11 November 1965, col. 360; 12 November 1965, col. 538.
15. As Wigg suggested, *George Wigg*, p. 326.
16. 720 *HC Deb.*, 12 November 1965, col. 632.
17. *New Statesman*, 19 November 1965.

18. 720 *HC Deb.*, 12 November 1965, col. 637.

19. Security Council Resolution 217 (1965), adopted 20 November 1965 by 10-0, with one abstention (France).

20. Security Council, *Official Records*, 20th Session, 1263rd Meeting, 17 November 1965; 1265th Meeting, 20 November 1965.

21. The views of this group were given wide coverage in the weekly *East Africa and Rhodesia*, edited by Mr F.S. Joelson.

22. 722 *HC Deb.*, 21 December 1965, col. 1912.

23. See Cmnd. 2093. Six aircraft – four Dakotas and two Pembrokes – were transferred to Northern Rhodesia, according to Mr Duncan Sandys, then Commonwealth Secretary. (684 *HC Deb.*, 21 November 1963, col. 124.)

24. 721 *HC Deb.*, 1 December 1965, cols. 1437-9.

25. 18 November 1965.

26. 10 December 1965.

27. 270 *HL Deb.*, 15 November 1965, col. 264.

28. See *Official Records*, 20th Session, 1397th Meeting, 16 December 1965. In his address, he reaffirmed that Britain did not intend to use force nor to impose majority rule. Most of the African delegations walked out in protest.

29. See 271 *HL Deb.*, 22 December 1965, col. 1148. 722 *HC Deb.*, 21 December 1965.

30. 722 *H.C. Deb.*, 20 December 1965, cols. 1691-1701.

31. *Commonwealth Prime Ministers' Meeting 1966, Final Communiqué*, Lagos, 12 January 1966, Cmnd. 2890.

5 DEALING WITH ILLEGALITY

'Rhodesia's future course cannot be negotiated with the regime which illegally claims to govern the country.'

Harold Wilson, 25 January 1966.

During the months following the Commonwealth Prime Ministers' meeting the Labour Government began to probe the possibilities of negotiating with the rebel regime. The initial attempt, made at the conclusion of the Lagos meeting, proved to be an abortive one. The pretence devised was that the Commonwealth Secretary, before returning from Lusaka, where he and Mr Wilson had been discussing the application of sanctions, would visit Rhodesia to confer with the Governor on the developments arising out of the Commonwealth meeting. The possibility that Mr Bottomley would also have talked to Mr Smith could not be ruled out, because of Mr Wilson's earlier statement that he (Mr Smith) was free to make any proposition to the Governor to bring the existing situation to an end.[1] As it turned out, the occasion did not arise, because the Smith regime chose to place what the Labour Government regarded as 'intolerable' conditions on the visit, which would involve recognition of the regime. In addition, they were not prepared to guarantee his safety during the visit, an assurance that became relevant after the regime's expulsion of three visiting Labour MPs, whose address to an 'illegal' meeting on 12 January had ended in violence to their person committed by Rhodesian Front vigilantes. In any case, the atmosphere for the proposed Ministerial visit was not improved by the speech of the 'Minister' of Internal Affairs, Mr William Harper, on 13 January, in which he said that the name of the British Government must be made 'to stink in the nostrils of the people of the world'.[2]

In place of Mr Bottomley's visit to Salisbury, the Rhodesian Chief Justice, Sir Hugh Beadle, came to London on 18 January, presumably as á result of arrangements made by the Governor. At that time, Sir Hugh was still regarded as a useful link between the illegal regime and the British Government, so his opinion was being sought for an assessment of how the Rhodesians were standing up under the impact of sanctions. But since he was in fact a supporter, albeit a furtive one, of the Rhodesian Front, he was likely to plead the cause of opening negotiations, which was what the regime were hoping for as a means of ending the sanctions, and to emphasise that there was no alternative political force with whom negotiations could be held.

Similar advice to get the talks started came from the Conservative party, some of whose members had been to Salisbury and returned convinced that the Smith regime were firmly in the saddle and unlikely to be toppled by any internal opposition. The party leader, Mr Heath, advised of these views, told a meeting of Commonwealth correspondents in London on 24 January that the Government should talk to anyone in Rhodesia who was prepared to return to the path of constitutional development, including Mr Smith and his party. Mr Heath was equally adamant that there could be no question of direct rule, either from the Commonwealth Office or from the Governor in Salisbury, because this would mean to all Rhodesians a set-back of forty years of progress towards independence. Instead, he proposed a return to legality based on the 1961 Constitution, with amendments necessary to reassure the Europeans that there was no threat of immediate majority rule and the Africans that there would be steady improvement and no retrogression on what had been achieved thus far. What Mr Heath seemed most concerned about was that the suspicion and bitterness evident among the Europeans would increase as a result of the application of the economic measures — a return to the case that sanctions should not be punitive or vindictive.

Although Mr Smith had repeatedly said, to visiting British politicians, to the Rhodesian public and to the Labour Government through the medium of the Chief Justice, that he was ready to reopen negotiations, no proposals were put forward as a basis and no terms, other than the retention of the independence illegally obtained, were mentioned. The suspicion and bitterness which so concerned Mr Heath were undoubtedly present, certainly among the members of the Rhodesian Front, which still commanded overwhelming European support, but so were a sort of Dunkirk spirit, a false bravado and what Mr Wilson once called an enormous capacity for self-deception. Having taken the plunge, the Rhodesian leaders could not afford to be seen to be surrendering to the former colonial Power. This was evident from the Harper outburst and from Mr Smith's television broadcasts (on 17 January and 10 February), in which he justified both the expulsion of the three 'extreme left-wing protégés of Mr Wilson' and the rejection of the Bottomley visit other than on the basis of recognition of the illegal regime; although on the latter he made the quite valid point that for the British Government to request the visit implied a far greater acknowledgement of the regime than the meeting of the Commonwealth Secretary at the airport by an illegal 'Minister'.[3]

The Carrot and the Stick

Mr Wilson's response to the various pressures upon him was marked by a certain degree of ambiguity. On the one hand, he was obliged to take account of the Commonwealth Prime Ministers' joint decision for firmer action against the rebel regime and, on the other, the forces both in Britain and Rhodesia urging the path of reconciliation. In an effort to meet these competing claims, he proposed, within the same week, a scheme for reopening the negotiations as well as a series of measures to extend the prevailing economic sanctions.

In a statement to Parliament on 25 January 1966, Mr Wilson set out the conditions under which Rhodesia could look forward to a return to constitutional rule and eventual independence. As he had said the previous December, while there could be no question of negotiating with the illegal regime ('legalise the swag of an illegal action'), the Governor was authorised to receive from the regime any proposals about the means by which the rebellion could be brought to an end. On the controversial issue of direct rule, to which the Tories took strong exception, he substituted the term 'interim government': an executive body which would be formed by the Governor, responsible to him, comprising the widest possible spectrum of public opinion of all races and constituting a representative government for reconstruction. Legislative power would be non-existent, because the alternative would be a Rhodesian Front parliament or, as Mr Wilson described it, a 'racialist' or 'semi-Fascist' parliament providing the legislative side of a representative government. The first responsibility of the interim government would be the maintenance of law and order, with the police and military forces coming under the direct control of the Governor. After this stage, the course of constitutional development towards independence would be based on the implementation of the Five Principles, to which Mr Wilson added a sixth (as a concession to European opinion), namely, that, regardless of race, there would be no oppression of majority by minority or of minority by majority. The means he envisaged for his scheme was a Royal Commission, acting in preparation for the constitutional conference which would be necessary before independence could be achieved.[4]

The other side of the Labour Government's offensive against the Rhodesian regime was an extension of the economic sanctions undertaken by Britain. The measures announced on 31 January 1966 had the effect of banning the remaining 5 per cent of British imports from Rhodesia, extending licensing control to exports of all goods from Britain to Rhodesia and blocking the illegal regime's efforts to raise credit. The latter measure gave the British Government the right to repudiate any debts of the regime incurred by raising credit overseas. It was also directed towards discouraging the purchase of the so-called independence bonds (the 4½ per cent tax-free, three-year, £1 bonds) that the regime were preparing to issue within a matter of days. The other measures, relating to the prohibition of trade, added little to the existing sanctions programme. In total, the ban accounted for some £30 million worth of British goods (on the basis of the 1965 export figures), and the three measures taken together amounted to 'tidying up' the restrictions already imposed by the Board of Trade and the Treasury.[5]

But the really crucial economic sanctions had still to come from Zambia, and so long as the British Government were not prepared to arrange for alternative supplies for the Zambian economy, the Smith regime could continue to rely on a captive market. The other significant loopholes, which were to widen increasingly as the other outside sources dried up, were the routes for the flow of exports, including oil, from South Africa and the Portuguese colonies. These the Labour Government also had no intention of disturbing. Nor would they support measures to sever cable, telephone, postal and radio links with Rhodesia, when the possibility of applying them was considered by the Commonwealth Sanctions Committee and the United Nations Security Council.

Not surprisingly, the Labour Government's new peace proposals were totally unacceptable to the Rhodesian Front. They were not prepared to acknowledge the illegality of their independence by renouncing it; and, as they had indicated before the UDI, they would not participate in either a broad-based government or a representative constitutional conference. It was difficult to believe that Mr Wilson, in making these proposals, especially the provision for 'interim rule' by the Governor, could not have been aware of their likely reception by the Rhodesians. It was possible that he was at this time convinced, as a result of the 'expert' advice of his civil service (Department of Economic Affairs officials were alleged to have had a dominant effect on policy),[6] that the Smith regime, about to collapse from the effect of the economic sanctions, would accept any terms that would allow them to participate, even in a less dominant role, in a future Rhodesian government. If he had then intended to negotiate with the Rhodesian Front, he would hardly have referred to their 'Parliament' as 'racialist' or 'semi-Fascist', irrespective of the accuracy of the terminology, nor described such negotiations as 'legalising the swag'. Undoubtedly, Mr Wilson was being provoked by the efforts of the Rhodesia Lobby to minimise the effect of the sanctions and to get recognition for the claims of the rebels. This was evident from his complaint that supporters of the Smith regime had intervened in the Hull by-election with leaflets printed in Rhodesia, and his reference to a meeting of the Monday Club's Rhodesia Emergency Committee as 'under Fascist auspices'.[7] However, there was a marked change in his attitude to the Rhodesian Front after his statement at the end of January 1966: references to the fascist elements were quietly dropped and the refusal to negotiate with the 'burglars' was got around by devising other means of contact with the illegal regime.

The division between the Labour Government and the Opposition over the extension of the sanctions measures arose mainly because of the Conservative party's concern that the negotiating possibilities would be diminished as the economic measures were increased. Having failed to get the Government's agreement to what amounted to unconditional negotiations, the Conservatives decided to send their spokesman on Commonwealth affairs, Mr Selwyn Lloyd, to Salisbury to investigate the possibilities of reopening the talks. His optimistic report on the situation did not seem to have been affected by the fact that during his visit the regime assumed sweeping powers of censorship over the Rhodesian Press and issued new sets of emergency regulations to control economic activities. In addition, he was not allowed to see the African nationalist leaders, Mr Nkomo and Rev. Sithole, because the security forces advised against it, the 'Minister' of Justice feared that the press coverage of the visit would raise the prestige of the African leaders and Mr Smith discounted them as of no consequence. Nevertheless, Mr Lloyd maintained that nothing he had seen suggested that Rhodesia was a police State. He returned convinced that if the situation were handled carefully, a settlement could be reached.[8]

But when it came to the actual terms on which an agreement was possible, Mr Lloyd had virtually nothing new or hopeful to offer. His agenda for the talks included most of the points already covered by the Five Principles — a blocking mechanism, more African seats, widening the franchise, safeguarding the entrenched clauses, 'movement' against racial discrimination and, again, a collateral treaty.[9] There was, however, no indication whatever that the Smith regime were prepared to implement any of these principles. Mr Lloyd's undue optimism was apparently based on his conviction that once the Labour Government's offer of 25 January were withdrawn, especially the provisions for direct rule from Whitehall (which it didn't include) and a constitutional conference, success was bound to follow. If nothing else, the Lloyd visit had the effect of uniting the divergent wings of the Conservative party, in itself an important achievement with the general election less than a month away. All were able to agree that negotiations with the Smith regime should be pursued, even if they differed on the nature of that regime and the application of the sanctions measures.

Electioneering

The differences between the two major parties on the Rhodesian issue, which appeared to have narrowed down to the question of whether negotiations should be conditional or unconditional (but which really involved the fundamental question of recognising an illegal action), were not sufficiently clear to have become an election issue of any significance. In fact, according to the Nuffield election study,[10] there was no evidence in the constituency reports or the opinion polls that Rhodesia was a vote changing issue. However, the UDI had made some impact on the British electorate and this accounted for a general awareness that Rhodesia was a problem that would require the attention of a future government. In 1964, the threat of a UDI had been deferred and both parties were on record as having warned the Rhodesians against illegal action. By 1966, UDI was a reality and the issue for those among the electorate concerned about it was which party was best equipped, on the basis of previous commitments, policies and experience to deal with it. On this score, Mr Wilson had most of the advantages: as Prime Minister, he had been in the driver's seat. His televised performances on the subject had conveyed an impression of confidence in handling the complex situation, of firmness in dealing with rebellion against the Crown, of prudence in not risking the lives of British forces and of humanitarian concern for the African majority. By refusing to negotiate with an illegal regime, he could impress those who didn't like to see Britain 'pushed around' by 'colonials', as well as those opposed to the appeasement of a white settler minority.

With a virtual monopoly of all the arguments, the Labour party left the Tories with little to say about Rhodesia in the electoral campaign. Mr Heath could accuse the Government of 'sweeping Rhodesia under the carpet' by not mentioning it, but since the electorate were not much interested anyway, this approach was not very productive. Sir Alec Douglas-Home and Mr Lloyd could push the Tory slogan 'talks now', but since they had no suggestions of what to talk about, this line was also not likely to sway any voters. On the contrary, it provided Mr Wilson with the opportunity of accusing the Tories of aiding and abetting the rebels by giving them the hope that a Conservative government in power would ensure their independence. Nor could the Tories make a real issue out of the sanctions measures. Since they had officially supported their application, they were in no position to call for their abolition; they could only argue that their purpose should not be to destroy the Rhodesian economy. What was left to dispute, so far as the Rhodesian issue was concerned, was the question of who was responsible for the prevailing situation. Even on this aspect, the Labour party had all the advantages on its side: there was no basis on which it could be accused of double-dealing or not speaking clearly with regard to Rhodesia's future status. It had been in Opposition when the Central African Federation was established and therefore could not be held responsible for its imposition, maintenance or dissolution. Nor could it have been involved in any of the Rhodesian claims of having obtained promises of independence from successive British Ministers. The Tories, on the other hand, having been in power when the events in question occurred, were bound to inherit any of the blame for what happened in central Africa. For the Conservatives, the irony of the situation was that they were in the position of having denied to the Europeans who dominated the Federation — the Huggins, Welensky, Whitehead Establishment — the very concessions that they were now all too ready to offer to the European extremists in the Rhodesian Front.[11]

Although the Labour party had no previous governmental commitments on Rhodesia to live down, where it could be faulted on grounds of inconsistency was on its pledge to implement African majority rule, maintained throughout the years of Opposition and then quietly buried by Mr Wilson and his Government upon assuming office. But since there was no significant African constituency in Britain, this reversal of policy could not be responsible for the loss of many votes, except among those who had fought consistently for the cause of African liberation, and even they were more likely to abstain than to switch their vote to a party advocating unconditional negotiations with a regime committed to perpetuate white supremacy.

Towards the end of the electoral campaign, the remaining issue between the two parties — 'talks now' — suddenly ceased to have any real significance as a result of Mr Wilson's revelation of having stolen the clothes of his opponents. While Labour party spokesmen (including Mr Bottomley) were still heartily denouncing Tory schemes for unconditional negotiations with the rebels, Mr Wilson disclosed to a press conference on 28 March that there had been a representative of the Commonwealth Office (Mr Duncan Watson) in Salisbury during the preceding few weeks (later clarified as 'a fortnight in March') to whom the Rhodesians could have expressed any views had they really wished to talk. However, while he was there, ostensibly for the purpose of dealing with the threat to expel the deputy High Commissioner (Mr Stanley Fingland) for alleged 'espionage activities', he had been informed by senior officials of the regime that they were not interested in talks with the British Government. This response had been confirmed by Mr Smith's statement, in a broadcast on 27 March, that it was now too late to hold talks; and, according to Mr Wilson, it made nonsense not only of what the Tories had said about negotiations during the election, but of 'the vague lead produced by Mr Selwyn Lloyd'.[12]

Thus the Labour party's volte-face on the issue of negotiations with the regime, although not officially announced until nearly a month after the election, had actually begun during the electoral campaign, when their official representative was empowered with full governmental authority to open talks with Mr Smith or any other member of his regime willing to participate. Their refusal to do so at that time may well have been attributed to what Mr Wilson called 'election fever' in Rhodesia, an emotional reaction against doing anything that might contribute to the return of the Labour party. In rejecting talks with the Labour Government, the Rhodesians were awaiting the verdict of the British electorate. If the Conservatives were returned to power, they were committed to reopen negotiations without conditions.

With their overwhelming electoral victory — a majority of 100 seats — the Labour Government now had a free hand to implement any policies which might have failed to survive on the basis of their former precarious majority. Their only commitments, in terms of an electoral mandate, were to the observance of the Five Principles and the implementation of the limited sanctions measures. Although the possibility of negotiating independence with the rebel regime had been qualified by an insistence upon a return to legality, this condition had apparently been modified during the electoral campaign, when talks were being attempted. The Labour Government were therefore faced with the choice of pursuing these talks with an illegal regime, or refusing to negotiate unless the rebels agreed to renounce their illegal status. While the latter possibility receded with every bellicose statement coming out of Salisbury, the choice became an increasingly unreal one. If the Labour Government could not get the rebels back to legality without the use of force, which they had already ruled out as a policy option, their only alternative was to tighten the screws of sanctions until the Rhodesians were prepared to make the concessions they were still so confidently denying. Consequently, the major weakness of the sanctions effort, the leakage of oil, was attacked on both the national and international fronts. But, at the same time, the talks begun by the Commonwealth Office representative were quietly pursued (Mr Hennings, replacing the expelled Mr Fingland, was authorised to follow up the initiative that Mr Watson had undertaken) and without any prior condition of a return to legality.

Blockading Oil

Within a week of their return to office the Labour Government were confronted with the problem of having to take immediate action to prevent a considerable shipment of oil reaching Rhodesia by way of the Portuguese port of Beira. Since the application of the oil embargo the previous December, the 'seepages and leakages' which Mr Wilson had then predicted might destroy the whole purpose of the sanctions had become an increasingly blatant reality. The South Africans had made no secret of their support for their beleaguered allies: 'friendship' lorries carrying 'gifts' of oil for Rhodesia, at a price, were observed daily on the route to the border between the two countries at Beitbridge. And the Portuguese, who continued to ship oil by rail from Mozambique, were engaged in building storage tanks in Beira in preparation for the arrival of new supplies by sea. Most of Rhodesia's oil supplies, prior to the UDI, had come through the port of Beira, from which the pipeline controlled by the Anglo-Portuguese Lonrho subsidiary, CPMR, supplied the Feruka refinery near Umtali, and also through the port of Lourenço Marques. Since the overland routes devised to beat the oil embargo were excessively costly and would not in any case have been sufficient to meet Rhodesia's long-term needs, the supplies received by sea through the Mozambique ports remained essential.

The Labour Government, aware that the entire oil sanctions programme would collapse if these routes were not cut off, had sent naval vessels to patrol the Indian Ocean, but they had no legal authority to intercept the ships of other nations bound for the ports of Mozambique. Nor had British diplomatic efforts with the South African and Portuguese Governments yielded any results. Both countries had rejected appeals to end their trade with Rhodesia and both had voted against every United Nations resolution on the subject. Since the Labour Government had been concerned throughout with preventing the extension of any United Nations sanctions against either of these countries, the pressure that they were able to exert was minimal. Furthermore, South Africa was one of their best trading and investment partners (then worth over £265 million of the former and an estimated

£1,000 million of the latter) and Portugal was one of their 'oldest allies'.

The crisis over the application of the oil sanctions began at the end of March 1966, with reports of the approach of a Greek-registered oil tanker, *Joanna V*, carrying crude oil to Beira destined for the Rhodesian refinery at Feruka. A second tanker, the *Manuela*, was also reported to be heading for Beira for the same purpose. This was the first test case: if these deliveries were allowed to get through there would be no limit to the amount of oil available to the Rhodesians in the future, since other tankers were already chartered and the CPMR Beira-Umtali pipeline still remained open on the decision of the Lonrho Company's Portuguese directors. For the Labour Government the immediate necessity, if they were not to lose face over their failure to implement the oil sanction, was to stop the tankers from unloading at Beira, and to do this they needed legal authorisation from the United Nations to intercept, since the resolution of 20 November 1965 was not mandatory. However, they were also faced with the problem of their own previous commitments, made at the time of the enactment of the oil sanction the previous December, not to impose a naval blockade around Beira and not to seek a Security Council resolution, under Chapter VII of the Charter, to implement it. Their decision was to take immediate action and to justify it later. An emergency meeting of the Security Council was called for on 7 April, and the move was defended by the claim that a resolution was forced upon Britain by other countries taking the initiative at the United Nations.[13] In a sense, the claim was a valid one, as it was throughout the years of the Rhodesian crisis, when successive British Governments were forced into action, mainly of a defensive nature, as a result of the initiative of other countries and with the objective of retaining control of the situation.

The Labour Government finally succeeded in getting their own limited commitment confirmed by the Security Council, but only after they had made it clear in advance that they would accept no broader one. The urgent meeting which they had requested on 7 April was delayed for two days, while the *Manuela* was nearing Beira, and while the president of the Security Council (the delegate from Mali) was consulting other African States on the resolution. The African members of the Council, in an effort to widen the scope of the prohibitions in the British resolution, proposed a series of amendments to extend the sanctions measures to include, among other things, the severance of postal, radio and other communications. All of these were defeated, by failing to obtain the required number of affirmative votes, and the British resolution was adopted by 10-0, with five abstentions. The

Labour Government thus had their authorisation to prevent 'by the use of force if necessary' the arrival at Beira of ships carrying oil destined for Rhodesia, and the Portuguese Government were warned not to receive at Beira oil destined for Rhodesia or permit oil to be pumped through the pipeline from Beira to Rhodesia.[14] However, the prohibition applied only to Beira; nothing was said of oil going to Rhodesia from Lourenço Marques, or indeed from any other route devised by the South Africans, although one of the African amendments (on which Britain had abstained) called on South Africa to take all measures to prevent a supply of oil to Rhodesia.

Within two days, the Labour Government informed the Security Council of action taken by the British Navy to prevent the tanker *Manuela* from reaching Beira. The *Joanna V*, having arrived at Beira, was not allowed to discharge her oil, and the CPMR pipeline to Feruka was temporarily closed down, with financial compensation to the company provided by the British Government. The Rhodesians were duly annoyed, as Mr Smith indicated in his broadcast on 16 April, accusing the Labour Government of breaking their promises not to use force, not to blockade Mozambique ports and not to refer the matter to the United Nations. They retaliated by closing down Rhodesia House in London and instructing the British High Commission in Salisbury to close down and repatriate the staff. But the latter was mainly for show, since Mr Smith was to announce ten days later that the decision to close down the 'embassies' (sic) in Salisbury and London did not mean that they were not prepared to talk.[15] Also for show was his claim that a new prospect of oil was under investigation, but that for security reasons he was unable to release any further information.

Parley with a Burglar

Mr Wilson, too, was ready for talks. When he made the announcement on 27 April, he claimed that what had been decisive in creating the situation in which talks could now take place had been the oil sanctions introduced in December and the action taken at Beira. What he did not explain was who had initiated the talks, although he was later to tell the Commonwealth Prime Ministers' conference in September 1966 that the discussions had started on Mr Smith's initiative,[16] perhaps with the hope of exonerating himself from the charge of encouraging negotiation with an illegal regime. But what he implied by linking the two events was that the limited measures taken by the Government to enforce the oil embargo had been so successful in their impact that the Smith regime had no alternative but to sue for peace. While this was obviously not the case, since oil supplies continued to come through the other sources organised by the South Africans and the Portuguese, there was a noticeable change in Mr Smith's attitude to the hitherto irreconcilable issue of conditional or unconditional negotiations when he stated in the Rhodesian 'Parliament', on the eve of Mr Wilson's announcement that talks would begin, that he had never laid down pre-conditions for talks. But he was also careful to reassure his European supporters that this did not mean that they would have to give ground: he would not insist that Mr Wilson acknowledge their independence and Mr Wilson would not insist that they give it up.[17]

Whether Mr Wilson had also dropped his condition for opening the talks — a return to legality — never emerged from his somewhat contra-dictory and at times apologetic statement to Parliament on the subject. If he had in fact done so, his attack on the Conservatives for having shifted their ground was a diversionary, if not meaningless, tactic. What he really had to contend with were his own previous commit-ments on the issue of dealing with the illegal regime: not to 'parley with Mr Smith', not to negotiate with 'a burglar', not to 'legalise the swag' and not to allow the continuance of a 'semi-Fascist Parliament' in Rho-desia. He was still saying on 21 April, the day before the Governor had arranged a meeting between Mr Smith and the two British officials, Mr Oliver Wright and Mr John Hennings, that, while there was a great deal they were prepared to forgive and forget, they were not prepared to legalise an act of rebellion against the Crown. Four months later, the talks were still going on and Mr Wilson was still maintaining that his Government could not have official dealings with an illegal regime, although they were willing to have these informal talks to determine on what basis they could get a return to constitutional rule.[18]

The 'talks about talks', as they became known, opened in London on 9 May 1966 and continued intermittently in Salisbury from the beginning of June until the latter part of August. The Rhodesians were represented by Sir Cornelius Greenfield, Chief Economic Adviser and responsible for co-ordinating the measures against sanctions; Mr Gerald Clarke, Secretary to the 'Prime Minister'; and Mr Stanley Morris, Chair-man of the Public Service Board and responsible for having arranged the *indaba* of the Chiefs. On the British side were officials of the Common-wealth Office and the Foreign Office, including Mr Duncan Watson, in addition to Mr Wright. Since the meetings were confidential, the only indication of how they were proceeding came from periodic statements from the two Prime Ministers during the intervals between the negotia-ting sessions. There was certainly no evidence of any progress from these sources. On the contrary, Mr Wilson's report to Parliament on 5 July stressed the Government's difficulties in reaching a solution that would be acceptable not only to the Rhodesian people and to the British Parliament but to the general community of nations. Throughout these months, he complained, they had been 'carrying the can' and sheltering Rhodesia from world opinion while remaining powerless, in terms of their ability to get the solution that they considered to be right.[19]

From the Rhodesian side, no progress was reported either. Mr Smith utilised the interval between the talks to reassure his supporters that they would never surrender and to tell the British to keep their 'cold, charitable shelter' to themselves. He even went so far as to reaffirm his position that there would never be African rule in his life-time, when he told the Rhodesian Front congress on 6 August that he was determined to keep Rhodesia in the hands of 'civilised' people and 'not only for the foreseeable future'.[20] An additional blow came with the regime's decision to introduce on 29 August the Constitution Amendment Bill, containing powers of preventive detention and making changes in the specially entrenched clauses of the 1961 Constitution. With this development, the British officials were instructed to conclude the talks and return to London. Responsibility for the breakdown was denied by Mr Smith, however, on the grounds that the British Government had already known of the Rhodesian Front plan to amend the Constitution, and that, in introducing preventive detention, they were merely bringing back what their predecessors in office had introduced in 1959. In addition, his regime had that same day been recognised by the High Court in Salisbury as the *de facto* government, in complete and effective control of the country.[21] Although the British side may well have used the opportunity of the constitutional illegalities to break off the talks, they had in any case to adjourn because the Commonwealth Prime Ministers' conference was due to open at the beginning of September and they could not be seen to be in the position of negotiation with the illegal regime.

While the talks about talks were not producing any noticeable results, the fact that they were taking place at all produced an outburst of disapproval from the United Nations, from the Commonwealth and from the Zambian Government in particular. The day after the talks had opened in London, a group of thirty-two African States sent a letter to the Security Council urging a meeting to consider the Rhodesian situation, and a joint draft resolution was introduced by the Mali, Nigeria and Uganda representatives which drew the attention of the

British Government to the harmful consequences which the current negotiations might entail for the establishment of a government based on majority rule.

In defence of the Labour Government's policy Lord Caradon insisted that they were not negotiating with the illegal regime; they were merely engaged in informal talks to explore whether a basis for negotiations existed. While responding to the new approach from Salisbury, they had made it clear that the principles to which they subscribed would be maintained and that there would be no betrayal of African interests. If, however, it were not possible to achieve a settlement in the interests of the Rhodesian people as a result of the exploratory talks in progress, they would need to reconsider their whole policy. Further action by the United Nations at that time, he warned, would be likely to prejudice the possibility of an agreement. Caradon won his point: the joint African resolution was lost, with New Zealand casting the negative vote on behalf of its Commonwealth ally.[22] But the British victory was a qualified one, since the supporters of the resolution succeeded in getting their recommendations approved where the veto could not deter them. Within a week, the Special Committee on Decolonisation, meeting in Africa, adopted a similar resolution condemning the negotiations with the rebel regime, with Australia replacing New Zealand as the sole defender of the British case.

Commonwealth Test

The Labour Government's negotiation efforts were also condemned by the Commonwealth Prime Ministers, at a conference which turned out to be one of the most bitter encounters ever experienced by a British government. The African delegates and their supporters were mainly concerned about the failure of the British to implement the principles endorsed at the Lagos conference the previous January and recalled, with a mixture of despair and contempt, the Prime Minister's prediction that economic sanctions would bring down the rebel regime 'in a matter of weeks rather than months'. The Zambian Government, in particular, represented by their Foreign Minister, Mr Simon Kapwepwe, took the opportunity of acquainting the other delegations with the economic and financial sacrifices that his Government had to bear – in terms of increased coal and freight charges, reduced copper exports, additional import costs – as a result of the British Government's failure to take adequate measures to end the rebellion. The British offer of 'contingency aid' (bringing the amount of assistance to some £14 million over the year) came nowhere near meeting Zambia's needs while the sanc-

tions programme was in operation. Their reply to Mr Wilson's suggestion that a Commonwealth effort should be organised to assist Zambia
to apply sanctions against Rhodesian exports was that they would not
wish to take bread out of the mouths of people living in many Commonwealth countries relatively poorer than Zambia for the sole purpose of
assisting them to end a rebellion that the British could end themselves
if they had the will to do so. Other African delegates joined the Zambians in demanding that if sanctions were to be effective, they had to
be made mandatory, and also comprehensive, by United Nations action.

But sanctions were a secondary consideration compared with the
issue of Rhodesia's political future. Most of the delegates (including the
Afro-Asian-Caribbean bloc, with the support of Canada) were strongly
opposed to the bilateral negotiations with the Smith regime, which
they considered incompatible with the commitment of the Lagos
meeting to convene a constitutional conference representative of all
sections of Rhodesian opinion. Nor could they accept any agreement
with the Rhodesians that did not guarantee that majority rule would be
established — the so-called NIBMAR pledge. On this issue they were in
direct opposition to Mr Wilson, whose negotiating position with the
Smith regime would be undermined by any such requirement, and who
had long since abandoned any pretence of insisting on African majority
rule as a condition for the granting of independence. The differences
between the two camps, with Britain supported only by the Conservative Governments of Australia, New Zealand and Malta (and Malawi on
the issue of force), appeared to be irreconcilable, so long as Mr Wilson
refused to give an unambiguous pledge on NIBMAR or agree to abandon his negotiations with the rebel regime on any other basis. Feelings
between the African delegations and the British became increasingly
bitter, with the Zambian Foreign Minister walking out of the conference and charging Mr Wilson with having become a racialist. It was
probably due to the mediation efforts of the Canadian Prime Minister,
Mr Lester Pearson, that any joint communiqué was possible at all.
While there were no dissentients, the differences of view recorded
revealed how wide the gap was between the two camps. Had it not
been for the view of most of the delegates that a breakup of the
Commonwealth over Rhodesia would only bring comfort to the Smith
regime, it might well have occurred.

While the final communiqué recorded the basic differences on the
use of force,[23] on the commitment to NIBMAR and on the negotiations with the rebel regime, it also revealed that the British Prime
Minister had been obliged to make some concession in order to preserve

the Commonwealth as an institution. As a result the British Government were committed to a programme which was similar to the offer which they had made the previous 25 January but apparently abandoned with the reopening of the bilateral negotiations. That programme envisaged that after the return to legality a broadly based government would be appointed by the Governor, who would also be responsible for the police and armed forces. With this interim government, Britain would negotiate a constitutional settlement directed to achieving the objective of majority rule on the basis of the Six Principles. The settlement would then be submitted to the people of Rhodesia 'by appropriate democratic means'. While such a programme was generally acceptable to most of the Commonwealth leaders (with the exception regarding NIBMAR), they recorded their reservations on the timing of the release of political detainees, which they felt should be immediate and unconditional in order that their leadership could participate in the interim government. They also expressed the view that the means employed for the test of acceptability, which Mr Wilson had refused to define, should be a referendum based on universal suffrage.

The time-table agreed by the conference for the implementation of this programme was that the British Government would communicate their intentions through the Governor to all sections of Rhodesian opinion and inform the illegal regime that if they were not prepared to end the rebellion and consent to the vesting of executive authority in the Governor, two consequences would follow. Firstly, the British Government would withdraw all previous proposals for a constitutional settlement and not submit to Parliament any settlement which conceded independence before majority rule.[24] And secondly, with the support of Commonwealth representatives at the United Nations, the British Government would sponsor in the Security Council, before the end of the year, a resolution providing for selective mandatory sanctions.

Although the Prime Ministers had also agreed that the Rhodesian situation would be kept under 'constant review' and that they would meet soon if the illegal regime were not brought to an end 'speedily', they did not meet again until January 1969. The conference of September 1966 was probably the last occasion on which the Commonwealth as a unit still had any hopes of achieving a solution to the Rhodesian problem. After that, not even the pretence existed that the British Government would enact any programme that would be effective in bringing down the Smith regime. At successive conferences, British Prime Ministers, whether Mr Wilson or Mr Heath, would be attacked by most of the Commonwealth leaders for their failure to end the rebellion, but the initiative would remain firmly under British control and the protests of the Commonwealth leaders who dissented would be increasingly diverted to other channels, such as the diplomatic, the United Nations and the Organisation of African Unity. As Mr Wilson admitted, at a press conference at the end of the meeting on 15 September, the Commonwealth had been tested in the heat of flames that week and it would never be quite the same again.

Three Points Outstanding

Once the Commonwealth conference was out of the way, no time was lost in resuming the negotiations with the rebel regime. Even before the conference was over, on 12 September, a senior official of the Commonwealth Office, Sir Morrice James, had been sent to Salisbury to confer with the Governor about preparing the way for further negotiations. A week later, the new Commonwealth Secretary, Mr Herbert Bowden (who had replaced Mr Bottomley, an outspoken critic of the Smith regime), accompanied by the Attorney-General, Sir Elwyn Jones, arrived in Salisbury, presumably for the purpose envisaged by the Commonwealth conference of acquainting the Rhodesian people, including Mr Smith and his regime, with the British proposals. But according to Mr Smith's interpretation of the visit, he had been approached by the British Government with a proposal that Mr Bowden should come to Salisbury to confer with him on the possibilities of a settlement. He had acceded to the proposal on the understanding that those discussions would be a continuation of the talks at Government level. As far as he was concerned, Mr Bowden was visiting Rhodesia as an emissary of the British Government, and as Commonwealth Secretary he no longer had any say in the affairs of an independent Rhodesia. Nevertheless, the British Government continued to keep up the pretence that the discussions engaged in by the Commonwealth Secretary would be held under the authority of the Governor.[25]

It didn't take Mr Bowden long — a matter of some nine days — to discover that there was very little prospect of settling the Rhodesian problem in the few weeks remaining before the time-table set by the Commonwealth Prime Ministers came into effect. When he told a press conference at the end of his visit to Salisbury on 28 September, that the areas of difference between the two sides had been clarified and that views had been frankly stated on both sides, that was a sure indication that no progress had been made. On the issue of a return to legality, Mr Smith was apparently still holding out against relinquishing the authority of his regime, and the control of his armed forces, to an interim government responsible to the Governor. Nor was there any prospect of agreement on the contents of the settlement, especially with the regime's refusal to agree to the entrenchment of the Constitution's provision relating to the number of African and European seats. There was even a repetition of the Rhodesian claim that an increase in the number of Chiefs in the Senate would be 'an immediate improvement in the political status of the Africans' (the Third Principle). All of the old schemes for a settlement were again trotted out by the British – a mission of Commonwealth constitutional experts or of Commonwealth Prime Ministers, a constitutional conference to draw up an independence constitution, an Act of Union between Rhodesia and the United Kingdom – only to be rejected in turn by the Rhodesians.[26] The door may have been left open, as Mr Bowden said before leaving Salisbury, but he was not optimistic about anything coming through it.

For political purposes, the timing of the first Bowden visit could not have been worse: it came in the middle of the Rhodesian Front annual congress, when Mr Smith had to be excused to go to Bulawayo in order to rally the support of his followers, and it preceded the Labour party annual conference, at which Mr Wilson would be answerable for any appeasement of the rebel regime. Compared with previous congress occasions, Mr Smith's address this year was noticeable for its relative restraint, perhaps as a result of warnings from Mr Bowden that any declaration of constitutional change, such as the adoption of republican status, would result in the breakup of the talks. In fact, his only reference to the negotiations was that the British Government should be able to accept the Rhodesian Front regime because the High Court in Salisbury had acknowledged them as the *de facto* government of Rhodesia.[27]

While Mr Smith was reassuring his party supporters, Mr Bowden took the opportunity of meeting his first Rhodesians outside the official talks. Since his political background had been based on the domestic front, as Chief Whip and Leader of the House of Commons, he had virtually no knowledge or experience of Rhodesian affairs. He was allowed to see about a hundred Europeans and Africans (but not Mr Nkomo or Rev. Sithole), whose visits, according to *The Times* correspondent in Salisbury, were duly noted by the security police. Of the Europeans he managed to see, Mr Bowden estimated that about 30 per cent had 'liberal' opinions and were opposed to the Smith regime, which may have been an accurate assessment of those whom he saw but certainly not of those who voted.

Mr Wilson had a less easy passage at his party conference, in early October, where a critical composite resolution condemned the Government's decision to negotiate with the rebels and called for mandatory sanctions against the regime as well as against countries failing to comply with them. The other resolution on Rhodesia, moved by the Locomotive, Engineering and Firemen's Union (ASLEF), also called for a settlement that would promote the principle of one man, one vote, but since it merely asked the Government to do all in their power to reverse the UDI, it was allowed to pass on a show of hands. A competing National Executive Committee statement, based on the Six Principles and the British proposals to the Commonwealth conference, was presented as an endorsement of the Government's policies. Although Mr Wilson did not participate in the debate, his reference to the subject, in his report on the Government's record over the preceding year, included the term 'principles' no less than eight times, in the course of explaining the determination of the Government to adhere to them, the willingness of the Opposition to surrender them and the insistence of the Commonwealth and the United Nations on the observance of them.

The unenviable task of putting the Government's case, contained in the NEC statement, fell to Mrs Eirene White, Minister of State at the Foreign Office and a former leading member of the Fabian Commonwealth Bureau, who had to endure slow hand-clapping and jeers during her reply to the debate. Other members of the NEC, especially those regarded as the left-wing spokesmen of the constituency Labour parties, must have been equally embarrassed at finding themselves collectively bound by the NEC statement. In reply to the demand for mandatory sanctions and a commitment to implement majority rule, Mrs White pledged that unless the Smith regime acceded to the British proposals, the Government intended to pursue the sanctions measures to ensure that they were made more effective, although comprehensive mandatory sanctions were ruled out on the presumption that they were not universally enforceable. Mr Smith had been given one more chance, she warned, and if he did not accept it, Britain would not continue sheltering Rhodesia from the international consequences of its folly.

The Government's policy survived the vote, by a majority of 3.0 million for the NEC statement and 2.5 million against the composite resolution. The latter probably suffered the loss of some votes by mistakenly calling for 'a return to direct British rule', which had never existed, but even so it managed to attract nearly 2 million supporters. The big battalions of the trade union bloc had saved the day for the

NEC. But the victory for the Government's appeal for 'one more chance' was a limited one: either an acceptable settlement had to be reached or the illegal regime had to be brought to an end.[28] Two years later, neither had been achieved and the party delegates responded accordingly by revolting against their own Government.

A greater show of party unity over the Rhodesian issue prevailed at the Conservative party's conference in mid-October. Since the earlier divisions had mostly occurred over the application of sanctions, with the leadership supporting only limited ones, all wings of the party could now come together in opposition to the Government's threat to resort to the United Nations for mandatory sanctions. However, the ambivalence of the Tory position was evident from the reply to the debate by the deputy leader, Mr Maudling, who had just returned from a fact finding mission to southern Africa. Although criticising the prevailing sanctions as damaging to the Rhodesian economy and to the British balance of payments, he did not propose that they should be abandoned altogether. Instead, he went on to attack mandatory sanctions as a disaster which would lead to a confrontation with the South Africans (who had just told him that they were determined to continue their 'normal' trade with Rhodesia) and would also unite the so-called 'moderate' elements which he had met with in Rhodesia solidly behind the Rhodesian Front regime. On the prospect of negotiations, Mr Maudling remained as optimistic as he had been during his visit to Salisbury that the gap between the two Governments was not too wide to be bridged and that a generally acceptable solution could be found on the basis of the 1961 Constitution, with additional safeguards from the Five Principles.[29] The inconsistency of this approach, as *The Times* leader pointed out the following day (14 October), amounted to 'proclaiming a principle but denouncing the only apparent means of enforcing it'. Furthermore, the proposal for negotiations was precisely what Mr Bowden had been attempting to achieve in Salisbury, but without any co-operation from the regime.

Two of the three months allowed for a settlement by the Commonwealth conference were to elapse before negotiations were resumed in Salisbury. In the interval, the British Government had prepared a set of final proposals, based on the points raised by Mr Bowden in the negotiations in September, which were delivered to the regime by the Commonwealth Office representative, Sir Morrice James, on 15 October. The following month (4 November), the Smith regime's reply was transmitted through the High Commissioner in Salisbury to the British Government. Questions and answers on the interpretation of the proposals and the Rhodesian reply continued to flow between London and Salisbury throughout November. On the first anniversary of the UDI, the British Government formulated three questions relating to the points on which the Rhodesians had refused to be moved: the entrenchment of the constitutional provisions for the number of African seats; the broad-based interim administration as a means of returning to legality; and the operation of the Fifth Principle before constitutional government was restored. Although the Rhodesian reply (17 November) was wholly negative and evasive, the Commonwealth Secretary was to return to Salisbury to consider the 'three points outstanding'.

While these manoeuvres proceeded, pressure was mounting for a direct meeting between the two Prime Ministers, particularly from the Conservative Opposition, from the South African Government (in the bluntest warning yet against sanctions by the Transport Minister, Mr Barend Schoeman) and from Mr Smith himself, now indicating willingness to meet Mr Wilson anywhere and at any time. Pressure was coming from the other side as well, from those opposed to such negotiations, including a considerable section of the Parliamentary Labour Party and the overwhelming majority of the Commonwealth, the OAU and the United Nations. In between was Mr Wilson, who had to decide which way to yield.

Within the Parliamentary Labour Party there were some 50-60 MPs who consistently opposed Mr Wilson's willingness to negotiate with the Smith regime and to consider an independence agreement before majority rule. The possibility that this was envisaged in the Government's final proposals of 15 October or in the confidential correspondence that followed, prompted these Labour rebels to sign a Motion on 7 November calling for the implementation of majority rule, at the minimum in ten years' time, and for the holding of a direct referendum on the test of acceptability. A second Motion urged that the application of the Six Principles be guaranteed by withholding independence until majority rule had been established.

Similar warnings were coming from the Organisation of African Unity and from the United Nations. On the same day as the Labour MPs' Motion, the Heads of State of the OAU, meeting in Addis Ababa, confirmed a resolution of their Ministerial Council denouncing the talks between the British Government and the regime as 'a conspiracy aiming at the recognition of independence illegally declared by the rebel settlers'. And at the United Nations, the General Assembly adopted two resolutions on the subject by the overwhelming majority of 86-2 (on 22 October) and 89-2 (on 17 November), with Britain abstaining on each occasion. Both resolutions expressed serious concern that the 'talks about talks' might jeopardise the inalienable rights of the African people to self-determination, and the latter recalled that the British Government had declared on several occasions since the UDI that they would not negotiate with an illegal regime on the future of Rhodesia.[30]

At the same time, however, pressure for resuming negotiations was coming from the Governor, Sir Humphrey Gibbs, who was reported to have been on the point of resigning if the British Government followed up their threat to resort to the United Nations for mandatory sanctions. While the Governor had ceased to exercise any authority in Rhodesia, having been stripped of his legal powers and also of the formal trappings of his office, he remained the last tangible symbol of the British presence in Rhodesia, to whom messages could be conveyed (by 'signing the Governor's book') from those still prepared to observe loyalty to the Crown. If he were to go, it would be a symbolic loss and a further blow to British prestige in Rhodesia. To prevent such an occurrence, a hurried visit to Salisbury was arranged for the Commonwealth Secretary on 25 November, during which he would also confer with Mr Smith, but still under the Governor's aegis. Apparently embarrassed by what had become public knowledge of his reluctance to play the martyr much longer (his car, staff, allowance and other perks had been taken away by the regime), Sir Humphrey had announced that he would never resign without the Queen's assent nor blackmail the British Government by threat of resignation. Nevertheless, he admitted that he was most anxious to confer with the Commonwealth Secretary to see if the remaining differences between the British Government and the Rhodesian Front on a constitutional settlement could be sorted out.

The Labour Government had been well aware, ever since receiving the regime's reply to their 'final' proposals of 15 October, and to their three questions of 11 November, that a very wide gap of principle would have to be bridged before there could be any settlement. As Mr Wilson said in Parliament on 23 November, he would not be prepared to commend a settlement which was in conflict with the Six Principles or failed to give 'copper-bottomed guarantees' that those principles would be carried through.[31] Three days later, the Commonwealth Secretary was in Salisbury conferring with Mr Smith and also with the Governor, who was supposed to be the purpose of his visit. After Mr Bowden's departure the following day, British officials put further questions to the regime, which were to be answered by 30 November.

It was upon his return from this meeting that the Commonwealth Secretary had referred to the points still outstanding between the two sides and had admitted that Mr Smith had made 'only minor concessions'. Nevertheless, even before the deadline for the Rhodesian reply, Mr Wilson sent the Commonwealth Office official, Sir Morrice James, back to Salisbury for the alleged purpose of clarifying issues which had arisen from the Commonwealth Secretary's report on his discussions. But, as it emerged later, the day of Sir Morrice's arrival in Salisbury (29 November) was the day on which Mr Smith received Mr Wilson's invitation to a meeting to work out a final settlement. It was also on the same day that Mr Wilson told the Commons that, while Sir Morrice had left for Salisbury the night before, he himself had no present plans to visit Rhodesia.[32] He was quite right, literally, since his plans were to meet Mr Smith aboard HMS *Tiger* off Gibraltar in the Mediterranean, and these plans he only revealed to Parliament on 1 December, the day of his departure.

In justifying his decision to meet Mr Smith, Mr Wilson claimed that the Commonwealth Secretary's report indicated for the first time a real possibility that a satisfactory agreement might be reached on the constitutional issues which would give full effect to the Six Principles. The report also indicated, for the first time, some 'sign of movement' on the question of the return to legality, although, according to Mr Smith's later version, only if a satisfactory constitutional settlement could be agreed. From these signs of movement, which coincided in time very neatly with the operation of the time-table of which Mr Smith had been made aware, Mr Wilson concluded that, notwithstanding all of the disappointments from previous efforts, one last attempt should be made to reach a settlement. While admitting that there was still a considerable gap to bridge, he nevertheless maintained that he would not have contemplated the meeting with Mr Smith unless he had reason to believe that they were 'within hailing distance' of a solution.[33]

The response to Mr Wilson's proposal for a 'summit' meeting was a rather mixed one. Among the Cabinet Ministers, according to his own account,[34] the Foreign Secretary (Mr George Brown) was 'decidedly enthusiastic and thought that a settlement was now possible'; the Chancellor (Mr Callaghan) and the First Secretary (Mr Stewart) strongly supported the idea that they should 'have a go'; and the Leader of the House (Mr R.H.S. Crossman)[35] said that, although they might have about fifty abstentions if they got a settlement, it would still be worth it, adding: 'Do not divert Harold from what I think he wants to do.'

More sceptically, the Lord Chancellor (Gardiner), while agreeing that Mr Wilson should meet Mr Smith in appropriate circumstances, was convinced that Mr Smith was not trying to get a settlement, but was engaging in 'a last-minute public relations exercise'.

From the date of this conversation – 26 November – it was evident that Mr Wilson had decided on the meeting with Mr Smith on the same day that Mr Bowden was negotiating in Salisbury, before the British officials had even put their questions to the regime and while Mr Bowden was aware that there were still major points of difference. Nothing was said by Mr Wilson of any opposition within the Cabinet, although it was known that several members, certainly Mrs Castle and Mr Bottomley, were opposed to any further efforts to placate the rebel regime.[36] His only reference to the subject was that 'on the Thursday (1 December) the Cabinet gave us their blessings', not that they had any choice at that stage, other than resignation, since the decision had already been made before the 'blessings' were sought. As for the Parliamentary Labour Party, Mr Wilson claimed that there was 'wild cheering' at a meeting he had called to enable the MPs to express their views. What pleased him most were the parting words (unspecified) of a deputation of Labour MPs active in African affairs. Once assured that there would be no sell-out or no agreement except on the basis of the Six Principles and the Commonwealth communiqué, they were alleged to have been 'very friendly'.[37]

If Mr Smith's agreement to have the meeting was, as Lord Gardiner had said, 'a last-minute public relations exercise', it was also possible that the same motive influenced Mr Wilson's decision. It was difficult to believe that he could have expected to arrive at any settlement that would be acceptable to the Smith regime and also be in accordance with the Commonwealth communiqué, let alone the Six Principles, which were imprecise enough to be violated in the spirit if not in the letter. The only thing to be gained by such a meeting, in the way of a public relations exercise, was to be seen to be having one, to be exonerated from the blame of having closed the door to negotiations. Even if a settlement failed to materialise, the pressures on Mr Wilson to try to obtain one would be lessened. It was also possible that he was still convinced that sanctions were eroding the will of the Rhodesians to resist any longer, and that with the threat of mandatory sanctions by the end of the year, they would be more amenable to an agreement. While there was certainly no significant public in Britain pressing for a settlement at any price, Rhodesia remained a nagging, obstinate problem, the solution of which would be an achievement for any

British Government. It was also an unwelcome distraction that consumed an inordinate amount of time and energy, which a Government facing a major economic crisis during the years 1966-7 could ill afford to waste. In addition, there was the incentive to put an end to 'carrying the can' for Rhodesia before world opinion, as reflected in the Commonwealth and the United Nations. To be continually reminded of bearing the responsibility for Rhodesia but lacking the power to enforce it was a constant humiliation which Britain had to endure so long as the issue remained a matter of international concern. Any or all of these factors may well have influenced Mr Wilson to have a last try at a settlement. But the chance for a settlement never really existed, because if he were to insist on a settlement on his terms, the Smith regime would never agree and if he were to concede to their terms, his own party would never accept it.

Notes

1. See 722 *HC Deb.,* 10 December 1965, col. 773.

2. *Rhodesia Herald,* 14 January 1966.

3. See Mr Smith's statement in *Punch,* 26 January 1966, in which he claimed that Rhodesia would not get its independence on 'any fair or decent terms'. He cited the Mutasa letter as evidence of the Labour Government's intention to substitute immediate majority rule for the 1961 constitutional system.

4. 723 *HC Deb.,* 25 January 1966, cols. 40-55.

5. Ibid., 31 January 1966, cols. 687-94.

6. According to Dudley Seers, in *Crisis in the Civil Service,* 1968, pp. 97-8. The DEA was established by the Labour Government after the 1964 election.

7. The Monday Club meeting in Central Hall, London, on 3 February 1966, was addressed by Lord Salisbury, Mr Paul Williams, Mr Julian Amery, Mr John Biggs-Davison, Mr Stephen Hastings, Mr Patrick Wall and Mr. Gerald Sparrow.

8. *Rhodesia Herald,* 16 February 1966.

9. For the report of his visit, see 727 *HC Deb.,* 27 April 1966, cols. 740-6.

10. David Butler and Anthony King, *The British General Election of 1966,* pp. 114-15.

11. See letter to *The Times,* 23 March 1966 from the Rhodesian Constitutional Association (including former members of the United Federal party) signed by Mr David Butler, Mr W.A.F. Burdett-Coutts and Mr N.A.F. Williams, making this suggestion. Sir Alec Douglas-Home's reply (29 March) was not very convincing in meeting the criticisms of Conservative policies.

12. Mr Wilson dismissed the proposals brought back by Mr Lloyd as containing no new points worth of consideration. (727 *HC Deb.,* 21 April 1966, col. 95.)

13. The Special Committee on Decolonisation, on 6 April, had condemned the measures taken by the British Government as 'totally inadequate'. The Government's case for the appeal was put by the Attorney-General, Sir Elwyn Jones, 727 *HC Deb.,* 27 April 1966, col. 843.

14. Resolution 221 (1966), Security Council, *Official Records,* 21st Year, 1276th, 1277th Meeting, 9 April 1966.

15. Rhodesia, *Parliamentary Debates,* vol. 63, 26 April 1966, cols. 2107-17.

16. Wilson, *The Labour Government, 1964-1970,* 1971, p. 279.

17. In a speech at the Bulawayo Trade Fair on 29 April 1966.

18. 733 *HC Deb.,* 8 August 1966, cols. 1017-24; also see 727 *HC Deb.,* 21 April 1966, col. 98, 27 April 1966, cols. 709-11.

19. 731 *HC Deb.,* 5 July 1966, cols. 253-7.

20. *Rhodesia Herald,* 7 August 1966.

21. The High Court ruling was given in response to appeals from Mr Leo Baron and Mr Daniel Madzimbamuto against detention orders, on the ground that the rebel regime had no legal powers to make such orders. See Chapter 8.

22. Security Council, *Official Records,* 21st Year, 1280th, 1285th Meeting, 18 May, 23 May 1966. The resolution was defeated by 6-1.

23. *Commonwealth Prime Ministers' Meeting 1966, Final Communiqué,* London, 15 September 1966, Cmnd. 3115.

24. Mr Wilson reported to Mr George Brown that he had not conceded NIBMAR and had got a 'three months plan' instead. (Wilson, *The Labour Government,* p. 286.)

25. *The Times,* 19 September 1966.

26. 737 *HC Deb.,* 7 December 1966, cols. 1377-9.

27. *Rhodesia Herald,* 24 September 1966.

28. *Report of the 65th Annual Conference of the Labour Party,* Blackpool, 1966.

29. *Report of the 84th Annual Conservative Party Conference,* Blackpool, 1966.

30. Resolution 2138 (XXI), 22 October 1966; resolution 2151 (XXI), 17 November 1966. Abstentions were 18 on the former, 17 on the latter.

31. 736 *HC Deb.,* 23 November 1966, cols. 1401-2.

32. 737 *HC Deb.,* 29 November 1966, col. 207.

33. Ibid., 1 December 1966, col. 625; 5 December 1966, col. 1054.

34. Wilson, *The Labour Government,* p. 307.

35. See the Crossman *Diaries* for his interpretation.

36. Ibid.

37. Wilson, *The Labour Government,* pp. 303-9.

6 THE *TIGER* DISASTER

'The mind boggles at the thought that a Labour Prime Minister would really have been prepared to perpetrate the outrage which the *Tiger* proposals represent.'

Leo Baron, September 1967.

The dramatic confrontation between the Labour Government and the rebel regime was staged on board HMS *Tiger* on 2 December 1966. The Prime Minister was accompanied by the Commonwealth Secretary and the Attorney-General; Mr Smith and Mr Jack Howman represented the regime; and the Rhodesian Governor and Chief Justice were also present. White Papers containing an account of the negotiations and of the working document prepared by the two sides were published by the British Government immediately after the meeting,[1] and a Rhodesian Blue Book version appeared a few days later.[2] The most perplexing aspect of the *Tiger* encounter was the complete misunderstanding that arose, after long and arduous negotiations on the contents of the working document, over Mr Smith's competence to accept it. Mr Wilson contended, and he claimed that Sir Morrice James had made this clear to Mr Smith, that both he and the Rhodesian leader had come to the meeting with full authority from their respective Cabinets to arrive at a final settlement. When Mr Smith denied that he had the power to commit his colleagues, the talks came to an abrupt conclusion. Mr Smith returned to Salisbury, doubtful about his acceptance of a document to which he had presumably agreed in the first instance, to obtain from his 'Cabinet' a final answer. Since his own position at the end of the negotiations amounted to a qualified, if not outright, rejection, it was not likely that his colleagues would react otherwise.

From the text of the White Paper it was evident that the Government's main concern was to establish that the requirements laid down by the Six Principles had been met. By far the most doubtful claim related to the First Principle — unimpeded progress towards majority rule — for which no convincing evidence was provided. The Second Principle — no retrogression — was allegedly met by establishing a blocking mechanism, in the form of twenty-five elected Africans (a three-quarters majority of both Houses being required to amend the entrenched clauses of the Constitution), and by providing for a right of appeal against the amendment of these clauses, in the first instance to a Constitutional Commission in Rhodesia and from there, as of right, to the Judicial Committee of the Privy Council. The Third Principle — immediate improvement in the political status of Africans — was envisaged as an extension of the 'B' roll franchise to all Africans over thirty years of age, an increase of the 'B' roll seats from fifteen to seventeen (the Europeans had fifty) and the creation of fourteen African seats in the new Senate, of which eight would be elected and six chosen by Chiefs. To meet the Fourth Principle, a Royal Commission would 'study and make recommendations' on racial discrimination, in particular land apportionment, and a Standing Committee would keep the problem under review. Under the Fifth Principle, the agreed settlement would be submitted to the people of Rhodesia as a whole by a Royal Commission, whose composition and terms of reference would be agreed by the British Government and the 'legal interim administration'. If the settlement were shown to be acceptable, the British Government would introduce legislation to grant independence and the two Governments would negotiate a treaty guaranteeing the independence constitution. Before this stage had been reached, however, with the restoration of 'legal government' the British Government would take action to bring about the immediate discontinuance of sanctions.[3]

Return to Legality

Where this elaborate exercise in creating constitutional devices that bore some relation to the Six Principles broke down was in connection with the 'return to legality' under an interim government, which was irrevocably bound up with the Fifth Principle, since it was inconceivable that a test of acceptability could be conducted with an illegal regime in power, censorship in force and the African leadership in detention. The regime's rejection of the settlement was allegedly based on their objections to a return to legality before they were assured of a constitution to their liking — what they called abandoning the substance of the existing 'Constitution' for the shadow of a mythical constitution yet to be evolved. In fact, Mr Smith went so far as to threaten that if they were to abandon their 1965 'Constitution' and the test of acceptability went against them, he would be prepared to declare a second UDI.

There was in fact no real basis for the Rhodesian Front claim that the terms for a return to legality required them to yield fundamental principles or surrender their power. The British Government had already conceded that the interim government period would last only four months, that no British forces would be posted in Rhodesia during that period, that Mr Smith would be Prime Minister, that the Rhodesian Front would still retain a majority in the 'broadly-based' government and that the five new members provided for would have to be approved by Mr Smith.[4] As for the myth of 'direct rule' by the Governor, on all matters of internal administration the Governor would act on the advice of his Ministers and security chiefs, all Rhodesians, acceptable to Mr Smith. The process of dismantling the police State apparatus before the test of acceptability would also be left to the Rhodesian Front. They would determine what 'normal political activities' would be permitted, what were 'peaceful' and 'democratic' practices, what 'intimidation' would be proscribed. The release of detainees would also be their decision, since the so-called 'impartial judicial tribunal' to review the detention of persons on security grounds would be appointed by the Rhodesian Government and contain only one British representative.

It was difficult to believe that the Smith regime could have rejected a settlement assuring them of no African rule in their lifetime solely on the basis of their objection to a formal 'return to legality'. But by basing their rejection on this ground, they could evade the real differences on the constitutional proposals, and so create the image of responsible men willing to compromise on constitutional reform but unwilling to surrender the powers which they had exercised for the preceding four decades. As Mr Smith claimed, in a televised press conference on 6 December, if Britain had put forward the present proposals thirteen months ago, he would never have had to resort to the UDI.

If the Rhodesian Front really had accepted the *Tiger* provisions, apart from the return to legality, they could have implemented them and then challenged the British to deny them their independence. But from the records of the negotiations, it was clear that Mr Smith had been evasive and contradictory on many aspects of the working document. Provisions that had once been agreed were later questioned and even rejected. The most obvious case was provision for entrenching the number of African seats in the Legislature, to which Mr Smith had allegedly agreed at his final meeting with Mr Bowden in Salisbury on 26 November 1966. But at the conclusion of the discussions on *Tiger* he was doubtful whether he could accept the provision at all. He had also reserved his position, at the very end, on the questions of whether there would be a return to legality before the test of acceptability and whether there would be a broad-based interim government more representative of Rhodesian opinion that the Rhodesian Front 'Cabinet'. Any remaining doubt about the regime's willingness to accept the proposals should have been dispelled by their statement on 6 December (the same day as Mr Smith's press conference), that they could not accept any limitation on their 'Parliament' to determine the number of constituencies; they could see no reason to increase the number of 'B' roll seats; and they regarded the right of appeal to the Judicial Committee of the Privy Council as inconsistent with their sovereignty.

In Britain, the Smith regime's interpretation of the *Tiger* negotiations was endorsed by the Conservative party, who also attributed the breakdown to Rhodesia's objection to British interference in their affairs during the interim government. But the main concern of the Tories was the application of mandatory sanctions, which would follow as a result of the failure to get an agreement, and the undertaking that no further proposals would be made for independence before majority rule. On this occasion, they were virtually united in their vote against the Government Motion supporting the decision to implement the commitment in the Commonwealth communiqué. While the Government's support in the Commons was sufficient to carry the Motion, in the Lords it was defeated by a majority of sixteen.[5] Ironically, many of the Labour MPs who regarded the *Tiger* proposals as a sell-out to white minority rule were obliged to vote for the Motion commending them in order to support the pledge on NIBMAR and mandatory sanctions.

Selective Retaliation

Within hours of the Rhodesian rejection of the *Tiger* proposals, the Labour Government announced their intention of implementing paragraph 10 (a) of the Commonwealth communiqué by sponsoring in the Security Council a resolution providing for selective mandatory sanctions. The British Minister, Lord Caradon, was instructed to request an early meeting of the Council and the Foreign Secretary, Mr George Brown, was to take personal charge of the British initiative at the United Nations. While the British Government had agreed to the inclusion in the Commonwealth communiqué of the sanctions option, they had succeeded in keeping control of the extent of the sanctions to be applied. This was evident from the different views that had emerged from the communiqué: although the Heads of Government were generally agreed on the need for stronger sanctions under Chapter VII of the Charter, most (not Britain) were convinced that mandatory sanctions of a general and comprehensive character should be applied under Articles 41 and 42, while others (Britain) favoured sanctions on selected individual commodities important to the Rhodesian economy. In addition, the British Government had imposed a second qualification, namely, that any new mandatory sanctions must not be allowed to develop into a confrontation, economic or military, with other States in southern Africa. This condition was to be imposed by Mr Brown when he put the British case before the Security Council on 8 December. In exchange for the British concession of including oil in the mandatory sanctions, he appealed for an undestanding from the other delegations of the importance of not allowing sanctions to escalate into economic confrontation with third countries — in effect, with South·Africa and Portugal.

The British draft resolution introduced by Mr Brown recognised that the situation in Rhodesia, resulting from the breakdown of the efforts for a negotiated settlement, constituted a threat to international peace and security and called upon all States to prevent the import of those commodities which were of critical importance to Rhodesia's foreign trade, including tobacco, asbestos, copper, chrome, pig iron and iron ore, sugar, meat, hides and leathers. Together, these products amounted to nearly 90 per cent of all Rhodesian exports.[6] The British resolution also called for a prohibition on the sale or shipment to Rhodesia of arms, ammunition, military aircraft, military vehicles, and equipment and materials for their manufacture and maintenance. In moving the resolution, Mr Brown pledged that if, with the support of the Commonwealth delegations, it were approved on the lines he had proposed, the British Government would proceed to the related further step which they had already undertaken to carry out in those circumstances: they would withdraw all previous proposals for a constitutional settlement which had been made to the Rhodesians; in particular, they would not thereafter be prepared to submit to the British Parliament any settlement which involved the grant of independence before majority rule.[7]

While the main concession in the British resolution had been the inclusion of oil, they had also yielded on a number of other amendments proposed by the African delegations, including a recognition that the Rhodesian situation now constituted a threat to peace; that the failure of any State to implement the measures constituted a violation of Article 25 of the Charter; and that all States should refrain from rendering financial or other economic aid to the rebel regime. However, the British delegation refused to accept responsibility for preventing 'by all possible means' the transport of oil to Rhodesia. They also opposed a ban on the import of certain commodities, such as coal and manufactured goods, because of the dependence of Zambia on this source for its supplies.

But the subject that caused the most controversy in the Security Council was the African amendment calling upon Britain to withdraw all offers previously made to the rebel regime and give a categorical assurance that independence would not be granted until majority rule had been established. The proposal, described by Lord Caradon as 'entirely out of place' and 'impinging on matters within the sovereignty of the British Parliament', was rejected by Britain, together with seven other members of the Security Council, who abstained from the vote. The refusal of the British delegation to include this undertaking in their resolution was a complete reversal of the pledge given by their own Foreign Secretary the previous week and a repudiation of the commitment contained in the Commonwealth communiqué, which was the basis on which the British Government had sought Commonwealth support for their resort to the United Nations for 'effective and selective' mandatory sanctions. The British resolution was finally adopted on 16 December, by a vote of 11-0,[8] since the general consensus seemed to be that selective mandatory sanctions were an improvement on those which had previously been only voluntary. But there was still a lingering doubt over just what obligations the British had assumed with regard to future negotiations with the rebel regime and the implementation of NIBMAR, since what Mr Brown had pledged on 8 December 1966 was repudiated by his Government's representative, Lord Caradon, a week later.

After the failure of the *Tiger* negotiations and the application of the conditions set out in the Commonwealth communiqué, the Labour Government's position was that, for the present at least, further negotiations with the Rhodesian Front regime were unlikely to yield an agreement. There was also the economic situation in Britain to contend with, which was particularly critical in 1967 — culminating in the decision to devalue the pound — and this preoccupation overshadowed the Rhodesian situation for most of the year.[9] So far as the British public were concerned, any interest in the issue, which might have been temporarily aroused by the *Tiger* confrontation, was rapidly dissipated in the aftermath of the Rhodesian rejection. No recriminations followed from Mr Wilson's failure, since he was seen to have tried, and certainly there was no groundswell for another effort. However, pressure on Mr Wilson to renew contacts with the rebel regime continued to come from his Conservative opponents, who never ceased to believe that an agreement was possible. For a period of nearly two years, there was a recurrent battle between the two parties over the issue of seeking a settlement. Despite all evidence to the contrary, the Tories were to maintain that the *Tiger* failure was due, not to the proposals as such, but to the Labour Government's conduct of the negotiations and their insistence on a return to legality.

If Mr Wilson had any intention of renewing the negotiations, and he implied that he did by the concessions he began to make in response to the continuing pressure from the Tories, he had first to rid himself of the commitment in the Commonwealth communiqué. By adhering to that pledge, to withdraw any previous offers conferring independence before majority rule, he would rule out the possibility of the Rhodesian Front responding to his overtures. To get around this dilemma, he introduced the condition that if there were a change of circumstances in Rhodesia (although what this might include was not specified), he would then appeal to the Commonwealth to seek a release from the terms of the communiqué. He also conceded that adherence to the NIBMAR pledge did not mean that the Government had altered their view that a substantial period of preparation would be required for majority rule, although he did not indicate whether independence would be granted during that period. As a further inducement, he opened up the possibility of the Rhodesians taking the initiative by inviting anyone in that country, obviously including Mr Smith, to approach the Governor with proposals for a settlement of the constitutional dispute.[10]

In spite of Mr Wilson's concessions, no signs of willingness were forthcoming from Salisbury. On the contrary, Mr Smith was again reverting to the old myth, long since demolished by his predecessor, Sir Edgar Whitehead, that Rhodesians had been led to believe that when they accepted the 1961 Constitution, part of the agreement was that if Federation broke up they would be given independence on the basis of that Constitution. On this ground, he maintained that the UDI had not been illegal: independence was something for which they had contracted with the British Government and were therefore entitled to. As for the British insistence on majority rule, according to his definition they already had it in Rhodesia: the party winning the majority of seats in Parliament was always called upon to form a government and they could only remain in office while they retained a majority in Parliament. In his view, that was majority rule and he was in favour of it.[11]

There was little encouragement to be derived from these excursions into unreality. But there was a noticeable change in Rhodesian tactics during the first half of 1967, which coincided with the concessions that the Labour Government were beginning to make in order to re-establish contact. Mr Smith responded to these overtures by maintaining that the Rhodesians had always been and still were prepared to talk, although no proposals were put forward. Instead, the time factor was invoked as a barrier: Rhodesia had already acquired new friends and was not to be deterred from proceeding with its own version of an independence constitution. As Mr Smith told his 'Parliament' on 17 May, as each day passed any possibility of talks deteriorated and the gap between the two sides widened. Already they had made a number of agreements with other countries, many of whom had accorded them *de facto* recognition by agreeing to trade with them. There were also certain constitutional changes which were imminent. A Constitutional Commission had been appointed in February 1967, under the chairmanship of Mr W.R.H. Whaley, to report on a new constitution for Rhodesia, and once the 'Government' acted on this report (which they refused to do because it envisaged parity between the races) there would be no turning back from that position either.[12] In effect, Mr Smith's case was that if the British Government were still interested in a settlement, they had better act before it was too late for Rhodesia to alter its course.

The British response to this approach was first to implement the new sanctions programme and then to dispatch a special emissary to test the atmosphere in Salisbury. The former was achieved by the enactment on 6 February 1967 of the Southern Rhodesia (Prohibited Trade and Dealings) Orders, which, together with the Southern Rhodesia (Petroleum) Order, would give effect to the mandatory sanctions resolution adopted by the Security Council on 16 December 1966. In moving the Orders, the Commonwealth Secretary, Mr Bowden, claimed that the mandatory sanctions resolution opened up a new phase in exerting economic pressure on Rhodesia: the commodities covered by the resolution comprised no less than 60 per cent of the country's total exports in 1965. If the embargo were fully implemented, Rhodesia's exports would be reduced by up to a further £30 million per annum. In an attempt to win the support of the Conservative Opposition for the measures, both the Attorney-General and the Lord Chancellor stressed that since the Government had succeeded in obtaining the full support of the Commonwealth and the United Nations, they could not now refuse to implement the resolution they had accepted. The Opposition, however, remained unconvinced, and their spokesman, Mr Maudling, maintained that sanctions would never work unless other countries, particularly South Africa, adhered to them. The Tories therefore expressed their disapproval by voting against the Orders (which were carried by a vote of 189-120); but in the House of Lords, where the Conservative leadership advised abstention, some 13 rebel peers defied the advice and recorded their opposition.[13]

Alport's Temporary Aberration

While condemning the extension of sanctions and the severance of relations with the rebel regime, the Tories were urging that talks begin with Mr Smith or, as Lord Harlech put it, with 'others exercising authority' in Rhodesia. Also in favour of such a move was a group of some 4,000 Rhodesians, including the former Prime Minisiter, Lord Malvern, who had signed a petition calling for the implementation of the *Tiger* proposals. But this possibility became increasingly remote as Mr Smith's statements revealed that substantive issues rather than the technical arrangements for a return to legality were the cause of the failure.

Whether or not Mr Wilson was influenced by the efforts of the Rhodesian citizenry or by his Tory opponents, he chose a former Conservative Minister, Lord Alport, to undertake an official mission to Salisbury. The choice of Lord Alport was an astute one, so far as silencing Opposition criticism was concerned, since he had served as Minister of State at the Commonwealth Office and as the High Commissioner during the last years of the Central African Federation. At the same time, he was an outspoken critic of the regime, having denied the possibility of any British Government concluding an agreement with the Rhodesian Front. With these views on record, it was surprising both that Lord Alport accepted the mission and that Mr Smith agreed to receive him.

On the terms of reference of the mission, Mr Wilson announced on 13 June 1967 that Lord Alport would be going to Salisbury for an exchange of views with the Governor, and that, while he was there, he would also be available to see representatives of all sections of Rhodesian opinion. On the Government's existing commitments, he confirmed that the position on NIBMAR remained unaltered : there would have to be a substantial change in circumstances before they would be prepared to approach the Commonwealth. As for the Six Principles to which they adhered, he pointed out that these had been increasingly violated by the regime since the *Tiger* meeting. There had been the

Emergency Powers Act, giving power to detain without trial; the tightening of the censorship laws and further evidence of interference with the judiciary.[14] Under these circumstances, the Alport mission began without much hope for any agreement.

Mr Smith confirmed this impression when he told a press conference in Salisbury that he had not been consulted about the British Government's decision to send Lord Alport. He found the choice of this envoy quite incredible because he could almost be described as a 'listed enemy of Rhodesia': he had been 'cold-shouldered' by the Federation Government for 'conniving with the British' on 'some pretty underhand tricks over the breakup of the Federation'; he had written a 'scurrilous book'[15] and he had indulged in offensive broadcasts from Francistown radio (operated by Britain) in neighbouring Botswana. Although suspicious of the projected visit, he was prepared to meet Lord Alport provided that his intentions were genuinely in the interests of Rhodesia. If, however, Mr Wilson was still insisting on NIBMAR then there was no hope of any settlement; and if Mr Wilson bungled this attempt, as he had the *Tiger* episode, he doubted whether there would be another opportunity, since time was running out and they had to get on with the business of adopting their new constitution.[16]

The Alport visit, which included meetings with a broad cross-section of the Rhodesian community, evoked a widely mixed reception. The controversy was sparked off by an outburst of personal abuse from the 'Minister' of Transport and Power, Brigadier Dunlop, who described Lord Alport as 'a failed Conservative Parliamentarian', during the course of a speech at the Sebakwe regatta on 11 July. For this 'acrimonious and personal' attack, he was censured by one of the 'B' roll African MPs (Mr P.J. Rubatika), who condemned the Government's departure from the high standards which they expected from 'a cultured and sophisticated community, especially in a multi-racial society'. But it was not clear whether the Brigadier's attack represented 'Government' policy, since Mr Smith, when questioned on the subject by another African MP (Mr P.E. Chigogo), replied that the 'Government' had 'no laid down policy on the visit of Lord Alport'.[17]

The main justification cited by the Brigadier for making this personal attack, apart from his having stemmed from British stock and served in the British Armed Forces, was that he wanted to 'punch home' to the British Government that their choice of an envoy was 'at best most unfortunate and at worst a studied insult'. At the same time, he wished to castigate those 'notorious Anthony-Eden-hatted businessmen', whose vast profits, as a result of the UDI, had been temporarily reduced and who, 'hoping to retain their profits, would gladly see their country's future sold for a dishonourable mess of pottage'. The question for him was whether these were the sort of people to whose views Lord Alport would give weight, or would he rather accept the opinion of 'down to earth Rhodesians of all races in town and country, whose roots were settled deeply in their country' (he had lived there only seventeen years) and who were determined to stay.[18]

Irrespective of whether Lord Alport was unduly influenced by the 'fifth-column' businessmen, his report on the visit appeared unduly optimistic for one who, at the time of the UDI, had ruled out the possibility of any negotiations with a Rhodesian Front regime. Apparently, the reason for his conversion was that he had been 'a witness at first-hand' of the strong desire of the Rhodesians for a negotiated settlement with Britain — a settlement which would involve give and take on both sides but which would accord with the principles accepted by both parties in Britain and contain proper safeguards for the future of Rhodesia as 'the stable and civilised community' which that country represented. Where Lord Alport envisaged some room for negotiations were the three features of the *Tiger* proposals — the blocking quarter of elected Africans, the cross-voting of the races and the right of appeal to the Judicial Committee of the Privy Council. The 'give', so far as the British negotiating position was concerned, was his assurance that the inclusion of a blocking mechanism against discrimination did not mean that it would operate in such a way as to procure 'the premature transfer of power from European to African nationalist hands'. He accepted, and he thought Rhodesia would be right to accept, that no British Government wished this to happen. But if Lord Alport expected any 'give' from the Rhodesian side on the three features of the *Tiger* proposals, he had only to recall Mr Bowden's words in Salisbury the previous November, namely, that there had always been three issues outstanding between the two sides.

On the basis of Lord Alport's report,[19] Mr Wilson concluded that it would be advisable for the Government to begin by authorising the Governor to undertake the preliminaries for negotiating a settlement. In taking this limited step, however, they fully reserved their position on NIBMAR on the return to legality and on the kind of broad-based government of national unity which would be essential for any progress to be achieved. In reaffirming the Government's stand on NIBMAR, he repeated that they would require a very substantial change of circumstances before they could appeal to the Commonwealth for a release from that pledge. He also warned that, in any renewal of conversations, the one thing that he would not be prepared to do would be to hand over Rhodesia to a 'partly Fascist regime', particularly in view of the very serious danger (which he was still cherishing) that when that happened they would get rid of Mr Smith, who, by Rhodesian standards, was a liberal, and would form a 'full-powered Fascist regime and a police state'.[20]

Mr Wilson was not deterred from following up the opening made by Alport either by a warning from the United Nations Special Committee against further negotiations with the illegal regime,[21] or by a Motion signed by nearly 100 Labour MPs opposing any compromise settlement with the Rhodesian Front and reaffirming the party's commitment to ensure majority rule before independence.[22] Communications between the two sides were proceeding, with the Governor in the role of a post-box from which letters from the regime could be legally received. Under the Governor's aegis, the British Government were seeking clarification of Mr Smith's interpretation of 'improving' the *Tiger* proposals. As the correspondence, which continued on through August 1967, soon revealed, the Rhodesian concept of improvement did not coincide with that of the British. Even the Fifth Principle (the test of acceptability), which had not been at issue during the *Tiger* meeting, presumably because the Rhodesians were confident that they could control the proceedings of a Royal Commission operating in their territory, was now being cited as an obstacle to a settlement. Their case was based on the doctrine of the popular mandate: since they had already obtained the support of the majority of the population (in fact, the white sector), there was no further need for a test of acceptability; whatever was acceptable to a Government confident of this support would also be acceptable to the people who elected them.[23]

Obviously, the British could not accept this sort of 'improvement' on the Fifth Principle. The majority of the Rhodesian people were the Africans and, in spite of the Rhodesian Front's claims, no evidence had yet been produced that they had obtained their support. So long as these circular arguments continued it was not likely that even an agenda for the talks would emerge. The Governor therefore took the opportunity of making the appointment of a new Commonwealth Secretary (Mr George Thomson) at the end of August 1967 the occasion for a meeting in Salisbury between the two sides. But before such a meeting could take place, reassurances were essential in several directions. Mr Smith and Mr Wilson had their respective party conferences to contend with, Mr Thomson was obliged to convince the African Commonwealth leaders that there would be no sell-out on NIBMAR and Mr Smith needed to consult the South Africans on the prospects of their continuing support for Rhodesia's illegally acquired independence.

The possibility of resuming any sort of meaningful discussions was also complicated by the intensification of guerrilla incursions during the months when the meetings were being planned. Mr Smith opened the diplomatic offensive on 28 August by sending a strongly worded protest to the British Government about the use of Zambia as a base for guerrilla attacks upon what he termed 'a friendly Commonwealth country', apparently under the delusion that Rhodesia was still a member of the Commonwealth. The procedure was a particularly odd one, since the British refused to receive a communication from an agent of an illegal government (the head of the residual mission in London) and the Rhodesians directed their protest to a country which bore no responsibility whatever for the actions of another sovereign State, irrespective of its former colonial status or its membership of the Commonwealth.

The Rhodesian protest set off a number of other diplomatic incidents, which worsened the already strained relations between Britain and Zambia, the latter now the threatened target of assault from both Rhodesia and South Africa. Zambia responded by appealing to Britain to intervene in its colony to restore law and order (which it was committed to do if it considered that this was the case) and to counter the invasion of the territory by South African forces. The British response was to ignore the Rhodesians, protest to the South Africans and warn the Zambians, none of which had any observable effect. The formal protest to the South African Government met with the reply that their forces would remain on Rhodesian territory so long as the guerrillas operating in that area included units of the banned African National Congress of South Africa. Their line of defence had become the Zambezi, and there was no intention of withdrawing the forces already posted there. (In fact, they were to be steadily reinforced.) The British reply to Zambia, which deplored the use of that country as a base for armed incursions into Rhodesia, had the effect of infuriating the Zambians, who took the warning as evidence that Britain was aligning itself with the Rhodesian regime against the countries which were aiming to overthrow it. So far as the Zambians were concerned, the British warning amounted to an acceptance and even an endorsement of the Smith regime's protest to the British Government.[24]

Nor was the atmosphere for renewed negotiations improved by the attempt of the Rhodesian Front congress, meeting at the end of September, to repudiate the *Tiger* proposals as a basis for any independence settlement. Not that Mr Smith had accepted the proposals either, but he was aware that for the British they would at least be the starting point on which any further discussions would be based. However, to reassure any supporters suspicious of conceding anything to the British, he reaffirmed that the 'Government' had set their course and that it was their intention to 'paddle their own canoe'. He left them in no doubt about his decision if he were offered the choice of going along the road they had already chosen or contemplating acceptance of anything that the British might offer them.[25] Although obviously for home consumption, Mr Smith's statement amounted to a flat rejection of the *Tiger* proposals (called for in the resolution he was allegedly opposing), since he was ruling out 'anything' the British might offer, and to do so in advance of negotiations was scarcely conducive to their success. But his immediate priority was to ensure the support of his party and this he had succeeded in doing, irrespective of the inconsistencies of his methods.

In Britain, only the Tories seemed undeterred about these ill omens from Rhodesia. As for the Labour party, no debate on the subject even took place at the party conference at Scarborough in October. Although there was a composite resolution on the agenda, it was conveniently never reached, despite protests from the delegates concerned about the Government's manoeuvres (including the meetings with representatives of the South African Government) in preparation for the Commonwealth Secretary's visit to Salisbury in November. Technically, the decision not to have any debate on the subject rested with the conference arrangements committee, responsible for the proceedings of the conference. But it was indeed unusual that for this subject, which had figured in nearly every party conference discussion of colonial policy since the 1950s and which had become an international issue involving the Commonwealth and the United Nations, the National Executive Committee could find no time for a debate.

No inhibitions on the subject prevailed at the Conservative party conference, meeting in Brighton in mid-October. Mr Heath was so convinced that a settlement could be concluded that he advocated the Commonwealth Secretary staying on in Salisbury until final agreement was reached. There was no real basis for this optimism, however, especially after Mr Smith's remarks to his party congress the previous month. Nevertheless, the Conservative party's conviction that a settlement was still possible was reflected in a conference resolution calling for the renewal of negotiations with Salisbury and also condemning United Nations interference in a problem subject to Britain's sole jurisdiction. Although there were some disappointed Monday Club spokesmen, who would have preferred an end to sanctions altogether and a recognition of the illegal regime's independence, most of the membership were able to accept the main objectives of the resolution.[26]

The Tories were so optimistic about the prospects of a settlement resulting from the Commonwealth Secretary's visit to Salisbury that they refrained from challenging the renewal of the sanctions Order when it was laid before Parliament at the end of October. Nevertheless, they still took the opportunity of expressing their doubts about the possibility of mandatory sanctions bringing about a return to constitutional rule in Rhodesia.[27] While the easy passage of the renewal Order was not unrelated to the expectations attached to the Thomson visit, Mr Wilson did not hold out much hope for its success. In the course of announcing the visit, he admitted that during the preceding two months, while the talks were being planned, the Rhodesians had thrown over in their public statements four of the Six Principles; they had never accepted the Fourth (on ending discrimination) and they were in the process of rejecting the Fifth (the test of acceptability). Nevertheless, he still retained some hope that, 'with statesmanship', they could reach agreement on the basis of those Principles. As an inducement for the Rhodesians to respond, he held out the assurance that there could be no question of early majority rule because of 'the state of African nationalist leadership', which was left undefined except for the speculation on how much it was the fault of the Europeans.[28]

The Thomson Visit

The British Government were also concerned about Commonwealth reactions to the impending talks in Salisbury. Mr Thomson, the Commonwealth Secretary, therefore used the occasion of his attendance at the Commonwealth Parliamentary Association meeting in Uganda at the end of October 1967 to assure the Commonwealth leaders that his Government would not be a party to any sell-out in Rhodesia nor abandon their commitment to the communiqué of September 1966. However, it was most unlikely that they would be won over by Mr Thomson's case for negotiations with the rebels, since they had already rejected similar persuasions from Mr Wilson at the Prime Ministers' conference and from Lord Caradon at the United Nations. Certainly the Zambians had grave doubts about the possibility of achieving any settlement which would ensure majority rule, as President Kaunda indicated at a private meeting with Mr Thomson in Lusaka after the conference. For Mr Thomson, it was a most unfortunate task, since he had to bear the brunt of resentment and hostility arising from the Africans' disenchantment with the Labour party. Most of the African leaders had formed close ties with, and received help and encouragement from, the Labour party during the years of their own struggle for independence. Mr Thomson had been a leading party spokesman on colonial issues and had worked with most of the nationalist movements in Africa. On behalf of his party, he had opposed Federation, fought against the imposition of the 1961 Constitution and supported the commitment to NIBMAR.. For the Africans he met at the conference in Uganda, he had been a symbol of the Labour party's record of opposition to colonialism and white minority rule; but that image had been shattered by the Labour Government's abandonment in practice of their commitment to majority rule.

At least Mr Thomson was saved from the final humiliation of a sell-out by the obduracy of the Smith regime. He was to be saved again, exactly a year later, for the same reason. The only surprise was that he expected anything else on either occasion, if he intended to uphold the Six Principles, let alone the NIBMAR pledge. From his report on the meeting, it was evident that Lord Alport had been seriously misled as to the nature of Mr Smith's 'improvements' on the *Tiger* proposals and therefore deceived about the possibilities of an agreement. The most important effect of these changes would be to remove the safeguards against retrogressive amendment (the Second Principle). Mr Smith's proposal that all African members of the Senate should be Chiefs would mean that the elected Africans would no longer constitute a blocking quarter to prevent discriminatory legislation or measures to impede majority rule. The other major alteration would remove the *Tiger* safeguard providing that amendments to the entrenched clauses should be subject to appeal to a Constitutional Commission, with the further right of appeal to the Judicial Committee of the Privy Council. Since these changes were fundamentally incompatible with the principles to which the Government were committed, Mr Thomson concluded that they had no alternative but to pursue the policy of sanctions and to stand by their pledge to the Commonwealth on NIBMAR.[29]

Sir Alec's Act of Faith

Mr Smith's renunciation of the Six Principles did not deter the Conservatives from launching their own settlement campaign, with Sir Alec Douglas-Home following in the footsteps of Mr Thomson. Just what Sir Alec expected to achieve after the recent rebuff to the Commonwealth Secretary was never clearly set out by the Conservative party. There was the Rhodesian claim that if the Conservatives had been in office a settlement would have been achieved[30] (although this had not happened when they were) and there was the Conservatives' contention that the failure to get a settlement was due to the Labour Government's conduct of the negotiations. The Conservatives were also preoccupied with what they considered to be the financial costs of the continuation of the rebellion. While this theme, not surprisingly, recurred in Monday Club pronouncements on the subject, as it did in those of the Rhodesian Front regime, it was increasingly heard from official front bench spokesmen of the party. Mr Bernard Braine, as one of these spokesmen, told the Conservative Commonwealth and Overseas Council on 30 January 1968 that it was ridiculous to continue along a course which cost the British Government at least £100 million a year on the balance of payments – a figure previously, and erroneously, quoted by Mr Duncan Sandys and denied in turn by the Prime Minister, the Chancellor of the Exchequer and the Commonwealth Secretary. The result of this course, according to Mr Braine, was to slow down Rhodesia's economic development, thus making life more difficult not only for the white minority but for the black majority, whose interests the British were supposed to be serving. He also revived the argument that the UDI was caused by the Rhodesian belief that a satisfactory settlement would never be secured from a Labour Government and that the *Tiger* negotiations had been conducted against a background of 'failure and futility'.[31] On all these counts, it was alleged, the Conservatives were better placed to succeed where the Labour Government had failed, and the visit of Sir Alec had been arranged to test this conviction.

Sir Alec's visit to Rhodesia was more than anything else an act of faith. He was convinced that the British and the Rhodesians were 'two sensible, civilised peoples' who ought to be able to work out a constitutional problem which, in his view, could not be insoluble. He based his optimism on the belief that the two sides had got very close to a political solution when Mr Wilson and Mr Smith had worked out the *Tiger* proposals. However, contrary to what Mr Braine had told the Conservative Commonwealth and Overseas Council, he admitted that he still didn't know whether it broke down because there was a failure of communications on the interim period or because Mr Smith and his colleagues did not like the constitutional part of it. While the former could be remedied, if it were concerned with the constitutional proposals — such as unimpeded progress towards majority rule — then that posed a much more difficult problem. His party had always maintained that that principle would be a condition of any settlement: no date or time-table would be laid down, as the *Tiger* provisions did not name one, but it would have to be written in as a guarantee.[32] Thus committed, Sir Alec held his talks with the Smith regime.

The outcome of those talks was never fully revealed, partly because Sir Alec was reluctant to admit that he hadn't got from Mr Smith the concessions necessary to justify the reopening of negotiations on the basis of the Six Principles, but also because the entire subject was buried by the overriding importance of the regime's decision to execute on 6 March 1968 three Africans condemned to death for offences committed before the UDI, in defiance of the Royal prerogative of mercy. Sir Alec had also to establish that his approach to the problem was not what the Conservatives might do if returned to office, since any indication that his party might be more generous in terms of concessions would only postpone the possibility of a settlement until the next British general election. Instead, he insisted that negotiations should be reopened 'within weeks rather than months', because it would be more difficult to get a settlement (as Mr Smith had threatened) after the Rhodesian constitutional commission submitted its report. Although he claimed to have found substantial changes since the Commonwealth Secretary's report the previous December, and to have worked out proposals that went a long way to bridge the difference between the two sides, when it came to spelling out the details it was evident that the fundamental differences still remained.[33]

After the hangings episode had ruled out any immediate resumption of relations, Sir Alec revealed that he had told Mr Smith 'straight' that he did not see how any British Government could accept a proposal that entrenched clauses, written into the constitution for the purpose of securing the minimum rights of Africans, should be controlled by Chiefs. However, when he explained that the whole purpose of his visit to Salisbury was to try to see whether he could obtain a 'braking mechanism', the essential difference between the two sides following the *Tiger* talks, the full extent of his failure, in addition to his misunderstanding, was revealed.[34] Presumably, by 'braking' mechanism, which was what the Smith regime wanted in order to slow down African advance, Sir Alec meant 'blocking' mechanism, which was what the Africans required to prevent retrogressive legislation by a European minority regime. (In 1972, Sir Alec was to chide a member of the African National Council delegation for not understanding this constitutional concept.) Whatever he chose to call it, he had to confess that he could not really say that the proposals contained 'a complete braking [sic] mechanism' of elected Africans. There was an amendment and an adjustment he should have required *if he had thought of it;* but he believed it could still be got. Any remaining doubts about what Sir Alec had got Mr Smith to agree to were dispelled by the Commonwealth Secretary's revelation that Mr Smith's proposals to Sir Alec still fell decisively short of the blocking quarter of popularly elected Africans to which he had allegedly agreed on *Tiger.*

Notes

1. *Rhodesia, Proposals for a Settlement, 1966,* Cmnd. 3159; *Rhodesia, Documents relating to Proposals for a Settlement,* 1966, Cmnd. 3171.

2. *Relations between the Rhodesian Government and the United Kingdom Government, November 1965 to December 1966,* CSR 49-1966.

3. See Cmnd. 3159, 3171, 1966.

4. According to *The Chronicle* (Bulawayo), 7 December 1966, Mr Smith claimed that Mr Wilson had suggested as possible members Sir John Caldicott, a former Federal Minister; Mr S. Sawyer, a former Federal Parliamentary Secretary; Mr. Frank Clements, former Mayor of Salisbury; Mr Garfield Todd, a former Prime Minsiter; Mr H. Holderness, a legal adviser on constitutional matters; and Mr Chad Chipunza, an African MP and supporter of the Federation.

5. For the debate on *Tiger,* see 737 *HC Deb.,* 7-8 December 1966, cols. 1371-703; 278 *HL Deb.,* 8 December 1966, cols. 1230-425. The Motion was carried by a majority of 109 in the House of Commons.

6. The British claimed that the voluntary sanctions prevailing since November 1965 had already reduced Rhodesia's exports by an estimated 40 per cent, from a level of £143 million in 1965 to a current annual rate of £80 million.

7. Security Council, *Official Records,* 21st Year, 1331st Meeting, 8 December 1966.

8. Resolution 232 (1966), ibid., 1340th Meeting.

9. The Labour Government denied that the maintenance of sanctions had any significant financial effect upon the British economy. They put the direct cost of payment by the Exchequer at £27 million between UDI and 30 November 1967; and the cost to the balance of payments at £40 million. (756 *HC Deb.,* 15 December 1967, col. 240.)

10. See 739 *HC Deb.,* 19 January 1967, col. 650; vol. 740, 2 February 1967, cols. 760-3; vol. 745, 20 April 1967, col. 152.

11. Rhodesia, *Parliamentary Debates,* vol. 66, 27 January 1967, vols. 804-8.

12. Ibid., vol. 67, 17 May 1967, cols. 1011-12.

13. See 740 *HC Deb.,* 6 February 1967, cols. 1219-300; 279 *HL Deb.,* cols. 1152-202.

14. 748 *HC Deb.*, 13 June 1967, cols. 305-9.

15. *Sudden Assignment*, 1965.

16. *Rhodesian Commentary*, 3 July 1967.

17. Rhodesia, *Parliamentary Debates*, vol. 68, 26 July 1967, col. 139.

18. Ibid., 20 July 1967, cols. 57-60.

19. Alport's report was announced in Parliament six months later. See 288 *HL Deb.*, 25 January 1968, cols. 581-5.

20. 751 *HC Deb.*, 25 July 1967, cols. 325-9.

21. The resolution was adopted 9 June 1967 by 17-1 (Australia).

22. *Africa Digest*, vol. XIV, no. 7, August 1967.

23. Letter from the Secretary to the Rhodesian 'Cabinet' (Mr Gerald Clark), *The Observer*, 20 August 1967.

24. See *Note to the United Kingdom Government from the Rhodesian Government*, 28 August 1967, CSR 45-1967.

25. *Rhodesia Herald*, 30 September 1967.

26. *Report of the 85th Annual Conservative Party Conference*, Brighton, 1967.

27. See Mr Richard Wood, 753 *HC Deb.*, 8 November 1967, vols. 1136-7.

28. 751 *HC Deb.*, 26 October 1967, col. 1885.

29. 756 *HC Deb.*, 12 December 1967, cols. 211-22. Mr Thomson's initial announcement of the differences between the two sides indicated that the proposed changes were in violation of four of the Six Principles. (See ibid., 14 November 1967, cols. 231-6.) In reply, Mr Smith denied that the principles were of any real consequence, because they 'could be interpreted in a dozen different ways'. He cited the First Principle (which he mistakenly called the Fourth) as meaning 'anything from five years to 1,000 years'. (See Rhodesia, *Parliamentary Debates*, vol. 70, 1 February 1968, cols. 357-63.)

30. See *Realites*, 4 August 1967, quoted in *The Times*, 5 August 1967.

31. *Rhodesia Herald*, 1 February 1968.

32. Ibid., 12, 14 February 1968.

33. Ibid., 28 February 1968.

34. 766 *HC Deb.*, 17 June 1968, cols. 752, 850.

7 AN ACT OF GRATUITOUS CRUELTY

> 'I have never ceased to be amazed at the number of Africans who still come forward and thank Government for restoring peace and normality to them.'
>
> Ian Smith, 13 December 1968.

If the Rhodesians had intended to pursue the talks begun by Sir Alec Douglas-Home, they chose an inopportune time to proceed with the execution of three Africans condemned to death for offences committed before the UDI and in defiance of the Royal prerogative of mercy. On 1 March 1968, while Sir Alec was telling his constituents in Perth that a negotiated settlement ought to be possible because the proposals worked out with Mr Smith went a long way to bridge the differences between the two sides, the Appellate Division of the High Court of Rhodesia was rejecting an application for a declaration that the three condemned Africans had a right of appeal to the Privy Council. Another application, for an order extending a temporary interdict for four months to allow a direct appeal to the Privy Council, was also refused. For the High Court, the Chief Justice, Sir Hugh Beadle, maintained that an application to the Privy Council would be wholly ineffective and would not prevent the execution of the appellants if the 'Government' decided to exercise their prerogative of carrying out the sentence. He also said that the granting of an interdict would have the effect of staying the execution of about 100 condemned men awaiting death, which would be 'an act of gratuitous cruelty' by increasing delay.

While the timing of the Rhodesian act of defiance could not have been worse so far as the negotiations were concerned, the decision to proceed with the hanging of the condemned Africans at that particular time was related to the culmination of the long process of court hearings on the cases, which involved the fundamental issue of the legality of the rebel regime. The fact that they had hesitated to execute any of the convicted Africans so long as their legal status was in doubt, for to do so without the Governor's assent would incur the onus of 'judicial murder', was an indication that they were still uncertain about the loyalty of the judiciary. Since the UDI, the judiciary had been acting under the instructions of the British Government to carry on their functions of dispensing justice but to refrain from actions which would further the aims of the rebellion. So long as the legality of the regime which they served was not challenged, this precarious balance could be maintained; but with test cases pending in the courts, the judiciary was obliged to come down on one side or the other.

The case of the three Africans condemned to execution had been under review since the previous September, after the 'Minister' for Law and Order, Mr Desmond Lardner-Burke, had announced the decision to proceed and the Officer Administering the Government, Mr Dupont, had signed the warrants. Two of the Africans (James Ndhlamini and Victor Mlambo) had been convicted under the Law and Order (Maintenance) Act in December 1964 for a petrol bomb attack on a car in which a European was killed and the third (Duly Shadreck) had been sentenced to death in September 1965 for the murder of a Chief. Although the Rhodesian High Court, in September 1967, had allowed an interim interdict granting a stay of execution, pending appeal to the Appellate Division, it had rejected a perpetual interdict on the ground that the Smith regime were the *de facto* government of Rhodesia and therefore rightfully exercised the authority to order the executions. The appeal against the High Court's decision reached the Appellate Division on 29 February 1968.

Before it was heard, however, another test case, involving the legality of detention under the Emergency Powers Act of November 1965, in which Mr Daniel Madzimbamuto and (in the initial stages) the European legal adviser to the African nationalists, Mr Leo Baron,[1] were involved, was decided on 29 January 1968 in favour of the rebel regime. Although, ironically, the Appellate Division found that the detentions of the two appellants were unlawful, it was for reasons not related to the constitutional question. The Court held that the Emergency Proclamations were valid but that the particular regulation under which the detention was continued was beyond the power to make regulations given by the Emergency Powers Act. It was for this reason that a Bill to amend that Act was introduced at the time of the Douglas-Home visit to southern Africa.[2] On the constitutional issue, however, as the 'Minister' for Law and Order summed up the judgement, the highest Court in the land had ruled that Parliament was the lawmaker of the country and that all Acts passed by it would be upheld by the Courts, at worst if they conformed to the 1961 Constitution but at best if they conformed to the 1965 'Constitution'; that all proclamations signed by the Officer Administering the Government were legal and of full force and effect, subject to the same qualification; and that all Rhodesians, because of this ruling, were obliged to obey the laws enacted by the

'Government' and not look over their shoulders for guidance from Britain.

With the *de facto* status of the regime established by the Madzimbamuto case, the result of the appeal of the three convicted Africans awaiting execution was a foregone conclusion. At the first hearing before the High Court the applicants had maintained that under the 1961 Constitution the final decision not to grant a reprieve had to be taken by the Governor and that this decision could not lawfully be taken by the Officer Administering the Government under the 1965 'Constitution'. Before the Appellate Division an additional plea was made that the long delay before execution amounted to inhuman treatment contrary to the provisions of the Constitution and that in view of this delay the death penalty should be reduced. Delivering the unanimous decision of the Court on 29 February, the Chief Justice stated that, as the effect of the judgement given in the constitutional case was that the present 'Government' could lawfully do anything that their predecessors could lawfully have done under the 1961 Constitution, they were clearly a successor in title to all the powers of the previous Government. Since the power to grant a reprieve under either the 1961 or the 1965 Constitution could only be exercised on the advice of the Executive Council, it followed that the present 'Executive Council' clearly had the power to decide whether the sentence should be carried out.

On the same day, to forestall the possibility of the Appellate Court granting a right of appeal to the Privy Council, the 'Minister' for Law and Order, in an affidavit before the Court, declared that the 1965 'Constitution' neither permitted nor recognised any right of appeal by any person in Rhodesia from a decision of the Appellate Division to any other court, including the Privy Council. It was in these circumstances that the judges of the Appellate Division, on 1 March, refused the application for a declaration that the three Africans sentenced to death had a right of appeal to the Privy Council and also decided unanimously that they could not make a declaration that a right of appeal to the Privy Council existed in the Madzimbamuto detention case.

The British response to this flagrant violation of the constitutional provision for appeal to the Privy Council was to invoke the Royal prerogative of mercy, commuting the death sentences to life imprisonment. Two days later, on 4 March, an application to the Appellate Division for an order staying the execution in accordance with the Royal reprieve was also rejected. This time the Chief Justice said that the new circumstance arising since the last application was that the British Government 'purported to use the prerogative of mercy', invoking the name of Her Majesty the Queen. However, he maintained that the 1961 Constitution, which granted full internal sovereignty to Rhodesia, divested the Crown of the power to exercise the prerogative of mercy, which was now the responsibility of the 'Executive Council' of Rhodesia. Since no other new issues had been raised and since it had been ruled by the Court that the 'Government' of Rhodesia was the *de facto* government and the successor to the Government under the 1961 Constitution, the application was dismissed.

While the judges of the High Court had gone along with the regime's case up to this point (except for Fieldsend's dissent in the Madzimbam-uto case), the impending split — over the constitutional right of appeal to the Privy Council — came on 4 March 1968, with the resignation of Mr Justice Fieldsend and a critical statement by Mr Justice Dendy Young, who subsequently resigned. In his request to the Governor to relieve him of his duties as a judge of the General Division, following the judgement by the Appellate Division, Fieldsend said that to continue in office in the light of the regime's declared intention not to recognise any right of appeal to the Privy Council amounted to acquiescing in the abandonment of the 1961 Constitution. Mr Justice Dendy Young, senior judge of the General Division, said in a statement in his Bulawayo court that the refusal of the Appellate Court to stay the executions was a denial of the right of the condemned men to test the validity of the provision of the 1965 'Constitution' which denied to the citizens of Rhodesia access to the Privy Council. He claimed that, while in the earlier constitutional case, the Appellate Division had by implication held this provision to be invalid, the effect of the later decision appeared to have extended validity to it.

It only remained for the 'Executive Council' to consider the petitions for clemency submitted to the Officer Administering the Government on behalf of the three condemned Africans. To have granted a reprieve would not have derogated from the sovereign powers claimed by the rebel regime, since the decision to do so would have been taken by Mr Dupont, on the advice of his 'Ministers', not by the Sovereign's representative, the Governor. At stake in the decision was not the legality of the regime, which had already been conferred by the courts, but the regime's relationship with Britain, which would be severely affected by an act of defiance of the appeals for restraint, Nevertheless, the regime chose to reject the final appeals, and on 6 March three Africans were hanged. Two other Africans, condemned to death in October 1964 for killing a sub-Chief, were also hanged within the same week.

In defence of their actions, the rebel regime issued a statement on the day of the first hangings declaring that, as far as the British Government were concerned, the three executed Africans, whom they had purported to reprieve, were merely pawns in the political game, to be manipulated in an attempt to undermine the authority of the Rhodesian 'Government' and to discredit the High Court. They accused the British Government of irresponsibility and cynicism, all the more to be deplored because they had brought in the Queen, and of unconstitutional action, in terms of the recent judgement by the High Court that internal sovereignty (including the prerogative of mercy) had been granted to Rhodesia under the 1961 Constitution.[3]

Comprehensive Retaliation

The reaction of the British Government and of the world community was one of horror and repugnance. In Britain, the Commonwealth Secretary expressed shock and outrage at the execution of men who, however serious their crimes, had been so long under sentence of death and had been denied time for their cases to be determined by the highest court of appeal. Nothing could remove or reduce the grave personal responsibility that rested on all those involved in the executions, he said; and as a first step the Government were taking action to remove the Chief Justice from the line of succession to the Governor. Although the Conservative party preferred to condemn all acts of violence in Rhodesia, their spokesman, Sir Alec Douglas-Home, also had to concede that it was difficult to see how talks with the regime could be reopened in the light of the executions. The Government's Motion on the subject, moved by the Prime Minister himself, expressed abhorrence of the executions carried out in defiance of the Royal prerogative of mercy and deplored the action of the regime in denying the reprieved men the right of appeal to the Privy Council.[4]

The Rhodesian action was condemned by most of the world community, including the Organisation of African Unity, the Commonwealth and various agencies of the United Nations. Papal intervention was also exercised, through the Roman Catholic hierarchy in Salisbury, in an effort to put an end to any further hangings. At the United Nations, protests were immediately recorded by the Special Committee on Decolonisation and by the Commission on Human Rights; and the Security Council was summoned to consider the situation on 19 March at the request of thirty-six African States. The Special Committee, which began hearings of petitioners on the day of the first hangings, adopted a resolution on 7 March, condemning the 'assassination' of the three Africans and deploring the failure of Britain to prevent such crimes.[5] On the same day, the Commission on Human Rights approved a statement denouncing the 'illegal killings' as 'a clear and extreme denial as well as a flagrant and gross violation of human rights and fundamental freedoms of the African people'. Like the Special Committee, the Commission also called for appropriate action by the Security Council and urged the British Government to take immediate steps to save the lives of the remaining 100 or more political prisoners unlawfully detained by the illegal regime.

With mounting pressure from the United Nations for British intervention in Rhodesia, the Labour Government were obliged to take some action, if only to avert action by other States. Since force had long since been ruled out, the alternative could only be more of the same. The British permanent representative at the United Nations was accordingly instructed to propose to the Security Council a resolution to give effect to comprehensive mandatory sanctions. But the task assigned to Lord Caradon was not an easy one, since he had to convince the delegates calling for immediate action by the Council that Britain would not agree to any resolution which either proposed the use of force or advocated a direct confrontation with South Africa. He had also to ensure that his Government remained free of the NIBMAR commitment, so that they would be able to hold themselves open for future negotiations with the rebel regime.[6] From the opening meeting on 19 March until the passage of the compromise resolution on 29 May, the British delegation insisted upon imposing these conditions. While they succeeded in preventing a vote on the rival Afro-Asian resolution, by holding in reserve their power to veto, they could not get their own resolution adopted for lack of the necessary affirmative votes.

The resolution finally adopted on 29 May 1968, by a unanimous vote for the first time in the history of the Rhodesian issue before the Security Council, contained paragraphs from both the British and the Afro-Asian draft resolutions (in the latter case, those not repugnant to the British delegation). From the British draft, the new resolution incorporated provisions for the total ban on all imports from and exports to Rhodesia (with the exception of humanitarian and educational materials); the prohibition of all funds for investment; the denial of entry to persons travelling on Rhodesian passports; the prevention of airline companies operating to or from Rhodesia; and the denial of facilities for promoting emigration to Rhodesia. To ensure the implementation of the sanctions measures, a committee, composed of all members of the Security Council, would be established. On the more controversial issues raised by the Afro-Asian draft, only recommendations remained and these, unlike the sanctions proposed, were not mandatory. The specific condemnation of South African and Portuguese assistance to the rebel regime became a mere 'deploring' of the attitude of States that had not complied with their obligations under Article 25. The demand for NIBMAR disappeared, leaving only an advisory opinion that the administering Power should ensure that no settlement was reached without taking into account the views of the Rhodesian people, in particular the parties favouring majority rule.[7] Nor was Britain required to undertake any special responsibilities for meeting Zambia's increasingly difficult economic position as a result of the extension of the sanctions measures. Only a general request for assistance to Zambia was included, even though Zambia was entitled under Article 50 of the Charter to special consideration as a victim of the trade boycott. The only real British concession to the Afro-Asians, possibly as a compensation for the abandonment of NIBMAR and the requirement to use force, was the provision in paragraph 13 urging all member States 'to render moral and material assistance to the people of Southern Rhodesia in their struggle to achieve their freedom and independence'. But even this commitment was qualified by the Commonwealth Secretary's subsequent statement that nothing in the resolution condoned the use of violence and that, in any case, paragraph 13 was not mandatory.[8]

Although the Labour Government had succeeded in getting their limited objectives endorsed by the United Nations, they nevertheless encountered considerable opposition from the Conservative party when they sought Parliamentary approval for the new sanctions Order implementing the Security Council resolution. Since the three-way split over the oil sanctions vote in December 1965, the Tories had managed to restore at least a semblance of party unity by adopting the position that they were against the imposition of mandatory sanctions. However, by June 1968 it was no longer a practical proposition to be against mandatory sanctions when Britain and the rest of the United Nations were committed to supporting them. If the Labour Government were to be criticised for their sanctions policy, it was much more relevant to question the piecemeal manner in which, in three stages, they finally arrived at a comprehensive programme of economic sanctions, which the Commonwealth leaders had urged in September 1966. But the Tories made no real distinction between the selective mandatory sanctions of 1966 and the comprehensive ones of 1968. Both were condemned as punitive and vindictive, as well as a burden on the Zambian economy and the British balance of payments.[9]

While the sanctions Order was readily carried by the Government majority in the House of Commons, in the Lords enough Tory 'backwoodsmen' (predominantly hereditary peers) were summoned to defeat the measure by a margin of only nine votes. However, the victory of the Conservative peers did not prevent the adoption of the sanctions Order, since the Government need only bring in a new Order for Parliamentary approval. As a non-elected chamber, the House of Lords could not expect to reverse the policy of a Government which could command a majority of 73 on this issue in a popularly elected House. It was mainly for this reason that the Tory leadership in the Lords had not challenged the mandatory sanctions of the previous year (6 February 1967), even though their party colleagues in the Commons had voted against it. If the act seemed gratuitous in Britain, it was not so in Rhodesia, where it was regarded as a moral victory for the Smith regime and a rebuff for the United Nations sanctions effort. Nevertheless, for the Conservative leadership, Lord Jellicoe maintained that the vote against the new sanctions was not a vote in favour of the illegal regime, but a vote in support of continued negotiation.[10]

In the Shadow of the Gallows

The resumption of negotiations, as Jellicoe had admitted, was the main objective of the Conservative party protest. Tory pressure to take up the proposals brought back from Salisbury by Sir Alec Douglas-Home had been temporarily diverted by the hangings, which followed within a week of his return. At that time, the Commonwealth Secretary had announced that, under existing circumstances, there could be no question of resuming contacts with the regime. He said this on 6 March, when the first hangings occurred, and repeated it on the 11th, after two more Africans had been executed. On the first occasion, he had received encouragement from Sir Alec's observation that it was very difficult to see how the British Government could reopen talks with the Smith regime in view of the executions. Mr Thomson's statement had also been confirmed by the Prime Minister, when he added that it was quite impossible to have dealings with people who flouted the rule of law. What particularly appalled him was the affidavit by the 'Minister' for Law and Order declaring that whatever the highest court (the Privy Council) decided, he would take no notice of it and would go ahead with the hangings.[11] Only a fortnight later, although the Government were still condemning the hangings, they were not ruling out the possibility of resuming negotiations. From the tone of the Prime Minister's statement to Parliament on 27 March — his attack on people who could not be trusted to carry out legal agreements (Mr Lardner-Burke and Mr Dupont) and on the regime's recent racialist legislation, including the African (Urban Areas) Accommodation and Registration Act and the proposed Property Owners (Residential Protection) Bill — it appeared that any future contacts with the regime were ruled out. This impression was underlined by his specifying that, in the prevailing circumstances, the Government did not intend to talk 'in the shadow of the gallows'. Nevertheless, he could still envisage talks with 'any responsible persons' who were prepared to discuss a settlement on the basis of the principles to which they were committed.[12] In essence, he was not saying 'never'.

Nor was the Smith regime ruling out any future contacts, although they were still smarting under what they considered to be British interference in their internal affairs. After the hangings had ceased and reprieves were issued on 13 March to thirty-five Africans sentenced to death, Mr Smith told a press conference on 16 March that the execution of 'murderers' recently carried out in Salisbury should not be used as an excuse to prevent talks which could lead to a settlement between Rhodesia and Britain. However, any constitutional talks they might have with Britain were completely separate and divorced from the maintenance of law and order in the country, which had always been an exclusively Rhodesian affair in which Britain had never had any constitutional jurisdiction. Recent British interference, 'covertly hiding behind the skirts of their Queen', he regarded as 'one of the most despicable acts ever committed by a government of Britain'. Consequently, any personal doubts he had about Rhodesia becoming a republic had been wiped out completely by 'the antics of Harold Wilson and his socialist Government'. Nevertheless, Mr Smith envisaged Rhodesia facing two roads for its constitutional future: the first was the Anglo-Rhodesian settlement route; the other the country's own constitutional commission. There could be no doubt in his mind that if the British Government were prepared to play their part and co-operate, the first road would prove the best and quickest means towards Rhodesia's goal of world recognition. But the first road would be taken only if the end result were in Rhodesia's interest. There was a time limit to this plan, and if the first road were closed, Rhodesia would reach a constitution via the second road, and thereafter it would be too late to go back once the die had been cast.[13]

The Second Road

Although Mr Smith may have preferred the first road, the prospects of getting the British to agree to any of the constitutional schemes devised by the Rhodesians, beginning with the report of the Whaley Constitutional Commission on 5 April 1968 and culminating in the Rhodesian Front's 'Yellow Paper' on 17 July, became increasingly remote. Nor was there any likelihood of Mr Wilson finding 'any responsible persons' in Rhodesia who were prepared to discuss a settlement on the basis of the Five Principles, all of which were violated by the proposals under consideration in that country. In fact, relations between the two countries, already embittered by the hangings and their aftermath, became increasingly strained as Mr Smith was obliged to outflank his right wing during the extended debates on the constitutional future of Rhodesia. Within the Rhodesian Front were those who, in the absence of a complete surrender of their principles by the British, were opposed to any attempt at a negotiated settlement, preferring to move on directly to an apartheid-style constitution and republican status. While Mr Smith may have shared these objectives, he was aware that to implement them at that stage would have precluded the possibility of getting any settlement with the British. At the same time, he had to preserve the unity of the Rhodesian Front, safeguard his position of leadership and convince the rank and file that he was not preparing to sacrifice party principles in order to comply with the British Government's conditions for an agreement.

Mr Smith had succeeded in preventing dissension within the Rhodesian Front, during the year between the appointment of the constitutional commission in February 1967 and its report in April 1968, by postponing any debate on the constitutional issue until the report was completed. He had also made use of the interval to threaten the British Government with the prospect that, unless they agreed to a constitutional settlement soon, the Rhodesians would go ahead and produce their own version. In fact, the fourteen-month-wait for the Whaley report turned out to be in vain. The proposals, even though they failed to meet any of the requirements of the Five Principles – particularly in their rejection of majority rule at any stage and their preservation of racial discrimination in land apportionment – proved to be unacceptable to the Rhodesian Front, and especially to the right-wing group that broke away to form the Rhodesia National party under the leadership of Mr Len Idensohn. The lesson that the British Government could derive from this move was obvious, as Lord Alport had pointed out:

how could Mr Smith contemplate negotiating with any government in Britain committed to eventual majority rule in Rhodesia when he could not even get the acquiescence of his own supporters to the report of a Rhodesian constitutional commission, composed mainly of 'strong Rhodesian Front men', which proposed the modified solution of eventual parity of representation between the races?[14]

The Rhodesian Front had their own conception of what a Rhodesian constitutional system ought to contain and this included the entrenchment of apartheid and the prevention of anything even approaching parity. In these circumstances, Mr Smith's dilemma was similar to that of Mr Nkomo, when the African nationalist party rejected the constitutional proposals in 1961 — 'no sane leader could disregard the voice of his people and supporters'[15] — and he behaved accordingly. During the months between the rejection of the Whaley recommendations and the adoption of the Front's own constitution, Mr Smith's pronouncements increasingly tended to reflect the voice of *his* supporters, especially on the crucial issue of majority rule. Not that these views were anything new, either to Mr Smith or to Rhodesian Front spokesmen, who had always denied the possibility of majority rule. It was only after Mr Smith came to realise that a constitutional settlement with Britain would be Rhodesia's 'first prize', in the sense that it would bring about international recognition and the end of sanctions, that such expressions were less in evidence, although never entirely absent.

The hardening of Rhodesian attitudes was not lost on the British Government either. In fact, coming right after the hangings, it provided a useful justification for the increase in the sanctions measures and conclusive evidence (at least for a few months) that no settlement would be possible under such circumstances. Although Mr Wilson and the Commonwealth Secretary had said after the hangings that they could not negotiate with a regime that 'flouted the rule of law' nor 'in the shadow of the gallows', the reasons produced after the furore over the executions had died down, at least in Britain, were more concerned with the retrogressive constitutional manoeuvres. Several of the Labour Ministers who had participated in the independence negotiations with the Smith regime were only now revealing that there never had been an acceptance of majority rule by the Rhodesian Front. Even the Lord Chancellor, Gardiner, who envisaged majority rule as 'many, many years ahead', admitted that apart from a very brief hour in the *Tiger*, Mr Smith had usually fairly frankly said that he did not believe in majority rule. He himself had been in the Cabinet room at No. 10 when Mr Smith had said that, if at any time it appeared that there were likely to be an African majority elected, obviously they would have to have the right to change the constitution in order to prevent it.[16] The Attorney-General, Sir Elwyn Jones, also took to quoting the sayings of Mr Smith. On the same subject, he noted that Mr Smith had said (at Bulawayo on 3 May 1968) that his regime must retain the ability to change the constitution, so that if in ten years or twenty years time their children found that the course along which they had set Rhodesia was drifting, then they would easily be able to reverse this so that it once more moved back on to the true course. As for getting any agreement on majority rule, he pointed out that Mr Smith had recently told a British newspaper that the only basis on which he could sell this to Rhodesians would be to try to get them to believe that it didn't really mean anything for the next hundred years.[17]

This was the tactic actually used by Mr Smith when he had to face the task of getting his supporters to agree to the official party proposals — known as the 'Yellow Paper' — emanating from the Rhodesian Front caucus sub-committee and the party's divisional chairmen's committee. However, although the proposals were designed as a compromise to meet the varying shades of opinion within the party, they did not go far enough towards full-scale apartheid to appease the extremist wing led by Mr William Harper ('Minister' of Internal Affairs) or Lord Graham ('Minister' of External Affairs). The essence of the Yellow Paper was a two-stage approach to 'separate development' over a period of five years. During the interim stage, there would be a national parliament elected on racial lines, with the Europeans elected on a European roll (and also on a common roll for which only they would be able to qualify in any significant numbers) and most of the Africans chosen by electoral colleges of Chiefs. The second stage would follow with the implementation of the scheme for 'provincialisation', providing for a national parliament and three provincial councils representing, respectively, the European and the African, the latter divided along the tribal lines of the Ndebele and the Mashona. Provincial representation in the national parliament would be based on the contributions made by each of the provinces to the national Exchequer on the basis of personal income tax. The main advantage of the scheme, so far as Mr Smith was concerned, was that in the interim period he would be able to confront the British with the alternative of either conceding a settlement or allowing Rhodesia, by default, to move on to the second stage of provincialisation.

It was on these grounds that the compromise solution came unstuck. From the vote on the adoption of the proposals, it appeared that the

Rhodesian Front were fairly evenly divided. The majority, perhaps out of personal loyalty to the leader, were willing to go along with the interim government (which was overwhelmingly dominated by the Europeans) with the prospect of either getting some concessions from the British during the interval or, failing this, moving on to provincial separation. But the minority, who lost out by only two votes in the party caucus and by only eleven votes at the party congress, opposed any further efforts to try to work out with the British a *Tiger* type of constitution, favouring the immediate implementation of separate parliaments for each of the races. Although Mr Smith won a narrow victory for his proposals, he failed to maintain the unity of his party. The first to go was Mr Harper, who resigned at the request of Mr Smith on 4 July, after the party caucus had narrowly approved the proposals. The same week, the former leader of the party, Mr Winston Field, also resigned, but allegedly for different reasons — the party's increasing trend to the right and dissatisfaction with the leadership's handling of the situation. The resignation of Lord Graham followed on 11 September, after he had failed to get the party congress to adopt the alternative set of constitutional proposals which he had circulated to the delegates. With him went a large section of the Salisbury constituents, which had tabled the amendment based on his proposals. Their objection to the Yellow Paper, according to Lord Graham, was that it gave way to 'the liberal in stage one and to the illiberal in stage two'.[18]

The split in the Rhodesian Front over the Yellow Paper turned out to be a mixed blessing for Mr Smith. Although he had got his proposals through the congress, it was evident that nearly half of his party disapproved of them and would remain a potential source of conflict. Nevertheless, he had gained the interim period of five years, during which he could approach, or be approached by, the British, and he had shed some of the more extremist members who had been one of the main obstacles to the renewal of negotiations. He had also been rewarded, as a result of his campaign efforts to sell the interim plan to the electorate in the Gatooma by-election on 19 September, by the victory of the Rhodesian Front successor to the banished Mr Harper over his opponent from the right-wing Rhodesia National party.[19]

A further bonus for Mr Smith came in the form of a ruling from the Appellate Division of the High Court on 13 September that the regime were the *de jure* government and the 1965 'Constitution' the only valid one. The judgement arose from an appeal made in the General Division of the High Court in July during the hearing of a case against thirty-two Africans alleged to have entered the country carrying arms of war and thus subject to the mandatory death penalty. The appeal followed the ruling of the Privy Council on 23 July (by a majority of four to one, with Lord Pearce dissenting) in the constitutional test case involving the continued detention of Mr Madzimbamuto, that the regime's emergency regulations providing for detention without trial had no legal validity. What the Privy Council decision amounted to was that the regime and the 'Constitution' of 1965 were illegal and that legislative and administrative action by the members of that regime (including detention) were themselves illegal. As in the hangings case the previous March, the 'Minister' of Law and Order once more intervened to nullify the effect of the decision by announcing that the judgement of the Privy Council in the Madzimbamuto case would have no force or effect in Rhodesia because appeals to the Privy Council had been abolished by the 1965 'Constitution'. The High Court followed suit on 8 August, first by the Registrar's refusal to receive the Order-in-Council signed by the Queen requesting the release of Mr Madzimbamuto and then, on the following day, by rejecting the Privy Council ruling on the ground that, since the Court was sitting on the basis of authority derived from the 1965 'Constitution', it was not in the same hierarchy of courts as the Privy Council and therefore not bound by its judgement.

It was this decision of the High Court that was confirmed by the Appellate Division on 13 September, with the Chief Justice (Beadle) not only conferring legality on the regime but predicting that sanctions would not succeed in overthrowing the Rhodesian 'Government' and restoring the British Government to control (in the sense of their former authority) and that there were no other factors which might have succeeded in doing so.[20] Although settling the constitutional position in Rhodesia, the judgement of the Appellate Divsion did not finally dispose of the case of the thirty-two Africans, whose appeal on the merits of their case had still to be heard. But the court ruling was followed by an announcement by the 'Minister' of Law and Order'[21] on 24 September that the Government had decided, 'from a position of strength', to abolish the mandatory death sentence from the Law and Order (Maintenance) Act. In future, it would be left to the judges, who had just given legal validity to the regime (or else resigned in protest, as had Mr Dendy Young following the High Court's ruling on *de jure* status, and Mr Fieldsend after the hangings decision the previous March) to decide on such a penalty in future cases.

Notes

1. Mr Baron was released on 24 April 1967, on grounds of health, and subsequently left the country. He became deputy Chief Justice of Zambia.

2. Rhodesia, *Parliamentary Debates*, vol. 70, 8 February 1968, cols. 623-8.

3. *Rhodesia Herald,* 7 March 1968. For the regime's case for the decisions, see the official journal, *Rhodesian Commentary*, March 1968.

4. 761, *HC Deb.,* 26 March 1968, col. 1546.

5. The vote was 20-1, with Britain abstaining on the ground that it could not accept the allegations regarding its responsibilities.

6. See Security Council, *Official Records*, 23rd Year, 1399th Meeting, 19 March 1968; 1415th Meeting, 23 April 1968.

7. Ibid., 1428th Meeting, 29 May 1968.

8. See 765 *HC Deb.,* 30 May 1968, cols. 2136-8.

9. The direct cost to the Exchequer was put at £34.5 million between the UDI and May 1968, a rate of about £14 million a year; and the extra drain on the balance of payments was put at about £50 million a year. On the capital side, a Rhodesian settlement would probably harm the balance of payments. See *The Times*, 14 October 1968.

10. 293 *HL Deb.,* 17 June 1968, col. 360.

11. See 760 *HC Deb.,* 7 March 1968, col. 659; 11 March, col. 978; 14 March, col. 1620.   *

12. 761 *HC Deb.,* 27 March 1968, cols. 1559-69.

13. Broadcast on 24 March 1968, *Rhodesia Herald,* 25 March 1968.

14. 293 *HL Deb.,* 18 June 1968, col. 553.

15. Statement to the press on the rejection of the 1961 Constitution, 17 February 1961.

16. 293 *HL Deb.,* 17 June 1968, col. 328.

17. *Daily Telegraph,* 26 April 1968, quoted in 766 *HC Deb.,* 17 June 1968, col. 744.

18. *Rhodesia Herald,* 12 September 1968. The vote on the proposals at the party congress was 217-206, with 70 abstentions.

19. Ibid., 20 September 1968. The vote was 870-65.

20. Ibid., 14 September 1968.

21. Rhodesia, *Parliamentary Debates,* vol. 72, 24 September 1968, cols. 1569-81.

8 THE SECOND ROUND

> 'The present regime in Rhodesia is unwilling to accept the odium that would attach to a refusal to negotiate altogether ... but it will find some excuse for rejecting any final agreement by which it loses the right to control African advancement.'

> Sir Robert Tredgold, *The Rhodesia That Was My Life,* 1968.

Even before the second road had been traversed, Mr Smith had begun to approach the first. This was evident from his admission to London Independent Television on 20 September 1968, that he was prepared to try to work out with the British Government a constitution that satisfied the Six Principles, using the *Tiger* proposals as a starting point. Although this offer was obviously directed at the British envoy from the Commonwealth Office (Mr James Bottomley), who had arrived in Salisbury that day, he was careful to reassure his European supporters that he could not accept the British view that elected Africans should have all the say in the proposed blocking mechanism (the Second Principle) and, as usual, that he did not envisage majority rule occurring in his life-time. With this position declared in advance, he agreed to meet Mr Bottomley, whose visit was related to the alleged political changes in Rhodesia, including the results of the Rhodesian Front congress and the Gatooma by-election, the removal of some of the extremist elements from the party and the judicial decision on *de jure* status. The visit was also intended as a follow-up to the secret meetings held the previous month between Mr Smith and Mr Wilson's legal adviser, Lord Goodman, which had been arranged by Sir Max Aitken, chairman of Beaverbrook Newspapers and a close friend and former RAF colleague of Mr Smith. With Sir Max as intermediary, Lord Goodman's task was to sound out Mr Smith on the subject of a possible agenda for negotiations with the British Prime Minister. What these confidential meetings came to was not revealed, but enough encouragement emerged to justify the visit of the Commonwealth Office representative a month later.[1]

The new initiative undertaken by the Labour Government had begun as a secret mission, with Lord Goodman hiding out in South Africa while Sir Max Aitken paid what might appear to be a not unusual social visit to his war-time friend, Mr Smith. It was unlikely that the appearance in Salisbury of the chairman of Beaverbook Newspapers would be regarded as connected in any way with the activities of the Labour Government. But Lord Goodman's presence in Rhodesia, once the way was cleared for his participation, was less easy to conceal, since he was a well-known adviser to Mr Wilson and was unlikely to be in Rhodesia for any purpose other than one devised by the British Prime Minister. Prior to this occasion, he had served Mr Wilson as a general 'fixer' in various negotiations and legal proceedings, none of which was remotely concerned with Africa or Africans. Presumably, his selection for this mission was based upon the premise that Rhodesia was merely another problem to which he could apply his obvious talents as a negotiator. It was also possible that his choice for the task was due to the fact that, having no political constituency to which he was responsible, he had no prior commitments which would either inhibit his freedom as a negotiator or offend those with whom he was obliged to negotiate. The ambiguity of the Five Principles left the Government's emissary with a wide range of options as to how they should be interpreted. But he was still obliged to ensure that any agreement with Mr Smith would be acceptable to Mr Wilson as a proposition which he could recommend to his Cabinet and his supporters in Parliament and justify before his colleagues in the Commonwealth and in the United Nations.

Following the initiative of Lord Goodman in August and the visit of the Commonwealth Office representative the following month, further talks (or 'probings', as Mr Wilson called them) were conducted under the Governor's aegis by the head of the British Residual Mission, Mr P.A. Carter, with Mr Smith, Mr Howman (who had replaced Lord Graham at External Affairs) and Mr Lardner-Burke. Further preparations were being made by the Commonwealth Secretary (or Minister Without Portfolio, as he was known after his office was combined with the Foreign Office on 17 October), in talks with the South African Foreign Minister, Dr Hilgard Muller, who visited London on his return from the United Nations. But no meeting between the Prime Minister and Mr Smith could be held until after the conclusion of the Labour party conference the first week in October. Mr Smith had narrowly survived his party congress in September, Mr Wilson had yet to confront his.

From Birmingham to Bulawayo

Mr Wilson's political future may not have been at stake at Blackpool, as Mr Smith's had been at Salisbury, but it was evident that a large section of the party was concerned about the rumours of preparations for yet another meeting with the rebel regime. There had been considerable opposition within the Labour party to the *Tiger* proposals, and the fact that Mr Smith had rejected these terms was an indication that they would not settle without further concessions. There was also a sense of frustration with the failure of the sanctions measures to bring about any change in the situation, either in the sense of toppling the regime or making them more amenable to changes which would comply with the British Government's conditions for an independence settlement. While there had always been some members of the party who had opposed any negotiations with the rebels, and some who had advocated the use of force, these views had become more widespread over the years since the UDI, particularly as a result of the increasingly repressive and racialist policies carried out by the illegal regime. It was inconceivable that Mr Wilson could not have been aware of the growing opposition within his own party to the policies he was pursuing in Rhodesia. It was no longer a case of a few rebels who could be dismissed as representatives of the party's 'Africa lobby', such as Mr Alexander Lyon or Miss Joan Lestor. But the obvious leadership for a rebellion against Mr Wilson's policy — those members who had fought for African majority rule over the previous decade — had been co-opted into the Government, either directly responsible for Rhodesian policy (such as Mr Thomson and Mr Foley) or preoccupied with their own Ministries and also bound by collective responsibility (such as Mrs Castle, Mr Anthony Greenwood, Mr Callaghan and Mr Healey, the latter two having served as Opposition spokesmen on colonial affairs).

By the time the Labour party conference came to consider the question of renewed negotiations with Mr Smith, the arrangements were already made for the meeting, although this fact did not emerge until the following week (when the Tory conference would be opening). Not that a conference resolution on the subject would have deterred Mr Wilson from doing what he had planned to do in any case. But it could provide a source of embarrassment for him to embark upon negotiations condemned by a majority of his own party in advance and then have to seek the final approval of the Parliamentary Labour Party for any settlement. Although in most instances where the views of the conference and the PLP were at odds, the latter tended to prevail, there was always the possibility that the effect of the party conference decision would be to increase the growing number of MPs already reluctant to endorse any deal with the Smith regime.

Even with a large number of party members critical of the Government's policy, it was not certain that they could carry a hostile resolution against the advice of the National Executive Committee. It may well have been the case that the NEC expected the composite resolution, moved by the Billericay constituency party, to be defeated, because it included among its recommendations a call for the withdrawal of the Government's commitment not to use force. However, the resolution also included two other points in particular which were of overriding concern to the party delegates: a reaffirmation of the NIBMAR pledge and a rejection of further constitutional negotiations with the rebels. Although bound by the Commonwealth commitment to NIBMAR and by the United Nations recommendation for moral and practical assistance to Rhodesians struggling for their freedom (also contained in the composite resolution), the Government could scarcely afford to reaffirm either on the eve of the opening of negotiations. But the resolution was skilfully worded and in such a way as to recall the party's commitments since the NEC's warning statement of 1963, thus making it awkward for the NEC to swallow its own words and for the delegates to vote against what they had once voted for. Even the less controversial recommendations — on practical support for Zambia as a 'moral obligation' and on funds for educational assistance to Rhodesian Africans — could cause some embarrassment to a Government that had yet to meet Zambia's economic needs or to convince the Smith regime that the purpose of aid to African education was to prepare them for exercising the franchise and for assuming positions of governmental responsibility. The additional proposal, for resettling elsewhere Europeans opposed to living under African majority rule (the Kenya solution) was not even given any consideration.

While the main case against the resolution, put by Mr Frank Chapple, a trade union representative not in the Government, was that it called for a withdrawal of the commitment not to use force, the NEC spokesman also qualified the NIBMAR pledge beyond recognition and justified the resumption of negotiations with the rebels. Instead of NIBMAR the Government's policy was that, in the exceptional circumstances of Rhodesia, they were prepared to grant independence before majority rule provided that certain essential conditions, embodied in the Five Principles, were fulfilled. As for renewing negotiations with the rebels, this was justified by the argument that if they came to terms it would be better to deal with them than to have no deal at all. What the 'deal' would consist of seemed to matter less than the fact that it would take place. For those delegates concerned about the failure of sanctions 'to bring Mr Smith to his senses', the only consolation the NEC could offer was that in the event of the United Nations deciding to use force to impose a settlement (which Britain would veto in any case), the Government would then face quite different legal, military and moral obligations, in line with their policy of collective security. But Mr Wilson's concept of collective security did not embrace the Rhodesian situation, which was considered the sole responsibility of Britain. His message to the conference was that the struggle against racialism was a world-wide fight; it was the dignity of man for which they were fighting; and if what they asserted was true for Birmingham, it was also true for Bulawayo.[2] However, the 'fight' would obviously not include the use of force. Although the NEC had hoped to get the resolution defeated on the basis of its reference to the use of force, it was in fact carried by nearly half a million votes, after an amendment to delete that single recommendation had been approved by a show of hands (an outcome that was disputed by many of the delegates). The Government had thus suffered their first defeat on the Rhodesian issue and the negotiations on which they were about to embark had been condemned in advance. Not to be deterred, Mr Wilson took the decision as 'a sharp but not unexpected vote against the platform'.[3]

If Mr Wilson gained anything from pursuing the negotiations against the will of his party, it was a victory over the Conservatives, whose party conference opened in the shadow of a blaze of publicity accorded to the meeting on board HMS *Fearless* at Gibraltar from 9-13 October. Not only did the Tories lose the usual press attention to their proceedings; they were also left with virtually nothing to say about Rhodesia while the meetings proceeded. Their persistent demand for a renewal of talks had been answered, but all too soon so far as the timing of their conference was concerned. Their opposition to sanctions could not be pressed at such a time, since their initial support for the measures was based on the assumption that they would bring the regime to the conference table. Nor was the Government's conduct of the negotiations vulnerable to criticism. The secret diplomacy favoured by Sir Alec Douglas-Home had been carried out over the preceding months, Mr Smith received the type of treatment accorded to a legal head of government (having an entire cruiser for accommodation) and the proposals remained 'on the table' at the end of the talks. While the negotiations were on, they could only hope for a successful outcome; and when they were over, they had the consolation that the door was still open for further consultation.

A Change of Circumstances

Mr Wilson's justification for going ahead with the talks, in spite of the opposition he encountered from his party, was that the time had come to test the sincerity of Mr Smith's statement to Sir Alec and other British visitors that he was ready for a settlement within the Six Principles (which he had been saying on and off over the preceding three years). Moreover, the Governor, who was becoming impatient, had pressed strongly for a summit meeting, because he had felt that the chances of success were higher than for some time. To rebuff him might lead to his resignation, which Mr Wilson alleged would have the effect of 'precipitating a serious political crisis in Britain'. Other factors influencing his decision were the departure of some of 'the more objectionable' members of the regime, the firmness with which Mr Smith had dealt with his recent party congress and the move to end mandatory death sentences for certain offences. His case for opening talks at that particular time (which showed that he had been taken in by Mr Smith's propaganda efforts) was the urgency of attempting to conclude a settlement before the regime produced a new constitution that would be 'hard-line in form, segregationist, and designed to ensure that majority rule would be postponed well into the next century'. Mr Wilson was convinced that if the British Government rejected any attempt to negotiate or any attempt to head off a series of 'totally reactionary and oppressive constitutional moves by the regime', then there would be many in the British Parliament and among the public — going beyond the usual fringe of Rhodesian Front supporters — who might find it hard to forgive them.[4]

Much of Mr Wilson's optimism about the changed circumstances within Rhodesia had no basis in fact. The disappearance of 'intransigent racialists' like Mr Harper, Lord Graham and Mr George Rudland still left in the Rhodesian Front 'Cabinet' men like Mr Dupont and Mr Lardner-Burke, who had defied the Crown and the Privy Council over the hangings, and several others, like Mr A.P. Smith and Mr Phillip van Heerden, who had been on the side of Harper and Graham in opposing the Yellow Paper in the party caucus the previous July. In any case, Graham's departure did not take place until two months after the decision (on 30 June) to send Goodman to Salisbury. As for regarding Mr Smith's firmness with his party congress as a change of circumstances, this represented a difference of degree not of kind and was more than anything else an exercise in self-preservation. The only distinction that could be drawn between Mr Smith's position and that of his opponents (nearly half the party membership at the congress) was over the matter of timing – the five-year interim before Rhodesia moved on to a system of provincialisation. If Mr Smith chose to speak in terms of 'merit' or 'civilised' rule, instead of the more blatant language of 'white' control used by his opponents, he was doing so in order to assure the British that there was still something to negotiate about. Even the dropping of the mandatory death sentence, which Mr Wilson also had seen as a change of circumstances, had been explained away by the 'Minister' of Law and Order as a tactic to encourage the 'terrorists' entering Rhodesia with arms of war to surrender instead of trying to fight it out with the security forces (who were suffering increasing casualties in the process), with the hope that the judges might not always exercise their regained prerogative of withholding the sentence of death.

In spite of the propitious omens seen by Mr Wilson, he took the precaution of warning that there could be no certainty, or even probability, that a meeting would produce a settlement. He also admitted, although he did not share the view, that at the Cabinet meeting to consider the project, 'one or two Ministers were dubious, more so than at the time of the *Tiger* discussions'. All that Mr Wilson himself had to go on at that point was that the answers given by Mr Smith to the ten-point summary of the British requirements for a settlement conveyed by the Aitken-Goodman team went further than anything they had thus far received and were certainly better than the proposals brought back by Sir Alec Douglas-Home the previous February. Furthermore, on two of the key issues – the blocking quarter and the right of appeal in constitutional cases to the Privy Council – Mr Smith's replies to Sir Max Aitken had been 'clear and satisfactory'. He had also confirmed that he fully understood that, as a condition precedent to holding the meeting, there could be no agreement which failed to honour the Six Principles in full.[5]

If Mr Smith's replies had been clear and satisfactory, particularly on the issue of the 'second safeguard' (against retrogressive amendment), they did not remain so in the course of the negotiations. The talks on the *Fearless* failed, as those on *Tiger* failed, because, as Mr Wilson conceded, there remained deep differences, mainly derived from fundamentally opposed outlooks about Rhodesia's future, which expressed themselves in disagreement about safeguards. This should not have come as a surprise to Mr Wilson, although he may have been deceived by the assurances brought back by Sir Max Aitken. As in the *Tiger* talks, what Mr Smith appeared to agree to in the preliminary negotiations he ceased to accept as a part of the settlement. Since there was no time limit set for the decision of Mr Smith and his colleagues, as there had been at the conclusion of the *Tiger* meeting, this left ample opportunity for raising anew issues which were supposedly settled in the earlier stages of the talks.

Both the *Tiger* and the *Fearless* proposals involved amendments to the 1961 Constitution for the purpose of meeting the objectives laid down in the Six Principles.[6] In the *Fearless*, the main retreat by the British Government was the abandonment of the *Tiger* provision for 'a return to legality', alleged (but erroneously) by both the regime and the Conservative party as the reason for the failure to get a settlement. Under the *Fearless* proposals, Mr Smith's regime, suitably 'broad-based', but still with a majority of Rhodesian Front members, would remain in power while the proposals were submitted to the test of acceptability, thus remaining in control of the security system and the media of communication. Even if the test went against the regime, a second UDI would not be necessary, because Mr Smith's administration would still be in power, although sanctions would remain in force. Other changes, which represented further British concessions to Rhodesian pressure, involved a weakening of the *Tiger* provisions for ending racial discrimination and for obtaining the release of detainees. In the case of racial discrimination, while the *Tiger* proposals provided for a Royal Commission to be appointed by the British Government after consultation with the Rhodesians on its composition, under *Fearless*, a commission 'of the necessary independence and high-standing' would be established by Rhodesian legislation. The British Government would only be 'consulted' on its composition and also on its terms of reference. While both *Tiger* and *Fearless* allowed continued detention and restriction during the test of acceptability, the former provided that this would not be authorised unless the reviewing authorities were satisfied that the persons concerned had 'committed, or incited the commission of acts of violence or intimidation'. According to *Fearless*, they need only be satisfied, 'having full regard to past activities' that the persons concerned were 'likely to commit, or incite or inspire to commit, acts of violence or intimidation'. Such cases would be reviewed by a judge of the Rhodesian High Court (now purged of any dissenters against the regime) or referred to an 'impartial tribunal', two of whom would be Rhodesian nominees and the third appointed by the Lord Chancellor.

Three features of the *Fearless* proposals were singled out by Mr Wilson as relevant to the 'substantial change of circumstances' which would justify the British Government raising with their Commonwealth partners the question of NIBMAR.[7] The first, and by no means new feature, was an extended programme for African education, particulary technical education, for which the British Government would contribute up to £50 million over ten years. Such a programme was expected to have an important bearing on the number of Africans able to qualify for the 'A' roll franchise, although in fact the technical type of education would not provide the educational qualifications essential for the 'A' roll franchise. Moreover, the Rhodesian Front had already made it clear, when a similar proposal for British aid was broached by the previous Government, that, while it was not their policy to increase African educational expenditure for the purpose of political advance, they would accept financial support for a programme of technical education, which would obviously not have the same effect.

Nor could the other two important features be regarded as contributions to a 'substantial change of circumstances'. One provided that the Royal Commission appointed for the test of acceptability should also enquire into the arrangements for the registration of eligible voters under the proposed widely extended franchise for the 'B' roll. This proposal had arisen as a result of the British Government's concern that the requirements of the literacy test for electoral registration (about as easy to complete as a British income tax return, according to Mr Wilson) could not be met by more than an estimated 50,000 Africans. In any case, African voters, irrespective of their numbers, would still be almost entirely limited to the election of the seventeen 'B' roll seats, since few could meet the 'A' roll qualifications. All that the Royal Commission was empowered to do was to 'enquire' into the registration arrangements, with a view to 'encouraging greater African participation in Rhodesian political life'. As for the proposal for a broad-based government, including Africans, to carry Rhodesia through the whole process of introducing the new constitution (also included in *Tiger* but rejected by the Rhodesians), such an administration would still have a majority of Rhodesian Front members and the Africans, as well as any other members from outside the Front, would have to be acceptable to the Smith regime.

According to the communiqué issued at the end of the talks, Mr Smith was to take the proposals back to Salisbury, without commitment, for consideration with his colleagues. The Commonwealth Secretary would be available to go to Salisbury if the Rhodesians felt that this would assist them in their consideration of the British proposals. Although the British position at the end of the talks was defined as 'no sell out, no slamming the door', both sides recognised that a very wide gulf still remained between them on certain issues.[8]

The wide gulf proved insurmountable and the Rhodesian attack on the proposals began as soon as Mr Smith returned to Salisbury. There was no longer the excuse of the 'return to legality', which had been used for rejecting *Tiger*, since this was not required as part of the settlement. Instead, other issues, presumably agreed in advance of the meeting, were now raised as obstacles. In particular, Mr Smith, in a broadcast on 16 October 1968, seized upon the 'second safeguard', providing for appeal to the Privy Council of amendments to the specially entrenched clauses of the Constitution, as a derogation from the sovereignty of the Rhodesian 'Parliament'. While he could see other 'undesirable points', this provision was 'so fundamental and so completely repugnant' that unless it were removed there would be no possibility of agreement. Since this was one of the points on which he had supposedly given a clear and firm assurance to Sir Max Aitken, the whole credibility of his negotiating position was cast in doubt. Although this was not by any means the only point of difference to emerge, as the subsequent conversations with Mr Thomson revealed, it was made use of, in a public relations exercise, to convince pro-settlement groups in Rhodesia and in Britain of the reasonableness of the Rhodesian Front's case.

Since the British Government had already indicated their willingness to examine alternative methods of providing a second safeguard, Mr Smith's objection to the *Fearless* provisions on this ground had no basis in fact. Some of these were revealed by Mr Wilson in the Commons debate on 22 October. In particular, he offered to dispense with a judicial-type review altogether if an undertaking were given that there would be no amendment of the entrenched clauses for a given period, e.g. the fifteen years mentioned in the White Paper. Such an arrangement could be embodied in a treaty between the two Governments, as had been suggested on a number of earlier occasions.[9] In addition, if this proposal were not satisfactory to Mr Smith, Mr Wilson had worked out another alternative, according to him, in the aircraft returning from Gibralter, which would begin in Rhodesia and also leave the last word with the Rhodesian people: namely, provision for a referendum of the entire electorate, 'A' and 'B' roll electors voting separately, with the requirement that a simple majority on each roll would be sufficient to validate the amendment.[10]

On the same day that Mr Wilson was setting out these alternative safeguards, the Smith regime submitted an *aide memoire* declaring that they considered the British proposal for a system of appeals in relation to amendments of the entrenched provisions of the Constitution to be completely unacceptable in any form. According to Mr Smith's version of the events (in a broadcast on 19 November), this message had been submitted prior to the British decision to send Mr Thomson to Salisbury. He also claimed that even before leaving Gibraltar, when Mr Wilson had proposed sending Mr Thomson for further discussions, he had insisted that if this objectionable feature were not dropped, there would be no point in the visit. Nevertheless, Mr Thomson was dispatched to Salisbury at the beginning of November, equipped with yet another scheme for an alternative second safeguard. At this stage it was difficult to determine which side was engaging in a public relations exercise. While the Rhodesians had originally maintained that if it were possible to reach agreement on the second safeguard, differences on other issues could be quickly resolved, they had refused to consider any of the alternatives proposed by the British. If the British case for sending a Minister to Salisbury were based on the belief that there was only one major obstacle to a settlement, they were soon disabused of the notion. Instead of one obstacle, Mr Thomson found himself faced with an additional eight and these were fundamental changes to the 1961 Constitution and the *Fearless* proposals, not mere details which could be quickly resolved.

It was not likely that the Labour Government would make any further concessions to meet the demands of the rebel regime,[11] since they had already incurred the hostility of a large section of their party and of the Commonwealth and the United Nations as a result of the *Fearless* offer. Although Mr Wilson continued to maintain that there was widespread agreement that the *Fearless* terms were right and ought to be accepted, he was obliged to recognise, after some fifty Labour MPs had voted against the proposals, that a considerable number of his supporters could not accept any settlement other than one based on NIBMAR. Nevertheless, he appeared to be more concerned with the fact that the Opposition were not disposed to criticise the proposals or attack the Government for their conduct of the negotiations. He also maintained that the Press welcomed them and considered them fair, although his evidence for this claim seemed to be limited to *The Financial Times* and *The Daily Telegraph*. From the latter, he chose to quote that there was a limit to what Parliament would accept: that limit had been reached in the *Fearless* proposals; and there was no more to come.[12] However, he overlooked that section of the Press which argued that that limit had been exceeded. The *New*

Statesman characterised the proposals as 'unimpeded progress to permanent minority rule'; and in the *Guardian,* Professor Claire Palley calculated that if African majority rule came at all, it was nearer the mark to predict 2004 as the earliest possible date than the seven to fifteen years quoted by Mr Wilson to justify the abandonment of NIBMAR.[13]

Fearless on the Table

As it turned out, the *Fearless* proposals weren't really acceptable to any of the constituencies involved in the Rhodesian dispute.[14] Perhaps the only enthusiasm generated by the offer came from the former ruling Establishment in Rhodesia, particularly the European business and financial communities, who had to bear the brunt of the hardships flowing from the decline in trade and the curtailment of foreign investment. Pressure for an independence settlement had always come from this section of the population, and it was to them that Mr Smith usually directed his professions of reasonableness on the issue of negotiations. But after the failure of the *Fearless* meeting he was obliged to account for the fact that, in spite of the sweeping concessions made by the Labour Government, there had still been no agreement. Just as in the aftermath of *Tiger* a group of Europeans had called for implementing those proposals, so after the rejection of the *Fearless* terms a similar call came for their adoption. Those favouring this course – including the Rhodesian Constitutional Association (containing many former UFP members) and the Centre party, with which it later merged – maintained that the proposals offered independence on terms that would safeguard the country from the danger of government being taken over by 'irresponsible hands'. To publicise their claim that *Fearless* was acceptable to the great majority of the Rhodesian electorate, they placed an advertisement in the *Rhodesia Herald* and *The Chronicle* (Bulawayo) calling for a referendum on the proposals, and also warning that the country's future should not be left in the hands of a few men. The leader of the Centre party, Mr Pat Bashford, charged the Rhodesian Front with perpetrating the 'monstrous lie' that the UDI had been necessary to prevent the imposition of majority rule and accused Mr Smith of rejecting constitutional safeguards for the sole purpose of wanting a lock he could pick and a promise he could break – in short, 'the right to cheat'.[15]

This attack on the Rhodesian Front and on the leadership of Mr Smith, taken up by representatives of the business community, was reminiscent of the warnings issued on the eve of the UDI. Like Mr

Bashford, they were also concerned that time was not on Rhodesia's side, and that the country was faced with a population explosion, growing poverty among the Africans and continuing economic and financial sanctions. The chairman of the Rhodesian Iron and Steel Corporation, Mr E. S. Newson, made the point that the steady and often spectacular progress that Rhodesia had made over the previous decades — while entrenched clauses remained a part of the Constitution — had only been possible because of a steady influx of foreign investment and a continuing expansion of external trade. But three years of sanctions had already made appreciable inroads into Rhodesia's export earnings; and their continuation would in a relatively short time ruin the country's tobacco, chrome, asbestos and ferro-alloy industries and ensure that their promising nickel industry was stillborn. In his view, the UDI had been a tremendously costly mistake and so long as the existing political differences remained Rhodesia could never hope to expand its economy at the necessary level to prevent economic unrest and ensure maximum utilisation of the country's rich resources.[16] A similar admission that sanctions had already severely damaged the Rhodesian economy came from the chairman of the Standard Bank in Rhodesia and a former High Commissioner in London, Mr Evan Campbell, who was concerned about the growing rate of unemployment throughout the country. What was needed, and would only be possible with a settlement that would bring an end to sanctions, was a massive injection of outside development capital to create the necessary job opportunities. But if there were no settlement, he warned, the result would be an almost bankrupt country dependent on the charity of their 'friendly neighbours', whose friendliness was wearing increasingly thin over the years since the UDI.[17]

This was the first real opposition the Smith regime had encountered since their decision to go ahead with the illegal declaration of independence, in spite of the dire economic forecasts announced at that time. In response, Mr Smith launched a fierce attack on the 'old gang', in league with the Argus Press, for trying to prepare the country for a sell-out. In particular, he condemned Mr Newson for divulging a considerable amount of economic information, thus breaching the understanding between the 'Government' and the country's financial and industrial community. Mr Campbell was also accused of being responsible for a breach of the understanding, and his allegations concerning unemployment and charity from friendly neighbours were denounced as a figment of his fertile imagination. In rejecting these appeals for a compromise over the *Fearless* proposals, Mr Smith claimed that instead he had a secret plan to use in the remaining time that was available to reach a settlement with Britain.[18] The plan was to remain a secret, however, and at a press conference early in the new year, he denied that there was any plan to put to the British Government.[19]

In spite of the deadlock between the two sides, the Labour Government continued to insist that the *Fearless* proposals remain on the table. But in return for the dubious eventuality of their being acceptable to the Smith regime, they were obliged to justify before their critics both at home and abroad the retention of an independence offer which was clearly incompatible with the NIBMAR pledge. The Prime Minister had already been reminded of the party's obligations in a letter of 25 November, signed by some thirty-five MPs, representing a wide cross-section of the Parliamentary Labour Party, reaffirming their uncompromising opposition to the *Fearless* proposals as a basis for a settlement. The MPs cited the Government pledge in the House of Commons in December 1966, not to submit to Parliament any agreement which involved independence before majority rule, as a doctrine commanding the overwhelming support of the party, as the conference in October had demonstrated. What most concerned the Labour MPs was that all the evidence in the form of speeches and legislation by the Rhodesian Front indicated that independence granted to them would inevitably result in 'unimpeded progress to apartheid'. Was it worth breaking faith with the Commonwealth and flouting the United Nations, they asked 'to rush into a shabby compromise, Munich fashion, with the squalid clique in Salisbury?'[20]

The question of breaking faith with the Commonwealth became an immediate reality when Mr Wilson had to confront the Prime Ministers' meeting in London at the beginning of the new year. This was the first meeting since September 1966, when the British Government had undertaken to implement the NIBMAR pledge and initiate a policy of mandatory sanctions if an independence settlement were not agreed by the end of that year. While the British refusal to consider the use of force had been the main point of dispute in 1966, by the beginning of 1969 most Commonwealth Governments had reluctantly to accept that this was no longer a policy option for the British Government, although they would continue to favour it themselves. It was perhaps for this reason that Mr Wilson described the contributions to the debate as expressed with 'a great deal more moderation' than in 1966. Only a few delegations, he claimed, a smaller number than previously, continued to urge the use of force. While admitting that there were still sharp divisions on this question, he also found, for the first time, a genuine awareness of the difficulty and complexity of the problem.[21]

The main point of disagreement at the 1969 conference was in fact about NIBMAR. Since it had become evident that no amount of pressure on the British Government would alter their policy on the use of force, the minimum demand for which most of the Commonwealth leaders would settle was the observance of the NIBMAR pledge. But this had been cast in doubt by the negotiations with the rebel regime on the basis of proposals that conceded independence under white minority rule and by the decision that these terms should remain on the table as a potential independence settlement. Mr Wilson, when reminded that he had promised at the 1966 conference that independence would not be granted before majority rule was ensured, continued to insist that, although the *Fearless* proposals remained on the table, there had been no change in the British Government's policy on NIBMAR. Although he was aware that those proposals were unacceptable to most of the Commonwealth, he himself did not take that view, because he considered that it would be right to give the Rhodesian people an opportunity to decide for themselves whether they wished for a settlement on the basis of the Six Principles. In the event of such an outcome, he would then consult his Commonwealth colleagues about the NIBMAR commitment.

The only point of agreement to emerge from what appeared to be an irreconcilable divergence of opinion on the feasibility of retaining both *Fearless* and NIBMAR was that a settlement would only be possible if it were based upon the democratically ascertained wishes of the Rhodesian people. While it was conceded that the process for ascertaining their views was the responsibility of the British Government, most of the Commonwealth leaders insisted that the only valid test would be an election or a referendum, although they were doubtful that adequate safeguards for free political expression could be provided with the rebel regime in power during the test of acceptability. Mr Wilson, however, remained committed, by the terms of the *Fearless* proposals, to the use of a Royal Commission for this purpose. Nevertheless, he did concede that it would be open to that Commission either to say that no genuine assessment was possible in the circumstances prevailing in Rhodesia or to recommend an alternative method, including a referendum, which would adequately test Rhodesian opinion. What Mr Wilson's conditions amounted to was that no settlement would be possible if the Royal Commission found themselves unable to adjudicate on the acceptability of the proposals or if the Rhodesian people, by other means, recorded their opposition to terms which conceded independence before majority rule.

Compared with the treatment of the Rhodesian issue at the 1966 meetings, the 1969 conference could almost be regarded as a qualified success.[22] In spite of the differences of opinion on method, the Commonwealth leaders were at least unanimous in their conclusion that, 'whatever the time needed to reverse it', the seizure of power by a small racial minority could be neither recognised nor tolerated.[23] There was less bitterness, or perhaps more resignation, over the British refusal to use force; sanctions were now comprehensive, and therefore potentially effective if universally applied; and NIBMAR still remained the final objective, although overlaid by Mr Wilson's qualifications regarding the Fifth Principle. Even the split caused by his insistence on leaving the *Fearless* proposals on the table soon became an irrelevance, since the Labour Government were spared from the consequences of Mr Smith ever picking them up.

As Mr Wilson had indicated at the Commonwealth conference, no time limit had been set for leaving the *Fearless* proposals on offer. It seemed to suit Mr Smith as well as Mr Wilson to maintain the appearance that a settlement was still possible, in spite of the irreconcilable differences revealed after the Thomson visit. Mr Wilson was able to assure the Conservative Opposition, who continued to press for negotiations, that these were available on the basis of the *Fearless* terms; and Mr Smith could tell his critics, who advocated putting the proposals to the electorate, that their chance would come, when a referendum was held on the new Rhodesian Front 'Constitution', to vote against that 'Constitution'. In the unlikely event of a majority choosing to do so, Mr Smith would allegedly concede defeat, a general election would ensue and they would then have the opportunity of returning a government which would put forward the type of constitution they preferred.[24]

The Death Knell

During the first half of 1969, the pretence that a settlement was still possible on the basis of the *Fearless* terms became increasingly thin as the Rhodesian Front proceeded to produce a 'Constitution' of their own (which Mr Wilson condemned as 'a complete and flat denial of at least five of the Six Principles'),[25] while carrying on a series of desultory exchanges with the British Government on what had become some nine points of difference between the two sides. Throughout this period the Prime Minister and the Foreign and Commonwealth Secretary (Mr Michael Stewart) continually asserted that if the *Fearless* proposals were not acceptable, it was for the rebel regime themselves to put forward an alternative that would be equally effective in guaranteeing the Six Principles. Although they awaited the 'secret plan' referred to by Mr Smith in his broadcast of 13 December, no communication was received until 23 January — a mere enquiry of clarification on the second safeguard and the reinstatement of Rhodesian civil servants — and no plan was ever forthcoming. Instead, three messages were received from the regime, through the head of the British Residual Mission in Salisbury (Mr P. A. Carter), who dismissed their memorandum of 13 February as not in any real sense a plan for a settlement, but simply a reiteration of the negative position adopted by Mr Smith and his colleagues at the conclusion of their talks with Mr Thomson in November 1968. Mr Carter also pointed out that his Government's hopes for a settlement had not been encouraged by the tone in which on several occasions Mr Smith had referred to the *Fearless* proposals, particularly regarding the second safeguard. Although the British Government had repeatedly made clear their readiness to consider alternative proposals for the safeguard, provided that agreement could be reached on the other outstanding differences, no such proposals had been offered by the regime. Similarly, the purported extension of the period for which an emergency could be declared from three to twelve months would inevitably be regarded as making agreement more difficult, since a proposal to extend that period to six months had been one of the major points of difference at the talks in Salisbury. While the British Government had not been encouraged by the tone of Rhodesian references to the second safeguard, they were even more alarmed by Mr Smith's attitude towards majority rule. As Mr Carter said in the concluding British exchange of 14 May, it could only be taken as destroying any possibility of a settlement consistent with the Six Principles.[26]

The Labour Government's contention that all of their efforts to get a settlement had been frustrated by the intransigence of the regime was considerably enhanced by the pronouncements coming out of Salisbury during the debate on the Rhodesian Front constitutional proposals, which extended from the announcement of the plan on 15 February 1969 until its adoption in the referendum of 20 June 1969.[27] In the course of the referendum campaign, Mr Smith not only admitted, but even boasted, that the new 'Constitution' was a 'racial' one and that it would 'sound the death knell of majority rule in Rhodesia'.[28] The proposed scheme established separate voters' rolls for the two races (the common roll was regarded as 'distasteful'); it limited African representation by setting income tax contributions as the qualification for increasing membership (fewer than 1,000 Africans paid only 0.5 per cent of the total personal income tax); it ruled out African majority rule by setting parity as the maximum representation obtainable; it enshrined the division of land between the races in the Land Tenure Act; and it provided that the Declaration of Rights would not be enforceable in the courts. It was, in fact, the 'death knell', not only for majority rule but also for a settlement with Britain.

The Labour Government awaited the outcome of the referendum before announcing the break. The Foreign and Commonwealth Secretary was still saying on 21 May (the day after Mr Smith's broadcast blaming Britain for the breakdown) that the *Fearless* proposals were a very fair offer,[29] perhaps hoping that the Rhodesians who favoured them would reject the new 'Constitution'. But those who chose this course (some 20,000 out of 76,000) may have done so because they preferred an even more extreme apartheid-style constitution. For the overwhelming majority of Rhodesians, the choice was for the Rhodesian Front plan, with 72 per cent for the 'Constitution' and 80 per cent for the republic. After the vote, Mr Stewart conceded that the constitutional proposals which the European electorate had just endorsed could never form the basis of an acceptable settlement with Britain (although Sir Alec Douglas-Home attempted to do just that in 1971), and that it would be totally unrealistic to suppose that there could be any useful discussion with the rebel regime. In the light of the results of the referendum, it would be impossible for the Governor to continue his duties as a representative of the Crown and it would serve no useful purpose to maintain the UK Residual Mission in Salisbury or Rhodesia House in London. Nevertheless, Mr Stewart still looked forward to resuming links whenever there were people in Rhodesia who shared their principles and with whom they could talk. When that day came, the *Fearless* proposals would still be available as a starting point from which discussions could begin.[30] Such an eventuality was, however, exceedingly remote, since the proposals had already been 'knocked off the table' by the verdict of the Rhodesian electorate, and Rhodesians sharing common principles with the British were in no position to exert any influence on the direction in which the country was moving under the new Rhodesian Front 'Constitution'.

The Foreign and Commonwealth Secretary's announcement of the break met with a mixed reaction, both at home and abroad. While there was a general sense of relief from the Labour party MPs, the Conservative Opposition lodged a vigorous protest about the loss of contact with the rebel regime. Their leader, Mr Heath, complained that the

Government were deliberately cutting themselves off from those in Rhodesia who were opposed to the existing system. The Tories were also concerned that the Government might be obliged to support the move for communications sanctions being canvassed by the African States and their supporters at the United Nations. They were united in opposing this action, and Sir Alec Douglas-Home spoke for the party when he urged the Government to use the veto to prevent such a step.[31] On this point, however, the Tories were pushing against an open door, since the Labour Government had previously rejected the measure as 'not contributing appreciably to the sanctions programme already in effect', and they were to do so again when it was proposed in June 1969.

As a result of this decision and of their generally cautious attitude at the United Nations, the Labour Government won a grudging abstention from the Tories on the annual vote to renew the sanctions Order in October 1969. In urging the abstention, Sir Alec admitted that since Britain could never be a party to the new Rhodesian Front 'Constitution', there would have to be a change of attitude in Salisbury before a negotiated settlement could be attempted. Even Mr Duncan Sandys, who was still expressing Monday Club sentiments on the futility of the continuation of sanctions, had to concede that Britain could never in any circumstances approve a Rhodesian 'Constitution' which entirely contravened the principles supported by all parties in Britain. Nevertheless, he remained convinced that if the Conservatives had remained in power there would have been no UDI. Conveniently forgetting his own stand against the Rhodesian demand for independence in 1964, when he had reminded them that they had a franchise which was incomparably more restrictive than that of any British territory to which independence had hitherto been granted, he now maintained that his party would have offered Mr Smith before the UDI a package similar to *Fearless* (which they had not done) and that, in such an eventuality, Mr Smith would have 'jumped at it'.[32]

While the Conservatives were convinced that the Labour Government had gone too far in breaking with Salisbury, at the United Nations there was a strong feeling that Britain had not gone far enough. An urgent meeting of the Security Council was therefore convened on 13 June, at the request of nearly sixty member-States, to consider the failure of the sanctions programme to effect any change in the situation prevailing in Rhodesia. But when a five-Power draft resolution, condemning the Rhodesian referendum and the racial 'Constitution', and also calling for the use of force and the extension of economic measures against South Africa and Portugal, was proposed, there were sufficient abstentions (some seven member-States, including Britain) to prevent its adoption.[33]

According to the British delegate, Lord Caradon, while his country agreed with several provisions of the resolution, including the non-recognition of the rebel regime, the illegality of the referendum and the so-called 'Constitution', and the maintenance of sanctions, they could not contemplate starting a war by invading Rhodesia. Nor could they extend economic sanctions, backed by a naval blockade, against South Africa, because to go beyond their arms embargo against that country would seriously harm Britain's trade and balance of payments position. Concluding on a personal note, Caradon said that he had resigned from the British delegation in 1962 because he had disagreed with the Government at that time on the issue of the need to consult all the people of Rhodesia on their constitutional future. He would not have hesitated to resign again rather than be associated with any dishonourable settlement which offended against the principle of consultation and consent. However, he did not disagree with the two main decisions he was now defending: that Britain could not send an army to start a war in southern Africa and that Britain could not justify an economic war against South Africa.[34]

Although the Labour Government (unlike their Conservative predecessors) had thus far been able to avoid the odium attached to the use of the veto, at the following session of the Security Council, convened at the request of Britain to condemn the rebel regime's assumption of republican status in March 1970, they were to cast their first veto on the Rhodesian issue.[35] The justification for the action, as the Foreign and Commonwealth Secretary told Parliament, was that disagreement in the Security Council led to the use of the veto by the British Government, supported by the Americans, on an 'extreme' Afro-Asian resolution, again condemning Britain for its failure to use force, and originally calling for the extension of sanctions to South Africa and Portugal. The compromise resolution which was finally adopted, he claimed, contained a number of practical and effective measures to increase the pressure on the illegal regime. These included the call to enforce more strictly existing economic sanctions, to sever the remaining consular, trade and other links with the regime and to increase the powers given to the Security Council Sanctions Committee.[36] Already he could report that, since the assumption of republican status on 2 March 1970, the regime's hopes of gaining international recognition had been dealt a severe blow by the closure of eleven of the thirteen consular missions remaining in

Rhodesia.[37]

The Labour Government maintained their boycott of the regime during their last year of office. The final communication acknowledged by the Government was the correspondence concluded by the head of the British Residual Mission in Salisbury in May 1969, recording the total deadlock reached in the series of exchanges. As a result of this policy, the Government succeeded in regaining the support of the Labour party conference, which had been denied them the previous year. At the Brighton conference in October 1969, there was overwhelming endorsement of the National Executive Committee statement (contained in *Agenda for a Generation*), which asserted that a Labour Government would refuse to settle the Rhodesian problem on terms which would deny the majority of the people of that country 'full human rights and unimpeded progress to majority rule'. In a composite resolution, the conference also condemned the Rhodesian Front's 'racial Constitution' and reaffirmed their support for economic sanctions as 'the best and most likely method of bringing about the downfall of the rebel regime'. While some conference delegates advocated recognition of the guerrilla struggle as 'the only effective means of ensuring the legitimate aspirations of the African people for majority rule', and others urged the Government to seek the agreement of the United Nations to take over responsibility for the territory until there was a democratically elected government, these deviations from Government policy did not affect the general consensus that Rhodesia was solely a British responsibility and that the use of force was an unrealistic proposition. Some encouragement for those calling for additional measures came from the NEC spokesman, Miss Joan Lestor, who urged the Government to support communications sanctions and also to use the Rhodesia Fund, which had been established to assist the education and training of Africans for responsibilities in government, to help get across to the British public what was at stake in Rhodesia.[38]

While the Government's refusal to consider any further dealings with the illegal regime had the effect of unifying their own party on the issue, it provoked a serious rift with the Conservatives. As Mr Heath said at the party conference in October 1969, a great divide had arisen between the two parties over the possibility of reaching a settlement with the Rhodesian regime. On the issue of sanctions, however, Tory policy continued to remain ambiguous. While Mr Heath maintained that his party had always been opposed to mandatory sanctions by the United Nations, on the ground that this took the matter out of the control of the British Government, he also admitted that he had never at any time proposed that sanctions (which were already mandatory) should be taken off before negotiations were reopened. But what the basis for negotiations at that stage could be was never spelled out by the Tories in the course of their efforts to reopen them.[39]

The final encounter between the two parties before the opening of the 1970 election campaign arose over what Mr Wilson, in a speech at York on 18 April, condemned as secret talks between the Conservatives and the rebel regime. Taunting the Tories with the challenge that if there were people in this country, with certain political views and with powerful economic sponsors behind them, who were still ready to contemplate a sell-out to racialism, they could no doubt take advantage of the cheap and empty ex-consulate premises in Salisbury for maintaining whatever continuing presence they felt appropriate. There had been allegations of informal contacts with an illegal regime, contacts behind the backs of the British Government, which he would not have expected of any responsible people, even in dealings with a sovereign government.[40] So far as the possibility was concerned of any settlement arising out of these manoeuvres, he was ready to declare that he would not be a party to any compromise on the principles laid down by the Government.[41]

Mr Heath's defence was that the purpose of exchanges with the Rhodesian regime was to enable the Opposition to carry out their duty of keeping fully informed on the situation in Rhodesia, of forming their own judgement upon it and of formulating their policy accordingly. He retaliated by challenging the Prime Minister to reveal the full details of the secret missions he had sent to Mr Smith, together with the terms his secret emissaries were authorised to offer. Refuting the allegation of 'ratting' on the Six Principles, he maintained that his party was working for an honourable settlement in accordance with the principles first agreed between Sir Alec Douglas-Home and Mr Smith and that this was the basis for any views expressed in private to Rhodesian leaders.[42] But what the views consisted of and who was expressing them to whom the Tory leader did not reveal, since Mr Wilson was able to charge him with failing to answer challenges, both in the Press and six times in the House of Commons, suggesting that there had been secret talks between his party and the illegal regime.[43] The Labour Government, on the other hand, maintained until the very end of their term of office that they had neither engaged in, nor had any intention of engaging in, any further communications with the rebel regime.

The 'great divide' between the two parties, to which Mr Heath had referred during the Tory party conference, was in fact no more than a difference of approach on the tactics to be adopted towards an illegal regime which had opted for Mr Smith's 'second road' to Rhodesian independence. The Tories' attempt to present an alternative solution to the Rhodesian problem in the general election of June 1970 was never a real possibility, since the Labour Government had in the course of their six years in office gone to the utmost limits of concession to accommodate the Rhodesians. Nor could they arouse much interest in a subject which by 1970 had a low electoral priority. As the Nuffield election study revealed, only a small percentage of candidates (7 per cent of the Conservatives and 4 per cent of Labour) even mentioned Rhodesia as an issue during the electoral campaign.[44] The policies of the two parties, as stated in their election manifestos, reflected the difference between a party that had been in power, and therefore bore the responsibility for the consequences, and one that, in Opposition, could afford the luxury of apportioning blame for the failure. What the distinction amounted to was a justification of previous endeavours and a promise of future efforts.

According to the Labour manifesto, the Government had made every possible attempt to bring about an honourable settlement consistent with the Six Principles, but to no avail, because the regime had introduced an apartheid-type constitution. The Tories, in accusing Labour of having failed to solve the Rhodesian problem, proposed to make a further effort to find a solution which would be in accordance with the Six Principles. While the Conservatives remained noticeably silent on the subject of sanctions, which Labour promised to maintain, the latter were equally silent on NIBMAR. In a negative sense, they were committed only to negotiate no settlement which did not guarantee unimpeded progress to majority rule. Although this commitment would not prevent them from conceding independence before majority rule, provided that guarantees of progress towards that goal were obtained, the possibility of obtaining such guarantees was ruled out by a Rhodesian 'Constitution' designed to prevent such an eventuality. This was a dilemma the Tories could conveniently ignore while in Opposition but one which they would be obliged to face up to after their return to office in June 1970.

Notes

1. See *Rhodesia Herald*, 21 September 1968.
2. *Report of the 67th Annual Conference of the Labour Party*, Blackpool, 1968.

3. Harold Wilson, *The Labour Government, 1964-1970*, 1971, p. 564.

4. Ibid., pp. 566-7.

5. Ibid.

6. For criticism of their failure to do so, see the Africa Bureau, *The* Fearless *Proposals and the Six Principles* by M.J. Christie, 1968.

7. 770 *HC Deb.*, 15 October 1968, col. 210.

8. *Rhodesia: Report of the Discussions Held on Board HMS* Fearless, October 1968, Cmnd. 3793.

9. Including the *Tiger* meetings and also during the negotiations in Salisbury in 1965.

10. 770 *HC Deb.*, 22 October 1968, cols. 1224-5.

11. The additional points of disagreement announced by Mr Thomson included: a refusal to allow the Privy Council to continue hearing appeals in other than constitutional cases (as well as in cases involving the entrenched clauses); an extension of the three-month period for which the Legislature could approve the proclamation of a state of emergency; an alteration in the number of elected Africans in the Senate or an increase in the 'A' roll in the lower House and the Europeans in the Senate; a reduction in the existing value of 'B' roll votes cast in elections on the 'A' roll (in the system of cross-voting) from 25 to 10 per cent; the abolition of the 'delimitation' formula drafted in *Tiger*, which provided that as the number of Africans on the 'A' roll increased, the Africans' chance of capturing 'A' roll seats should increase proportionately; an extension of the criteria which the Judicial Tribunal should apply when considering whether detainees should be released to cases where others might respond with violence to their release; and a refusal to consider the reinstatement of public servants who felt bound to leave Rhodesia in order to remain loyal to the Crown. (773 *HC Deb.*, 18 November 1968, cols. 898-900.)

12. 22 October 1968, quoted in *Wilson*, p. 570.

13. 14 November 1968.

14. The Commonwealth Sanctions Committee issued a statement on 25 October 1968 warning that there would have to be a substantial and guaranteed change of circumstances to justify a review of Mr Wilson's pledge on NIBMAR. The UN General Assembly also called for a reaffirmation of NIBMAR, in resolution 2379 (XXIII), adopted 25 October 1968 by 92-2, with 17 abstentions (UK); and resolution 2383 (XXIII), adopted 7 November 1968 by 86-9 (UK), with 19 abstentions.

15. *Rhodesia Herald*, 26 November 1968.

16. Ibid., 27 November 1968.

17. Ibid., 10 December 1968.

18. Broadcast of 13 December 1968.

19. 7 January 1969, *For the Record*, No. 6, January 1969.

20. *The Times*, 26 November 1968.

21. Wilson, *The Labour Government*, pp. 593-7.

22. According to Mr Wilson's report to Parliament. See 776 *HC Deb.*, 21 January 1969, cols. 246-52.

23. *Commonwealth Prime Ministers' Meeting, 1969, Final Communiqué*, London, 15 January 1969, Cmnd. 3919.

24. New Year message. *Rhodesia Herald*, 1 January 1969.

25. 778 *HC Deb.*, 18 February 1969, cols. 204-5.

26. *Rhodesia: Report on Exchanges with the Regime since the Talks Held in Salisbury, November 1968*, Cmnd. 4065, June 1969. See also *Statement on Anglo-Rhodesian Relations, December 1966 - May 1969*, CSR 36-1969.

27. See *Proposals for a New Constitution for Rhodesia*, 1969 which replaced the 'Yellow Paper'.

28. *Rhodesia Herald*, 8, 29 May 1969.

29. 784 *HC Deb.*, 21 May 1969, cols. 443-5.

30. 785 *HC Deb.*, 24 June 1969, cols. 1219-24.

31. Ibid., cols. 1220-1.

32. 788 *HC Deb.*, 16 October 1969, cols. 623-4.

33. The draft resolution was defeated on 24 June 1969, by 8-0, with seven abstentions. A similar resolution, 2508 (XXIV), which Britain voted against, was adopted by the General Assembly on 21 November 1969 by 83-7, with 20 abstentions.

34. Security Council, *Official Records*, 24th Year, 1479th Meeting, 19 June 1969.

35. On 17 March 1970: the vote was 9-2 (UK, USA), with four abstentions.

36. Security Council resolution 277 (1970), adopted 18 March 1970 by 14-0, with one abstention (Spain). The British draft resolution obtained the support of only four other delegations.

37. 798 *HC Deb.*, 19 March 1970, cols. 615-17.

38. *Report of the 68th Annual Conference of the Labour Party*, Brighton, 1969.

39. See *Report of the 87th Annual Conservative Party Conference*, Brighton, 1969.

40. Mr Heath had sent a secret and personal message to President Nixon in February 1970, saying that when the Conservatives won the general election, they would as a matter of policy re-establish a residual mission in Salisbury. See Anthony Lake, *The 'Tar Baby' Option*, 1976, p. 141.

41. 798 *HC Deb.*, 26 March 1970, cols. 1647-50.

42. *The Times*, 20 April 1970.

43. 800 *HC Deb.*, 23 April 1970, col. 633.

44. D.E. Butler and M. Pinto-Duschinsky, *The British General Election of 1970*, 1971, pp. 62, 438.

9 THE SALISBURY SELL-OUT

'I could not in my view have negotiated better terms in November for the Africans than I was able to get then from Mr Smith ... I could not do so now.'

Sir Alec Douglas-Home, 23 May 1972.

'These terms were, in my view, so favourable that, had we not agreed to a Commission to test opinion, I should have had no hesitation in asking then and there for the support of the British Parliament.'

Lord Home, *The Way the Wind Blows*, 1976.

If the Labour party, while in office, could have been accused of going back on the NIBMAR pledge, the Conservatives, after 1970, were equally vulnerable to charges of having abandoned the principles to which they were committed when previously in government. During the last few years of Conservative rule, when the issue of Rhodesian independence arose as a result of the dissolution of the Central African Federation, successive Ministers — Mr Butler, Mr Sandys, Sir Alec Douglas-Home — laid down a number of conditions to be met by the Rhodesians before they could move forward to independence. These conditions, subsequently taken over by the Labour Government and formulated as the Five Principles, were mainly concerned with an increase in African representation, a widening of the franchise and the elimination of racial discrimination. It was because no Rhodesian leader, neither Sir Edgar Whitehead nor his Rhodesian Front successors, Mr Field and Mr Smith, would, or perhaps could, agree to implement these changes that the Conservative Government (until October 1964) maintained their refusal to grant unconditional independence. Had the Conservatives remained in office after 1964, it is extremely doubtful whether they would have been any more successful than their Labour party successors in preventing the UDI. Although the Tories could scarcely disown as an Opposition the principles they had established while in power, their interpretation of those principles during the years of Labour rule amounted to a dilution and a weakening of their original meaning. This was evident from the proposals they envisaged in their private contacts with the rebel regime and from their constant pressure on the Labour Government to settle on terms that could only remotely be embraced by the Five Principles. This retreat from principle did not go unnoticed by the European leaders in Rhodesia, who could afford to postpone a settlement on the Labour Government's terms, however generous these might have been, with the expectation that they would be conceded even more with the return of the Conservative party to power. As it turned out, the Rhodesian gamble paid off. What had been prescribed by the Conservative Government in the 1960s was to be abandoned in the 1970s: the 'wind of change' was to give way to the preservation of white supremacy.

Before the general election the Tories had committed themselves to making one more attempt to reach a settlement with the rebel regime. Their purpose, as Mr Heath had stated in a speech in Glasgow on 6 March, would be to determine whether the Rhodesians placed sufficient value on the connection with Britain to induce them to agree to a settlement. This undertaking was reaffirmed in the Queen's Speech at the opening of the new Parliament on 2 July 1970, but by this time Mr Heath, now encumbered with the responsibilities of office, was careful to add the qualifications that the Government did not propose to take 'hasty steps' and that a settlement would only be possible on the basis of the Five Principles.[1] However, a step in that direction had already taken place the previous day, when the Foreign Secretary had met with the South African Foreign Minister, Dr Muller, in London. Although the Foreign Office denied that any message had been sent to Mr Smith through the South African Government,[2] the following week Mr Smith was in South Africa conferring with Mr Vorster.

The new Conservative Government had also to face up to the reality of the sanctions measures which they had inherited from their predecessors. In Opposition, the Tories had repeatedly stated their disapproval of mandatory sanctions, although their voting record on the subject was a mixed one. In office, they were obliged to recognise that mandatory sanctions were in existence as an international effort, initiated by a British government, and that they constituted a means of pressure to get the rebel regime into negotiations. Even before the general election Mr Heath had been obliged to admit that he had never suggested taking off sanctions before negotiations. After taking office, however, his defence for retaining sanctions was extended beyond the link with the opening of talks. Although repeating the Tory complaint that sanctions had not brought about the desired objective, in so far as they had failed to restore constitutional rule, he conceded for the first time that it was undeniable that they had had an impact on the Rhode-

sian economy.[3] Whether this impact was sufficient to wring any concessions from the rebel regime was still uncertain, but in any case sanctions
were to remain pending negotiations, and since the Government did not
contemplate taking 'hasty steps' in that direction, they would be obliged
to seek Parliamentary approval for the annual renewal of the sanctions
Order when it expired that year.

The Conservative Government's volte-face on the sanctions issue did
not go unchallenged by their rank and file supporters, who had been
conditioned over a period of five years to oppose the mandatory or
'punitive' sanctions then in effect. For some, particularly the Monday
Club wing of the party, any sanctions were anathema, even as a means
of pressure to induce the regime to seek a settlement. This view was
particularly in evidence at the party conference in October, when the
weight and prestige of Sir Alec Douglas-Home's role in the party had to
be invoked to rally the support of the conference to defeat a resolution
calling for the immediate end of sanctions. Sir Alec chose to attack the
problem with the carrot and the stick: sanctions would remain for the
time being but Mr Smith would be approached before long. While revi-
ving all the old arguments of past years, put forward by Mr Heath and
Mr Maudling as well – that sanctions had not achieved their aim, had
been breached by others, had cost Britain money and trade and had
caused most suffering to the Africans – he conceded that it was questionable whether lifting them at that point would induce a mood to
compromise. It was also arguable whether any basis for negotiations
within the established principles could be found, as a result of the
constitutional changes introduced by the Rhodesian Front. Although
he confessed that he could not tell what the chances of success would
be, he hoped that Mr Smith was aware that the fates were unlikely to
give either of their countries another chance. The challenge to the
Rhodesians was to respond by devising a constitution that would
provide opportunities for all races in a genuine multi-racial society.[4]

The response from Mr Smith, at the end of his visit to South Africa,
was immediate as well as encouraging. Obviously, there was no possibility that he would agree to Sir Alec's call for a multi-racial society. But
he was still anxious for another chance at a settlement, as he indicated
in an interview with the Johannesburg *Sunday Express* on 18 October.[5]
Although his expectations were that he was more likely to get one from
a Conservative Government than a Labour one, he nevertheless warned
his supporters not to jump to the conclusion that Rhodesia's problems
were over simply because there was a Conservative Government in
Britain. However, one gain he could record was that that Government

had publicly recognised Rhodesia as a sovereign, independent republic by proposing to negotiate with them in the position in which they found them.[6]

By accepting the Rhodesians as they were, the Conservative Government were also accepting the 1969 'Constitution' as a basis for the negotiations. Although Sir Alec had admitted that this was a much greater obstacle to agreement than the previous Constitution, he never proposed that it should be set aside as a condition for the talks, because to do so would have ruled out their taking place. So long as Mr Smith insisted on retaining his racial 'Constitution' and Sir Alec his Five Principles, no agreement would be possible, since the two were clearly incompatible and one would have to go.[7]

This was the main ground for the Labour party's scepticism, if not hostility, towards the whole effort. Although it could scarcely make much of an issue of negotiating with a police State, as Mr Wilson attempted to do at the party conference in October 1970, it could legitimately object that since the Rhodesians had opted for a racial 'Constitution', there was very little left to negotiate about. If the exercise were undertaken merely to appease the Rhodesia Lobby in the Tory party or to win support for the renewal of the sanctions Order, as Mr Wilson also alleged,[8] then it could be dismissed as a manoeuvre in the cause of party unity. However, more was involved than party political considerations or having another 'go' because there was a new government in Britain. The move could have harmful repercussions both in Rhodesia itself and in the world community, which was engaged in a sanctions programme directed at bringing about the downfall of the rebel regime. Even though the talks were likely to end in failure, they would gravely damage Britain's image at the United Nations and in the Commonwealth, unless it could be established that they were taking place within the framework of the Five Principles.[9]

British Interests

Although the Conservative Government succeeded in appeasing their rank and file supporters with the prospect of renewing contact with the Smith regime,[10] the day after they had obtained approval for renewal of the sanctions Order they were confronted with the same hostile reaction at the United Nations as they had encountered from the Labour Opposition at home. The dispute arose over an Afro-Asian draft resolution, submitted to the Security Council on 10 November 1970. While the resolution contained a number of recommendations with which the Government were in accord, such as the maintenance of the sanctions programme and the withholding of recognition from the illegal regime, it was on the issue of NIBMAR that they, like their predecessors, recorded their dissent. As their permanent representative, Sir Colin Crowe, said in opposing the resolution, since his Government were committed to seeking a settlement of the Rhodesian dispute in accordance with the Five Principles, they were not prepared to enter discussions with their negotiating position dictated from outside. In establishing the case for the continuity of British policy, he reminded the delegates that his predecessor, Lord Caradon, had taken a similar stand on NIBMAR by rejecting its inclusion in the resolution of 16 December 1966, on the ground that the Labour Government could not accept this commitment in a United Nations resolution. Although the Conservative Government's delegation were obliged to veto the draft resolution for the same reason, they were prepared to give their support to an alternative resolution endorsing the sanctions programme to which they were now converted.[11]

The Conservative Government were to encounter similar opposition to their Rhodesian policy at the conference of Commonwealth Prime Ministers in Singapore the following month. By the time the conference convened in January 1971, they had incurred the hostility of most Commonwealth Governments as a result of their efforts to reopen negotiations with the illegal regime and their decision to resume the sale of arms to South Africa, hitherto banned, in accordance with United Nations resolutions, by their predecessors. The latter decision had also been condemned by the Organisation of African Unity, meeting in Addis Ababa on 1 September 1970, and by the conference of Non-Aligned States in Lusaka the following week. At the Commonwealth meeting the two subjects became inextricably linked because South African forces were operating with Rhodesian troops in anti-guerrilla warfare on Rhodesian territory.

Not since the London meeting of September 1966 had there been such a concerted effort to force a reversal of British policy, on this occasion on two counts. Whereas Mr Wilson had had to fight off a call for the use of British force to end the rebellion, Mr Heath was confronted with a demand for a reaffirmation of the NIBMAR pledge and a reinstatement of the embargo on arms to South Africa. His adamant defence of Conservative policy in southern Africa nearly resulted in what Mr Wilson described as his 'presiding over the liquidation of the Commonwealth'. Mr Heath admitted as much when he told Parliament that such strains as there were at the conference were imposed by an attempt to bind 'certain countries' over their own policies. That attempt he claimed to have resisted in the cause of 'British interests', in contrast with Mr Wilson, who allegedly 'gave way at every Commonwealth conference and then found himself bound by NIBMAR, which he knew was impossible and which was against his will'.[12]

As a result of the divergent views prevailing at the conference, the only possible agreed communiqué was one which contained no binding commitments, other than a directive to the Commonwealth Sanctions Committee to continue to review the situation.[13] On southern Africa in general, the conference merely noted the obvious – that tensions in that region were likely to increase rather than decrease unless there were fundamental changes in the conditions then prevailing. NIBMAR was quietly buried, with the obvious understatement that earlier discussions on the subject were 'recalled'. As for the Five Principles, to which the Conservative Government were supposedly committed, all that remained was a unanimous reaffirmation of the importance of the Fifth – that any proposals for a settlement would need to be acceptable to the Rhodesian people as a whole. The main concession from the British side was agreement to a Commonwealth Declaration of Principles (based on a Zambian draft, but diluted by amendment) which, in its recognition of racial prejudice as 'a dangerous sickness threatening the healthy development of the human race' and racial discrimination as 'an unmitigated evil of society', could be interpreted as a condemnation of the Rhodesian regime.[14] As a reaffirmation of the principles on which Commonwealth membership was based, the Declaration could be regarded as an effort to preserve that institution after the crisis it had experienced. So far as the Rhodesian situation was concerned, however, virtually the same principles had been enunciated at Lagos in 1966 and five years later they had yet to be realised.

Although the Conservative Government had survived the Commonwealth conference without incurring any hindrances to their pursuit of negotiations with the illegal regime, the one obligation they had recognised at the Singapore meeting – that any proposals for a settlement had to be acceptable to the Rhodesian people as a whole – was to result in the defeat of their entire effort. For nearly a year they prepared the groundwork for a summit meeting with the Rhodesian Front leaders that would mark the final stage of negotiations begun at the diplomatic level and continued through the medium of a special emissary. The first step had already been taken in Pretoria, where the British Ambassador had established communications with the rebel regime. Further progress had been impossible, however, until the Government had got the Commonwealth conference out of the way. Once that was over, there would be a clear period of at least a year in which to proceed with their plans. There would continue to be United Nations censure of the negotiations, but even this embarrassment had been lessened by the Government's decision to withdraw from the Special Committee on Decolonisation in February 1971 and to reject an invitation from that Committee to participate in its debate on Southern Rhodesia in April. The Government's position at home was also secure for the year, since their party conference did not have to be placated until October and the sanctions renewal Order would not become due again until the following November. Nor was there any cause for Opposition censure, so long as the purpose and content of the negotiations remained confidential. In any case, the Opposition leadership had little ground for criticism at that stage, having engaged in secret negotiations with the illegal regime themselves and having used the services of the same emissaries. Except for the occasional Parliamentary question about the progress of the talks, which elicited only evasive replies or denials, there was no pressure on the Government to abandon their course of action. They could even lay claim to public support for their policy, on the basis of a Gallup poll taken towards the end of November 1970, showing that 62 per cent of the electorate (including a majority of Labour supporters) favoured having the talks, although there was no indication whether they would have done so had they been aware of the basis on which the negotiations were taking place.[15]

The Rhodesians had also been awaiting the conclusion of the Prime Ministers' conference, perhaps with the hope, as Mr Smith said, that Mr Heath's determination to defend British interests would result in the breakup of the Commonwealth.[16] By March 1971, they had begun to show some signs that they were in earnest about proceeding with the negotiations. Mr Smith told the *Daily Telegraph* correspondent in Salisbury that prospects for an agreement with Britain had improved, since the Conservatives had a better understanding of Rhodesia's problems and its achievements. Settlement was the only logical and possible course between the two countries, he claimed, because they had got themselves into a 'stupid position' and had to find a way out of it. Another sign of movement was that when the Parliamentary session opened in March 1971, two of the Rhodesian Front's most offensive racialist measures – one allowing the creation of racially exclusive residential areas and another empowering urban authorities to provide separate public amenities – had been temporarily postponed. Preparations were also going ahead on the diplomatic front. One of the key members of the Rhodesian Front hierarchy, Colonel Knox, diplomatic representative in Lisbon, had been recalled to Salisbury to confer with Mr Smith. He was then to visit South Africa, where the secret exchanges had been going on between the Rhodesian diplomatic representative and the British Ambassador.

Secret Diplomacy

For the following three months, while negotiations were proceeding, complete secrecy on the subject was maintained by both sides. In Parliament, Government spokesmen would only admit 'preliminary exchanges' or 'exploratory discussions', without any indication of the contents or the participants. The Foreign Office statement that Lord Goodman, Mr Wilson's negotiator before the *Fearless* meeting, had visited Rhodesia at the Foreign Secretary's request was not made until 16 June, and Sir Alec's confirmation of the exploratory discussions was announced on 12 July, in reply to a Parliamentary question. What Sir Alec did not reveal was that Goodman had been secretly dispatched to Salisbury in April, through the good offices of his press colleague, Sir Max Aitken, who had also served as a go-between for Mr Wilson in 1968. Nor had there been any indication from the Rhodesian side that talks had taken place, since Mr Smith told the *Rhodesia Herald* on 15 April that contact with Britain through correspondence was the correct method of handling the situation at that stage. On the basis for any future negotiations, his position was that the Rhodesian 'Constitution' did not require amendment, but if it could be 'improved' in the interests of Rhodesia, he would be amenable to discussing it.

Mr Smith's simultaneous dismissal of the Five Principles as of no consequence did not discourage British plans for a return visit by Lord Goodman, this time accompanied by officials from the Foreign and Commonwealth Office. The mission was again a 'secret' one, although after Lord Goodman had returned to London the Press reported that the visit had taken place and that Sir Max Aitken had also met Mr Smith in June, apparently to encourage him to continue with the talks and to assure the Goodman team that he was serious about wanting a settlement. One indication that he was emerged from a press interview on 14 June, in which he admitted that the shortage of foreign currency was aggravated by sanctions and that the best thing for Rhodesia would be for sanctions to come to an end.

The Aitken intervention was followed by Goodman's third visit to Salisbury at the end of June, no longer with any pretence of conceal-ment. What remained shrouded in secrecy was the contents and the progress of the talks. All that Sir Alec would reveal to Parliament on the subject was what he had often said before, that any settlement would have to be within the Five Principles.[17] However, Mr Smith's recent denial of those principles left little cause for optimism on that basis. In addition, Mr Smith's sincerity in wanting the talks to continue was again thrown into doubt by his statement to the BBC on 15 July that there was less reason for Rhodesians to negotiate than at any other time, because they were more sure of themselves than ever before and their economy was now 'booming'. With these views on record, it was not surprising that by the beginning of August Sir Alec had arrived at the conclusion that what he had to be certain of before meeting any official representatives from Rhodesia was that they were talking the same language. He had good reason to be not quite sure yet that they were.[18] Although he was not satisfied that sufficient progress in the negotiations had been made to warrant his intervention, he sent Lord Goodman and his team back to Salisbury the following month to continue the talks.

No progress was possible, however, while the Rhodesians were engaged in their own internal political feuds and manoeuvres. With a by-election coming up in the first week of August 1971 (at Mabelreign), the Rhodesian Front leaders were exceedingly anxious that their talks with the Goodman team should not give their political opponents any cause for accusing them of making concessions to the British. That there was still considerable opposition to continuing the negotiations was evident from the large vote (42 per cent) polled by the right-wing Independent candidate in the by-election. The Rhodesian Front only just managed to hold the seat, which they had won by a majority of over 1,200 votes in the 1970 general election, by the narrow margin of some 68 votes. After such a close call, Mr Smith was careful to remove any impression that he either had been, or intended to be, bought off by any British offers, although by raising the financial issue he could also hold out the promise that British money would be forthcoming if a settlement were reached. In such an eventuality, the British would make a 'gift' towards the development of the Tribal Trust Lands, not only for academic education, which he considered a wasteful expenditure, but for balanced development of the African areas – in essence, a contribution to 'separate development'.[19]

While Mr Smith had been saying in August that some significant progress towards ending the dispute had been made,[20] when he addressed the Rhodesian Front congress on 8 October, he claimed that since August (including the period of the Goodman visit) progress had been insignificant. As on previous occasions, he had something to offer for all shades of opinion. For those favouring settlement, he said that the terms under consideration were better than those offered by the British Government at previous meetings, just as the terms on *Tiger* had been better than those before the UDI and the terms on *Fearless* better than those on *Tiger* — an astute commentary on the increasing rate of British concessions. For the opposing forces, he had the assurance that Rhodesia would not deviate from its principle that government must be retained for all time in 'civilised hands'. And those sceptical about the possibility of a settlement were told that there were still basic and major difficulties between the two sides; that they were closer to an agreement than ever before; and that the final gap was 'fraught with tremendous problems'.

Although Mr Smith managed to retain congress support for his varied offerings, he did not escape some harsh warnings from the new party chairman, Mr Desmond Frost, who told him that if he couldn't settle with the British this time he should slam the door forever and get on with governing the country in accordance with party commitments. Mr Frost felt it his duty to report that the public (the European electorate) distrusted the 'Government's' intention to implement their election promises and would no longer tolerate such affronts to their doctrine of separate development as mixed public facilities and amenities, uncontrolled African influx into the towns and the withdrawal of legislation to prevent the infiltration of other races into European areas. Even the African population explosion was blamed on the 'Goverment's' excessive subsidisation of African social services and lack of initiative in introducing measures to limit the birth rate. As the conscience of the party, Mr Frost claimed that the foundation of the Rhodesian Front was the survival of the Europeans in Rhodesia. Without racial harmony that concept was lost and the feeling of the European that he was being crowded out of his own area (one-half of the country) wouldn't help the 'Government' preserve that harmony.[21]

While Mr Smith had been given one more chance to settle with the British, the Conservative Government had to produce some evidence that a settlement was still possible if they were to retain the support of their party conference in October and of their Parliamentary Party when it came to the renewal of the sanctions Order in November. Since the negotiations were being conducted in an atmosphere of secrecy, there was little that Sir Alec could reveal at that stage except that, as a result of Lord Goodman's visit in mid-September, 'useful progress' had been made, 'exploratory discussions' were continuing and officials from the Foreign and Commonwealth Office would be returning to Rhodesia shortly. But it was obvious that no further efforts towards a settlement could be undertaken until after the Rhodesian Front congress, and for this reason the return of the British officials to Salisbury was arranged for the latter part of October. So long as the Conservative Government could keep the negotiations going at some level, they could hold off the censure of their party critics, anxious for a settlement and the end of sanctions. This they managed to achieve at their party conference at Brighton in October by avoiding any debate on Rhodesia at all, in spite of the thirteen motions on the subject submitted by delegates.

However the Conversative Government may have chosen to appease their followers, they did not escape the censure of the Opposition. At the Labour party conference at Blackpool at the beginning of October, Mr Wilson alleged that the protracted negotiations on Rhodesia had been clearly designed for the benefit of the Conservative party conference and the Parliamentary vote on the Order renewing sanctions. Although the proposals under discussion in Salisbury were still confidential, he referred to rumours in the Press, *The Financial Times* in particular, that Mr Smith appeared to have found a formula capable of persuading the Government to accept his position on no African rule in his life-time. In contrasting his own party's record, Mr Wilson maintained that the Labour Government had refused to contemplate any settlement that did not fully honour the Six Principles, the first of which required unimpeded progress to majority rule. When they had said that it must be related not to clock or calendar, they still insisted that it must be in measurable time, in ten or fifteen years, not geological time.

Mr Wilson's stand was firmly backed by the party conference, and the National Executive Committee took the unusual position of asserting that the conference resolution on Rhodesia was not strong enough, a reversal of the line taken when Labour was in office. Their spokesman, Mr Denis Healey, pledged that the Labour movement would fight to the end any sell-out to the white racialists in Rhodesia. They would insist, if an agreement were reached, first, that the Africans genuinely accepted it; and secondly, that if would be impossible for Mr Smith to default on the promises he had made, as he had done over the previous years.[22]

By the time the party conferences were over and the British officials had returned to Salisbury, Mr Smith was already defaulting on the principles which were supposed to form the basis of the negotiations.

In this case, his timing was particularly bad, if he really had any intention of working out a settlement. On the very day that the British arrived, on 21 October, the church heads of some twelve denominations were meeting in Salisbury to protest against the regime's 'unjust attempt' to evict several thousand African farmers from church land, in particular, the Epworth Methodist Mission and the Chisahawasha Roman Catholic Mission, to the Tribal Trust Lands, in accordance with the segregation provisions of the Land Tenure Act. The British negotiators, this time without Lord Goodman, were placed in the impossible position of having to work for an agreement to eliminate racial discrimination while the opposing side was engaged in intensifying it. Before the officials departed on 27 October, the head of the team, Sir Philip Adams, maintained that the episode of the African evictions had not been either 'a hastener or an impediment' to what they had been talking about.[23] Nevertheless, the British were clearly disturbed by this omen of the regime's intentions, irrespective of any inhibitions imposed by an agreement. This was later confirmed by their insistence on inserting into the settlement terms a clause postponing the African evictions from church land, although only until a commission of enquiry had reported on the subject.[24]

There was still no sign of an agreed settlement document when the sanctions renewal Order became due in November 1971. Although the Rhodesian Press had reported a breakthough at the time of Lord Goodman's September visit, with details allegedly narrowed down to a solution of the First Principle and the African franchise, Goodman had firmly denied before his departure on 21 September that any settlement document existed.[25] Nor was the return visit of the British officials the following month an encouraging one, coinciding as it did with the extension of racial discrimination through the Land Tenure Act. Under these circumstances, the Foreign Secretary faced the choice of either abandoning the negotiations as an impossible project, thus risking a revolt of his party over the renewal of sanctions; or going to Salisbury himself for one last effort before admitting defeat, in spite of his decision not to intervene personally until a settlement had been agreed at the official level.

Predictably, the Foreign Secretary's announcement of his intention to go to Salisbury on 14 November came on the eve of the debate on the sanctions Order. His party supporters were so optimistic about the prospects for the forthcoming meeting that they refrained from challenging that Order, apparently anticipating a rapid dismantling of the whole sanctions programme following the agreement. There was no comparable reception from the Labour Opposition, however, which took the view that so long as the 1969 'Constitution' remained in force there was no possibility of a settlement implementing the Five Principles. There was ample evidence to back up their charges, in view of Mr Smith's statements during the negotiations that he had never accepted the Five Principles nor the possibility of majority rule.[26] However, a Labour Government had also negotiated with Mr Smith when he was making similar pronouncements about the Five Principles and majority rule and when racialist and repressive legislation was already in effect in Rhodesia. In Opposition, their demands for African representation in the negotiations and for the provision of external guarantees went far beyond anything that they had required when in office. Nevertheless, the fact that Sir Alec had chosen to go to Salisbury was regarded as 'a tactical victory for Mr Smith', as *The Times* put it,[27] because by doing so he was recognising the Rhodesian situation as it was in 1971. If there were any justification for this concession, it was provided by the Tory Peer, Lord Alport, who said in the Lords debate on the sanctions Order that unless Sir Alec went he would never convince himself or be able to convince a vociferous section of his supporters that the idea of an honourable settlement with the Rhodesian Front was simply a political mirage. It was not within the art of the possible in politics, and however ingenious the terms, a settlement could not represent anything better than 'a *de jure* recognition of the republican, apartheidist, anti-British, pro-Afrikaner political solution' which Mr Smith's policy and party represented.[28]

Like Sir Alec, Mr Smith was also cautious about predicting a successful outcome of the meeting. In a broadcast on the UDI anniversary, he welcomed the Foreign Secretary's visit as 'a significant step in the right direction' but warned against undue optimism, because they would now be dealing with the most vexed and difficult issues which had thus far defied solution. Nevertheless, he was confident that Rhodesia was in a stronger negotiating position than it had ever been on previous occasions, since the British had accepted the Rhodesian constitutional system as the point of departure. Although admitting that it would be in the best interests of Rhodesia to settle the dispute with Britain, he had no intention of giving way on the basic principles and policies to which his party was committed. Under these conditions, a settlement could only come about as a result of the British giving way on theirs.

The negotiations, which extended over a period of ten days, were mainly concerned with the 'real obstacles' to which Sir Alec had referred when announcing his decision to go to Salisbury — the barrier to African advance beyond parity of representation and the prevailing system of apartheid — although other problems, such as a Declaration of Rights, constitutional safeguards and the release of detainees, also figured in the discussions. In between the meetings, Sir Alec made the usual round of visits established by his predecessors, seeing leaders of the various communities, such as business, the church, minor European parties, African MPs, the Asians and Coloureds and even some of the detainees, including Mr Nkomo. Most of those he saw were in favour of a settlement with Britain, although the various solutions they proposed could not have had much in common with what the Rhodesian Front had to offer and, in any case, their opinions were of no more than academic interest, since they were excluded from the negotiations. Secrecy was maintained throughout the talks, with the usual Press rumours of near breakthrough or near breakdown. The latter predominated during the last few days, when it appeared that the British side was near to departing because of the failure to find a formula that would embody the guarantees they were seeking to obtain and the Rhodesian Front were equally determined to evade. Some last minute modifications were eventually devised, for on 24 November the agreement was signed.[29] Mr Smith's comment on the occasion of the public announcement of agreement was that Rhodesia had 'the happiest Africans in the world'. When asked whether majority rule would occur, he merely laughed and several of his Rhodesian Front colleagues joined in.[30] They were soon to find the test of acceptability a less humorous proposition.

Perhaps the most ironic aspect of the whole episode was the supreme confidence with which both sides looked forward to the endorsement of the settlement. It was possible, although incredible, that Mr Smith really was convinced that the Africans would welcome the proposals. For those who would not, there were always the security forces to ensure that they did not upset his calcualtions by engaging in 'intimidation'. A similar euphoria pervaded the British delegation. Lord Goodman, a self-confessed amateur on African affairs, believed that if the proposals were fairly explained to the Rhodesian people (95 per cent of whom were Africans), it was extremely unlikely that they would reject them. Even the British Press was not immune to the initial optimism about acceptance, although they may have arrived at the same conclusion from quite different premises. The *Sunday Times* correspondent in Salisbury, for example, devoted a full page to explaining 'Why the Africans Must Say "Yes" '.[31] In addition, two opinion polls showed that a large proportion of the British public approved of the settlement: 52 per cent in an Opinion Research Centre poll and 46 per cent in a Gallup poll. However, on further questioning, the former poll revealed that those who thought it was a bad settlement and the 'don't knows' (45 per cent) outnumbered those who thought it was a good one (41 per cent); and the latter showed an almost equal division between those who believed that Mr Smith could or could not be trusted (37—35 per cent, with 28 per cent 'don't knows').[32]

The Great Debate

This initial optimism was soon dispelled by the mounting opposition, most of all in Rhodesia itself, but also in Britain and throughout the world community, as the full implications of the arrangement were realised. The great debate in Britain, which caused the sharpest party divisions on an external issue since the Suez crisis, centred around the argument whether the Five Principles had been honoured or abrogated. This had been the test to which the *Tiger* and *Fearless* proposals had been put and had been found, in accordance with varying interpretations, either satisfactory or inadequate. Since there had been an increase in British concessions with each successive version of a settlement, if there were considerable doubt about *Tiger,* and even more about *Fearless*, it was inconceivable that the Home-Smith terms could be regarded as anywhere near approaching the requirements laid down in the Five Principles, however imprecise they might be. In effect, the measurement of the agreement by the yardstick of those Principles, by which the Government arrived at a positive result and the Opposition a negative one, proved to be a meaningless exercise in semantics. By any valid or realistic criteria, the agreement represented a virtual abandonment of African interests and a victory for the racialist dogma embodied in the Rhodesian Front's 1969 'Constitution'.[33] While the Labour Government had previously conceded the former, the Conservatives could now be charged with responsibility for the latter.

Nevertheless, the official Opposition line was to condemn the settlement on the ground that it had failed to conform with the Five Principles. A resolution of the National Executive Committee on 24 November reiterated that no agreement should be submitted to the British Parliament unless it were within the framework of the Principles,[34] and an amendment was put down in Parliament declining to approve the scheme for that reason. It was not difficult for their spokesman, Mr Denis Healey, to demonstrate how flimsy was the pretext that any of the Principles had been observed, either in the spirit or in the letter.[35] However, the Opposition's second line of attack — that the proposals provided even less of an opportunity for African advance than *Fearless* — was of little consequence to the large number of Labour MPs, including the former Commonwealth Secretary, Mr Bottomley, who had opposed *Fearless* because of its inadequacies on that score. The Labour party was also on weak ground in attacking a settlement conceding independence before majority rule, since their own Government, pledged to NIBMAR, had made several offers of independence to a white minority government. Although there was also Opposition criticism of the role of Lord Goodman (Lord Walston, a former Minister at the Foreign and Commonwealth Office, complained that this was a job for a statesman or a politician not a 'negotiator'), the Labour Government had also used his services as a negotiator of the *Fearless* proposals. Even Lord Caradon, who had consistently defended those proposals, as well as the Government's repudiation of NIBMAR, before the United Nations, could now say that Goodman had produced the worst constitution he had ever known — a constitution under which millions of Rhodesians were 'for ever and ever denied participation in the government of their own country'. The result was a settlement which Mr Smith had succeeded in making unworkable and Lord Goodman had succeeded in making unintelligible.[36]

Perhaps the most effective case against the agreement was its negotiator's defence of it. Admittedly, Lord Goodman did not feel triumphant or enthusiastic about it, but he felt that it was the best they were able to achieve. The real difficulty they had experienced was that the difference of approach between the two sides, on issues of principle and social morality, made it necessary to shelve all such considerations and restrict themselves wholly to the technical issues. While he was under no illusion that his side had persuaded Mr Smith to a more liberal way of thought, he was convinced that if the results of their efforts were accepted in good faith and if they were prepared to take certain political risks, the agreement offered the only hope for the emancipation of Rhodesia from the certainty of 'horrible and violent insurrection'. In refuting charges of a sell-out, he denied that the British had anything left to sell, certainly not the African, who was already in bondage as a result of the sell-out in past years.[37]

The main grounds for the charge of a sell-out, as Lord Alport had pointed out, were that it was extremely unlikely that there would ever be majority rule and that, with the pressure of sanctions removed, there would be nothing to prevent the regime from repudiating the whole agreement except 'a renegade Chief Justice, a discredited Bench

of judges and a small band of unrepresentative African MPs'.[38] Even if
the good faith of the regime were observed (Goodman's 'political risk'),
there were still enough obstacles impeding African advance to assure
the perpetuation of European minority rule. In Rhodesia the key to
political power had always been the franchise, with its income, property and educational qualifications set at a level beyond the means of
most of the African population. For the African Lower Roll, which
elected only some eight African members (in a House of fifty Europeans and eight representatives of the Chiefs), the income qualifications,
although reduced somewhat by the agreement, were even higher than
those under the 1961 Constitution and approximately double the
national average income of Africans in employment. In any case,
however many Africans qualified for the Lower Roll, there would be
no increase in the number of MPs they could elect. For the new African
Higher Roll, which was supposed to be a concession allowing for increased African representation in the House of Assembly, the qualifications were the same as those for the European Roll. While the Europeans, with an average income of over $R3,000 per annum would
have little difficulty in qualifying, the Africans, with an average income
of less than one-tenth of that amount and excluded from most occupa-
tions providing the required income of $R1,800, could not hope to
qualify in any significant numbers. There was also the educational
barrier, for even those Africans earning the lesser qualification of
$R1,200 would also need to have had four years' secondary education.
It was the established policy of the Rhodesian Front, as Mr Smith
had repeatedly said during the previous negotiations, not to expand
African education for the purpose of increasing their number on the
voters' roll. This was evident from the 'new plan' for African education
implemented in 1966, which limited secondary education to a maximum of 12½ per cent of the African school population, and even they
had no assurance of the educational facilities being made available.

With these franchise qualifications, the prospects of additional
African seats being created until even parity with the Europeans was
achieved were exceedingly remote. Although the settlement had done
away with the income tax contribution as the determining factor for
increasing African representation, in its place was a scheme which
provided that two additional African seats would be created when the
number of voters registered on the African Higher Roll was equal to
6 per cent of the number of voters registered on the European Roll.
Further African seats would become due, two at a time, for each such
proportionate increase of 6 per cent in the number of voters on the

African Higher Roll until thirty-four additional African seats had been created, thus resulting in parity in the House of Assembly. However, only half of the new African representatives would be directly elected, with the other half provided by electoral colleges of Chiefs. Even at parity, the number of directly elected Africans would still be only a quarter of the membership of the Assembly.

The provisions for going beyond parity were so hedged about with restrictions as to make it doubtful whether any, let alone all of them, could ever be achieved. At parity, a referendum would be held (following a general election) among all the enrolled African voters to determine whether the seats filled by indirect election should be abolished and replaced by an equal number of seats filled by direct election. After the completion of the referendum (and also an election if the referendum resulted in the establishment of new directly elected seats), an independent commission would be appointed to ascertain whether the creation of ten Common Roll seats (elected by Higher Roll voters only) was acceptable to 'the people of Rhodesia'.[39] The commission would report to the Assembly within a year and a law to give effect to its recommendations would have to be passed in accordance with the requirements for amending the 'Constitution'. This entire procedure – a general election, a referendum among African voters, the possible election of the new African members, the commission of enquiry, the amendment process in the Assembly and another general election – would have to be gone through before majority rule was possible. At several stages, beginning with increased European immigration and ending with the blocking European vote in the Assembly, ample impediments were available to prevent it ever occurring.

In view of these conditions, it was not surprising that the agreement contained no mention of when majority rule would be attained. The various estimates put forward by its defenders as well as its critics ranged from ten to a hundred years or more. Lord Goodman made the incredible claim that the Rhodesian Front predicted the ten years, although it was inconceivable either that they believed it or would dare to say so publicly even if they did. He himself thought that such an estimate was 'fanciful', although he admitted that it would have been better if they could have contrived to get it in fifteen or sixteen years. But it was his 'firm and fervent belief' that it would be achieved in much less time than the sixty-four, or more likely eighty-four, years estimated by Professor Palley as the earliest possible date, based on the assumption of scrupulous honesty from Mr Smith and his successors.[40]

The honesty or good faith of the Rhodesian Front in observing the agreement was largely irrelevant, since its provisions would effectively exclude Africans from attaining majority rule. The argument about how many years was in fact meaningless, as Mr Smith and his colleagues had recognised on the occasion of the signing of the agreement. The only legal access to political power was through the franchise, and this was generally barred to the Africans by European control of the economy, which denied them the jobs and the property, and the educational system, which prevented them from obtaining in any significant numbers the opportunities freely available to Europeans. Nor would the extra £5 million a year over ten years contributed by the British taxpayer have any significant effect on preparing the African for political participation, since the money would be applied to 'purposes and projects agreed with the Rhodesian Government', and their priorities were development of the Tribal Trust Lands on the model of South African Bantustans. Even for the Africans who managed to qualify as voters, there was the additional threat of white immigration, which would bolster the numbers on the European voting roll, thus making it more difficult for them to achieve the 6 per cent required for the addition of the two new African seats. Increased white immigration also meant that the new Europeans, many of them illiterate and unskilled, would be available for the training and the jobs denied to educated or qualified Africans. With the impediments already built into the constitutional settlement and with the Rhodesian Front firmly in control of policies to supplement them, any attempt to predict the time required for majority rule was, as Mr Wilson had said on another occasion, a delusion which wasted valuable time and misdirected valuable energies.

The other provisions of the settlement, hailed by the Conservative Government as major concessions won from the Rhodesian Front, were of virtually no consequence in improving the political status of the Africans (the Third Principle). The Declaration of Rights was to be justiciable, thus allowing appeals to the courts (now purged of any dissenters) in cases of their violation. But existing legislation, including the repressive laws of the preceding decade, would remain in force and not subject to challenge in the courts. The state of emergency, in effect since the UDI, was also to remain, with a mere reduction of three months (from twelve to nine) in the time required for renewal by the Assembly. And so long as a state of emergency continued to exist, the Declaration of Rights would not be enforceable. Even without a state of emergency, the rights accorded by the Declaration were restricted by so many limitations as to make them meaningless. Almost any right could be overriden in the interests of public safety, order, morality, the economic requirements of the State or 'the stage of social or economic development for the time being reached by the various descriptions of persons affected'.

Nor was there any evidence that 'progress towards ending racial discrimination' had been achieved. Although the Rhodesian Front agreed to a review commission (with one African member out of three) to examine the question, its powers were limited to making recommendations to the Rhodesian 'Government' on such issues as existing legislation, including land tenure. But the long-term prospects of any end to racial discrimination were ruled out by the saving clause that any changes in existing legislation required to give effect to the recommendations of the commission would be subject to 'considerations that any government would be obliged to regard as of an overriding character'. With this loophole (another example of Goodman's 'political risk') any Rhodesian government would be able not only to retain but to intensify racially discriminatory legislation, and still be acting within the terms of reference of the commission and of the provisions of the Declaration of Rights. Mr Smith confirmed this when he said that he did not believe that the new Declaration would mean any dramatic change in the way of life in Rhodesia: although 'blatant discrimination' was out, it was still possible for discrimination to continue as long as this was 'justifiable and reasonable'.[41]

So far as the detainees were concerned, their protection under the Declaration of Rights was non-existent, since they had never been, nor would they have the right to be, charged or tried by any court for their alleged political offences. The only concession was that their cases would be reviewed, but by the existing tribunal, headed by a judge of the High Court, and not until after the test of acceptability had been completed. By postponing the new special review until this time, the Rhodesian authorities were effectively silencing any political opposition that might come from that quarter. Even with a British-appointed 'observer' (acceptable to the Rhodesians) present at the special review, the recommendations of the tribunal would be based on their interpretation of whether a release could be made 'without prejudice to the maintenance of public safety and public order' and their decisions would be binding on the detaining authorities. For those who had been in detention even before the UDI and for those whose cases had already been reviewed (and rejected) by the Beadle tribunal, the proposed special review by the existing tribunal offered little hope of improvement.

With such provisions included in the independence settlement, it was no longer relevant to question whether the guarantees against 'retrogressive amendment' (the Second Principle) were adequate, since the Rhodesians had already obtained all the concessions they required to retain European minority control without any need for amending or revoking the agreement. But they still had to prove that such an agreement was, in accordance with the Fifth Principle, 'acceptable to the people of Rhodesia as a whole'. Mr Smith was confident that it would receive the overwhelming support of the Europeans and the Africans, and optimistically forecast that the whole operation would be over by March or April of the following year.[42] It was indeed over by then, but not in the way he expected.

The mounting opposition to the agreement in Britain and in Rhodesia itself was supported by most of the African States, the Commonwealth and the United Nations. The verdict in Lusaka, from spokesmen of the exiled ZAPU and ZANU, was that the settlement was a total sell-out of the people of Zimbabwe: nothing better could have been expected from talks from which the Africans had been excluded and nothing short of NIBMAR would be acceptable to them. A statement from the OAU on 26 November referred to 'an outright sell-out for generations to come of some five million Africans' and called upon the people of Zimbabwe 'to take matters into their own hands and assert their rights by whatever means'.[43] Both President Kaunda and President Nyerere accused Britain of creating a second South Africa by giving moral support and recognition to oppression, to the violation of human rights and to Rhodesia's move along the road to apartheid. The Zambian President, more in sorrow than in anger, regretted the most unfortunate coincidence that a man such as Sir Alec Douglas-Home, who had been in the British team that negotiated the Munich agreement with Hitler, should end his political career with 'a despicable settlement with people renowned for racial bigotry and hypocrisy'.[44] Contrary to Lord Goodman's claim that the settlement was the only hope of saving Rhodesia from the certainty of 'horrible and violent insurrection', most of the African leaders were convinced that it only made such a result inevitable. This was evident from the OAU's appeal to Africans in Rhodesia to resort to whatever means possible to prevent the enactment of an agreement which permanently barred them from access to political power.

At the United Nations, the Conservative Government were also under fire for having engaged in bilateral negotiations with the illegal regime on the basis of the prevailing constitutional system.[45] On the

day that the agreement was concluded in Salisbury, the British delegation requested a meeting of the Security Council so that they could
make a statement on the objectives of the settlement. The following
day their representative, Sir Colin Crowe, after a lengthy discourse on
the inability of Britain to influence directly an internal situation of
which it disapproved, and in a country which had been virtually self-
governing and possessed its own forces for nearly half a century, maintained that the proposals were in accordance with the Five Principles to
which successive British governments had been committed. While
commending the agreement as marking a real change of direction away
from the 1969 'Constitution' in terms of unimpeded progress to majority rule, Sir Colin admitted that the application of sanctions had not
bitten so hard as to compel Mr Smith to capitulate and accept an
imposed settlement. Like Lord Goodman, his case was that, since they
were powerless to impose the sort of settlement they would prefer,
they had to be satisfied with the only sort Mr Smith would accept. The
alternative, in his view, was 'a dark cloud of growing racial discrimination
creeping northwards', which was bound to turn Rhodesia into a satellite
of the apartheid system unless it were halted or reversed.

Not unexpectedly, the British case for a settlement with the Smith
regime failed to convince most of the UN delegates. In the General
Assembly, a resolution adopted on 20 December 1971 and opposed by
Britain rejected the proposals as contrary to the 1960 Declaration on
the Granting of Independence to Colonial Countries and Peoples, and
urged the Security Council to consider appropriate measures to enable
the people of Zimbabwe to exercise self-determination.[46] When the
Security Council attempted to comply ten days later, with a draft
resolution also rejecting the proposals and requesting Britain not to
transfer to the Rhodesian regime any of the attributes of sovereignty,
the resolution was defeated by a British veto. Before the final vote,
however, separate votes were taken approving five key recommendations – relating to consultation with the African leadership (10-0),
expression of the right of self-determination (14-0), NIBMAR (10-0),
universal suffrage (14-0) and a referendum based on one man, one vote
(10-0).[47] Just over a month later, when the Security Council convened
in Addis Ababa, a similar draft resolution was defeated by the same
margin, with the British Government casting their fifth veto on the
subject. This time their representative insisted that while there was no
disagreement between his Government and the Security Council on the
ultimate objective of majority rule in Rhodesia, the means of achieving
it remained in dispute. The British means, which the United Nations

had overwhelmingly rejected, were their settlement proposals, and these were being put before the Rhodesian people for their verdict.[48]

Notes

1. 801 *HC Deb.*, 2 July 1970, col. 81.
2. *Financial Times*, 14 July 1970.
3. 801 *HC Deb.*, 14 July 1970, col. 1362.
4. *Report of the 88th Annual Conservative Party Conference*, Blackpool, 1970.
5. The interview was astutely timed to coincide with the visit to London of the OAU mission, headed by President Kaunda, to exert pressure on the British Government in the opposite direction.
6. Television interview, 23 October 1970.
7. This was the view of the Conservative Peer, Lord Alport, who claimed that no settlement was possible except on the basis of a British surrender, at the conclusion of his visit to Rhodesia. (*The Times*, 19 October 1970.)
8. See *Report of the 69th Annual Conference of the Labour Party*, Blackpool, 1970.
9. The Labour party case against the negotiations was put by Mr Healey and Mr Thomson during the debate on the sanctions Order. (806 *HC Deb.*, 9 November 1970, cols. 38-42, 94-5.)
10. Only 21 MPs voted against the Order, although an estimated 130 did not vote at all. Before the vote the Government announced an end to the postal surcharge and the invalidity of Rhodesian divorces in the UK. They also revealed that they had sent a communication of a preliminary nature to Mr Smith through the British Ambassador in South Africa.
11. Security Council resolution 288 (1970), adopted 17 November 1970 by a unanimous vote. General Assembly resolution 2652, (XXV), adopted 3 December 1970 by 79-10, with 14 abstentions, also opposed negotiations.
12. 810 *HC Deb.*, 26 January 1971, col. 326.
13. *Commonwealth Prime Ministers' Meeting, 1971, Final Communiqué*, Singapore, 22 January 1971, HMSO, *A Year Book of the Commonwealth*, 1972.
14. An amendment to the Zambian draft added the qualification that a State would deny assistance which 'in its own judgement' would contribute directly to the pursuit or consolidation of racialism.
15. The poll appeared in the *Daily Telegraph*, 20 November 1970.
16. *Rhodesian Commentary*, November 1970.
17. 821 *HC Deb.*, 12 July 1971, col. 16.
18. Ibid., 2 August 1971, col. 1079.
19. Speech in Bulawayo, *Rhodesia Herald*, 8 August 1971.
20. Speech in Salisbury, ibid., 13 August 1971.
21. Ibid., 8, 9 October 1971.
22. *Report of the 70th Annual Conference of the Labour Party*, Blackpool, 1971.
23. *Rhodesia Herald*, 28 October 1971.
24. See Guy Clutton-Brock, *Let Tangwena Be*, 1969, for the repeated appeals from the Chief of the Tangwena people for intervention to halt their eviction from land they had occupied for generations, and for the court trial of the case.
25. *Rhodesia Herald*, 21, 22 September 1971.
26. For the Labour Opposition case, see Mr Healey, Mr Lyon and Mrs Judith Hart, 825 *HC Deb.*, 10 November 1971, cols. 1094-180.
27. 10 November 1971.

28. 325 *HL Deb.*, 10 November 1971, col. 420.

29. *Rhodesia: Proposals for a Settlement*, Cmnd. 4835, 1971; *Anglo-Rhodesian Relations: Proposals for a Settlement*, RR 46-1971.

30. *Rhodesia Herald*, 25 November 1971.

31. David Holden, *Sunday Times*, 28 November 1971.

32. The ORC poll appeared in the *Evening Standard*, 10 December 1971, and Gallup in the *Daily Telegraph*, 13 December 1971.

33. See *Rhodesia: Proposals for a Sell-Out*, Southern African Research Office, with a foreword by Mr David Steel MP, 1972.

34. *Report of the 71st Annual Conference of the Labour Party*, Blackpool, 1972.

35. 827 *HC Deb.*, 1 December 1971, cols. 478-90.

36. 326 *HL Deb.*, 1 December 1971, cols. 454, 518.

37. Ibid., cols. 326-9.

38. Ibid., col. 401.

39. The commission was to consist of a judicial officer as chairman and equal numbers of Europeans and Africans appointed by the Government after consultation with all parties represented in the Assembly.

40. *Sunday Times*, 28 November 1971.

41. Interview in *Rhodesia Herald*, 7 December 1971.

42. Ibid.

43. *The Nationalist* (Tanzania), 27 November 1971.

44. *The Times of Zambia*, 4 December 1971.

45. In the Special Committee a draft consensus adopted 22 June 1971 and a resolution adopted 2 July 1971 deplored the talks between Lord Goodman and the regime as contrary to previous General Assembly resolutions condemning negotiations on the basis of independence before majority rule. The Assembly resolution 2769 (XXVI), adopted 22 November 1971 by 102-3 (UK), with 9 abstentions, also called for the participation of the African leaders in any negotiations for independence.

46. Resolution 2877 (XXVI), adopted by 94-8, with 22 abstentions.

47. The draft resolution was defeated 30 December 1971 by 9-1 (UK). Britain abstained on each of the separate votes on five paragraphs.

48. The draft resolution was defeated 4 February 1972 by 9-1 (UK), with 5 abstentions.

10 THE TEST OF ACCEPTABILITY

'If people genuinely prefer hope to present realities they are entitled to do so.'

Pearce Commission, May 1972.

The initial optimism with which both the British and the Rhodesian Governments regarded the outcome of the test of opinion on the terms of the settlement rapidly dissipated during the period of nearly two months between the signing of the agreement and the commencement of the work of the commissioners. This interval was later to be cited by the Rhodesian Front as one of the main causes of the rejection of the settlement, rightly so in the sense that it provided time for reflection on the terms and time for the Africans to mount a massive campaign against their implementation. By far the most impressive opposition came from a new group – the African National Council – established in a remarkably short time for the purpose of informing the African population about the effect upon them of the settlement terms.[1] The new ANC (the same initials as the old African National Congress banned in 1959), contained a number of members of the former African nationalist parties, many of whom had been detained or restricted, and had as its chairman Bishop Abel Muzorewa, head of the United Methodist Church in Rhodesia. At a press conference on 16 December 1971, which set the tone for the campaign that was to be relentlessly pursued for the succeeding three months, the chairman described the settlement as 'a constitutional rape of Africans by both the Rhodesian and British Governments' and tantamount to a sell-out of the African majority to 'perpetual oppression and domination by the privileged white minority'. For the Bishop the most effective case that could be made against the terms was the fact that a racialist regime had accepted them, and on the basis of this criteria alone the Africans would be well advised to reply with an emphatic 'no'.[2]

The ANC had thus launched its offensive even before the commission had been named, which was not until the last day of 1971. In addition to the chairman, Lord Pearce, who had been chosen for his acceptability to Mr Smith as the only British judge to have pronounced on the legality of the actions of an illegal regime, the deputy chairmen were a former Governor of Sierra Leone (Sir Maurice Dorman), a former Tory MP and ambassador to the USA (Lord Harlech) and a former governor of Malawi (Sir Glyn Jones).[3] Most of the commissioners (originally sixteen but increased to twenty) had served as colonial officials in British territories. Their background was one of paternalism towards native populations, their ideological outlook had been formed during an era of colonialism and their experience, often as District Commissioners, had much in common with Rhodesian officials engaged in similar activities.

Within the framework of their terms of reference — to ensure that the proposals were fully understood and acceptable to the Rhodesian people — the commissioners had a wide margin of choice as to how they would proceed. As they were later to admit in their report, 'the dividing line between exposition and advocacy is thin but immensely important': their task was to explain the proposals, not to argue the case for adoption or rejection. It seemed to them that it was legitimate to state that the settlement had the approval of the British and Rhodesian Governments and to quote British Ministers to the effect that if the terms were rejected there would be no possibility of amending them. On the other hand, they thought it wrong to attempt to give answers to questions which the negotiating Governments had not themselves answered, e.g. the likely period before majority rule.[4] If any criticism could be directed against the proceedings of the commissioners (even though they arrived at the correct conclusion), it was that they erred on the side of caution. With the exception of the few who openly commended the terms, the restraint which the others observed in 'explaining' a settlement which they must have known would permanently exclude the Africans from political power was a truly remarkable achievement.

The Pearce Commission, like the Monckton Commission of the previous decade, began with the blessings of the European community and ended with a verdict favourable to the Africans. During the course of its two-month survey of Rhodesian opinion it succeeded, at one time or another, in incurring the hostility of all the parties concerned. Its task was an unenviable one, as testing opinion in a police State was bound to be, since the Smith regime set the limits of 'normal political activities' and controlled the media of communications and the security forces. Under such conditions, there was always the possibility that its activities would be so constricted as to prevent a meaningful and accurate assessment of opinion.[5] However, the initial hostility and suspicion with which the Africans in Rhodesia and the Labour party in Britain had viewed the appointment of the Pearce Commission,[6] on grounds of its membership and the circumstances under which it was obliged to operate, soon gave way to a defence of its duty to carry out a fair test of Rhodesian opinion. By the end of January, the Commission was under fire instead from the Smith regime for failing to fulfil their expectations of docility. In a letter to the British Foreign Secretary, Mr Smith criticised the Commission for declining to consult with Rhodesian civil servants on how to test African opinion. The letter also referred to the deterioration in the security situation, asserting yet again that this would have been avoided if the Commission had begun its survey earlier.[7]

The security situation had indeed deteriorated since the arrival of the Commission in Rhodesia, but not for the reasons alleged by Mr Smith and also Sir Alec Douglas-Home: the former blaming the well-known strongholds of international communism and the latter, the minorities on the right and left dedicated to destroying the settlement.[8] While much of the disorder was a result of the Smith regime's prohibition of the normal political activities guaranteed under the settlement, it was also due to the fact that for the first time in a decade the Africans were suddenly given an opportunity to express their grievances in the presence of representatives of the colonial Power. Some of these grievances were genuinely political, relating to the Africans' exclusion from political participation and the banning of their leaders, but others were economic and included demands for better wages and employment opportunities, as in the case of the protest strike by mineworkers at Shabani. In the disturbances in the townships in Salisbury, Gwelo, Umtali, Bulawayo and Que Que, which occurred during the fortnight after the Commission's arrival, some 15 Africans were killed, about 50 wounded and hundreds detained by the security forces. Among the detained were the former Prime Minister, Mr Garfield Todd, and his daughter, Judith, and several officers of the newly formed ANC, including the secretary-general, Mr Josiah Chinamano. In many cases, the detentions were brief, but long enough to prevent those detained from meeting the commissioners in the areas in which they were taking their surveys. As Lord Pearce described the situation, in a statement issued on 20 January 1972, 'if people are detained simply to silence them, then even in existing conditions it is not allowing normal political activity'.

Whether the violence was spontaneous or provoked by the security forces, often using tear gas on groups of peaceful demonstrators, the result was the same: opposition was ruthlessly suppressed, its organisers terrorised by the use of force or arrest. Those blamed for the disturbances were accused by Mr Smith of playing directly into the hands of the authorities. As he said in his reply to Lord Pearce's statement, 'what greater proof could anyone have of their lack of maturity, lack of civilisation, their inability to make any constructive contribution?'[9] Certainly those caught up in the thirty-day detentions (over 1,100 by 27 January) were prevented from making any contribution at all. In spite of this curtailment of normal political activities, however, it was already evident that the settlement proposals would not be acceptable to the Rhodesian people as a whole and that the Smith regime would resort to every means to prevent the Pearce Commission from recording this obvious conclusion.

Normal Political Activities

The concern in Britain that the Pearce Commission would be prevented from carrying out the task assigned to it by the settlement terms prompted the Conservative Government to send a special envoy from the Foreign and Commonwealth Office (Mr Philip Mansfield) to confer with the British liaison officer in Salisbury and with the Smith regime on the conditions prevailing in Rhodesia. The Labour party had already protested about the refusal of the Rhodesian authorities to allow Sir Dingle Foot, a former legal officer in the Labour Government, to enter the country to advise the ANC. Together with the Liberals, they had also condemned the arrest of Mr Todd, who was to have come to London to address a public meeting, and to broadcast on the reactions of the Africans to the settlement. However, the presence of the Foreign and Commonwealth Office representative in Salisbury had singularly little effect on the situation, particularly since the arrest of Mr Chinamano, and his wife, Ruth, occurred the day after his arrival. According to Mr Smith's version, the arrest of the Todds and several African leaders were cases of preventive detention, under the 1970 Emergency Powers Regulations. Like Sir Alec, he was convinced that the protests against the agreement came from the extremist minorities out to blind or divert Rhodesians from a true appreciation of where their interests lay. In these circumstances, his regime were not prepared to relinquish responsibility for maintaining law and order, which Sir Alec had already conceded they had the right to do, provided the minimum of force was used.[10]

Having failed to get any satisfaction from the Government on the conditions under which the Pearce Commission was obliged to operate, the Labour party continued to press for a party delegation to observe the procedure for testing opinion in Rhodesia. The Government, however, had already indicated their preference for an all-party Parliamentary delegation for this purpose, on the grounds that it would be wrong to transfer British political differences to Rhodesia or for British political parties to propagate their views on the proposals while the test of acceptability was being conducted. Nevertheless, after assurances from the Labour and Liberal parties that they would not engage in such activities while in Rhodesia and would be willing to participate in an all-party delegation as well, Sir Alec Douglas-Home approached Mr Smith to make the necessary arrangements. Although it was doubtful that the regime would agree to receive representatives of political parties opposed to the settlement, their refusal was based on the allegation that some of the proposed Labour members (Mr Healey and Miss Lestor) and the Liberal Whip (Mr David Steel) had encouraged or actively supported 'terrorist' movements in Africa.[11] Thus, Mr Smith was left with the decision on who could enter a British colony and, as a result, no delegation, either party or Parliamentary, was able to observe the proceedings of the Pearce Commission. A few MPs, however, managed to get in on private visits (including Mr Foley and Mr Lyon of the Labour party) and their reports confirmed the Commission's concern about the infringements of the agreement on normal political activities.

In spite of these infringements, the Commission was determined to carry on its enquiry, and the chairman gave an assurance on 7 February that the task could be usefully completed. In the course of its proceedings, it encountered from both the African opponents and the European defenders of the settlement severe criticisms of the manner in which the survey was being conducted. The African National Council was particularly concerned about the fact that some of the commissioners, who were obliged only to explain the proposals, were actively campaigning for a favourable response. There was also the case of the Commission having withdrawn the forms on which Africans were to have recorded their verdict on the settlement, apparently on the advice of the regime, which couldn't fail to notice the resemblance to a referendum. In addition, the Commission's distribution of a free pamphlet containing a simplified version of the Government's White Paper and with the Union Jack on the cover, was regarded as an endorsement rather than an explanation of the proposals. The stark choice offered by the pamphlet was that if the proposals were accepted, then the dispute would end and Britain would declare that Rhodesia was independent; but if they were not accepted, then things would continue as they were and (with an ominous note) 'how this would turn out no one could easily say'. How things would turn out with the acceptance of such a settlement was glowingly portrayed as 'steady steps' towards African majority rule: the total number of African Members chosen in various ways would in time equal and then outnumber the Europeans; the African Members could then choose the government, make new laws and change old ones. Admittedly, all this could not happen at once and no one could say how many years it would take. Nor did the pamphlet say anything about the obstacles or 'braking' mechanisms which the Europeans could invoke to prevent any of these 'steady steps' from occurring. While the pamphlet could safely relegate all these events to a distant future (what Mr Wilson called 'geological time'), its promises on the Declaration of Rights were blatantly lacking in credibility. For those Africans detained or restricted it was not much consolation to be told that 'if you have done no wrong in the eyes of the court you have a right to be free' or 'you may go to lawful meetings and say peacefully what you feel or think'. And for those who did not find the Declaration easy to comprehend, there was the advice that to understand it they would need the help of men with special training in the law. As Caradon had remarked earlier, Lord Goodman had indeed succeeded in making the proposals unintelligible.

The Pearce Commission was also receiving complaints from the Rhodesian Front, concerned that things were not working out as expected at the time of the agreement. In a statement to the Commission on 4 February, the party chairman, Mr Desmond Frost, threatened that, without reciprocal co-operation from the Africans, there was no guarantee that his party would continue to support the proposals. The African response he described as tantamount to a 'slap in the face' for the Europeans, resulting in a hardening of European opposition to the settlement. He also repeated the party's charge that the delay in the arrival of the Commission had resulted in agitators and self-seekers intimidating the African to such an extent that the good relations between the two races had suffered a serious set-back. His party's advice was that the sooner the Commission departed, the sooner Rhodesia could return to the peace and tranquillity that it had enjoyed for the previous decade.

By the time the Rhodesian Front gave evidence to the Pearce Commission the verdict was already going against the regime and this trend undoubtedly accounted for the change in tone of their statements. Mr Frost's doubt about the party continuing to support the proposals was a far cry from Mr Smith's confident prediction that by March or April the whole exercise would have been completed, with the legal blessings of the British Parliament. Although the Rhodesian Front were fully in control of the conditions under which the test of opinion was being conducted, they had still been unable to ensure a result in their favour.

This was indeed the 'slap in the face' so resented by Mr Frost and his party supporters. Most unexpected was the startling success with which the ANC, within such a brief period of time and with such obstacles to surmount, succeeded in getting across the message, even in the Tribal Trust Lands from which it was banned, that the proposals had nothing to offer in the way of improving the status of the Africans or altering the minority rule under which they lived.

The ANC's formal rejection of the terms was made on 28 January 1972, in evidence to the Pearce Commission which demolished every claim that the Rhodesian Front, as well as Sir Alec Douglas-Home and Lord Goodman, had made in favour of the settlement. The essential point was that there could never be majority rule, because the Africans were denied the wages, property and education essential to qualify for the vote, as a result of the discriminatory legislation which would continue to prevail under the terms of the agreement. The proposed safeguards, the Declaration of Rights, the commission of enquiry were all regarded as inadequate and no more likely to succeed as a protection of human rights than the ill-fated Constitutional Council established under the 1961 Constitution, whose advisory opinions had been repeatedly overriden by the Rhodesian Front regime. Nor was the offer of British economic aid an inducement to accept the proposals, since the ANC view was that the principal beneficiaries would be the regime and European industry, in terms of foreign exchange, and much of the money would be used to promote 'separate development'.

While the ANC's rejection of the settlement could have been predicted from their statements since the previous December, less expected was the virtually unanimous verdict from the less politically active or articulate Africans. The first sign of this trend was the rejection of the terms, on 24 January 1972, by the Rhodesian Electoral Union, the eight African MPs elected by the tribal leaders. If anyone could have been considered as a safe 'yes' vote, it was the representatives of the Chiefs, who were paid for their support of the regime. Although they did not, like the ANC, go so far as to hold out for NIBMAR, they did object to the granting of independence before parity was reached. Surprisingly, in view of their reputation as stooges, they expressed their doubts about the regime's good faith in taking any measures to bring an end to racial discrimination. They also complained that Africans were not consulted during the settlement negotiations, and urged the British Government to recall the Commission (whose presence was blamed for the violence that had occurred) and convene a representative conference to discuss the future of Rhodesia.

Another shock for the Rhodesian Front was the reaction of the Chiefs. Before the Commission had arrived in Rhodesia the regime had instructed District Commissioners to explain and commend the proposals to Chiefs, Councillors and Headmen in their districts. Although the Council of Chiefs, in a joint statement to the Pearce Commission, had accepted the proposals, they had criticised certain features of the settlement, such as the franchise, racial discrimination and the Land Tenure Act. When they were interviewed in their own chiefly areas, however, the majority of them lined up with their people in the rejection of the settlement or chose to remain silent. In assessing their evidence, the Pearce Commission concluded that the Chiefs could not speak for their people on such political matters as the settlement proposals and that a private acceptance of the proposals not validated by the approval of their people could not commit the people. Even so, the commissioners found that of the total of substantive and acting Chiefs whom they interviewed, twice as many rejected the proposals as accepted them (87-44). The written evidence from Chiefs revealed an almost identical pattern: out of twenty letters, fourteen were rejections and six were acceptances. In the private sessions, the majority of Councillors also rejected the proposals and the Headmen supported the Chiefs in their rejection. Since these results had occurred in spite of the banning of political meetings in the Tribal Trust Lands, they could not be written off as the work of 'intimidation', particularly when private evidence had confirmed public declarations. Apart from the reservations expressed by the commissioners in Matabeleland North (with only 7 per cent of the African population) and in Victoria (where there was no evidence that the proposals were positively acceptable to the people as a whole), the Commission could only conclude that the population in the TTLs appeared to be consistent in their rejections.

The results from Africans outside the TTLs followed an identical pattern and most of the reasons given for rejection were similar to those expressed by the ANC. An overwhelming majority of the relatively privileged African Purchase Area farmers (who owned some 'immovable' property but not enough to qualify for the vote) unequivocally rejected the terms, as did the members of the African Farmers' Union, who were also concerned that the key word 'immovable' before property 'took it all away from the African voter'. Other groups recorded as rejecting the settlement included the African Trades Union Congress, the National African Federation of Unions, the African clergy, African teachers and African women. The large majority of African opinion in the urban areas (19 per cent of the total adult African popu-

lation), with the possible exception of domestic servants, were opposed
to the settlement. No very clear pattern emerged from the Africans
living in the European areas. The Commission therefore felt considerable doubt as to the acceptability or otherwise of the proposals among
this section of the population, which contained workers on European
farms who, like the domestic servants in the urban areas, had considerable pressure on them to record their agreement. From the numerous
African associations who submitted written evidence to the Commission, the result was equally overwhelming, with 110 rejections and only
7 acceptances.

On the other side, the Europeans, apart from a small minority, were
in favour of the settlement. By far the most important consideration
for the Europeans was the economy rather than the proposals themselves. In what amounted to the greatest tribute thus far paid to the
sanctions measures, they claimed that Rhodesia would thrive economically only if there were a settlement with Britain. This was certainly
the view of those in commerce and industry and also of the European
trade unions. The other main reasons given for acceptance were so irrelevant to the actual terms of the proposals as to cast doubt on either the
understanding or the honesty of those Europeans who professed them.
If the Africans could be accused by Mr Smith of not knowing what a
constitution was, the Europeans could equally be charged on the basis
of some of their replies. If it was not a matter of ignorance, it could
only have been a case of saying what the defenders of the settlement
would like to hear. The main concern, after the economy, was majority
rule. On this subject, the Europeans, while admitting that they did not
really welcome it, claimed that they realised it had to come and that
the more gradual and peaceful the road to it the better. The proposals
were even regarded as essential for the African, who was expected to be
better off this way than under permanent European control or immediate African rule. Since the Europeans had been assured by Mr Smith
that the proposals would ensure that government remained in 'civilised
hands', it was extremely unlikely that the European electorate, who
supported the Rhodesian Front for this reason, would favour any settlement which really did provide for majority rule, even by 'gradual' or
'peaceful' means. A similar lack of comprehension was shared by the
few Europeans who rejected the proposals on the grounds that they
had nothing to offer the European, that they did not guarantee the
retention of government in 'civilised hands' and that they involved
outside interference in Rhodesian affairs. The only other Europeans
who rejected the settlement did so from the opposite point of view,

on grounds of conscience: not enough had been conceded to the African. How many were represented in each of the two European groups who said 'no' was not revealed, since only one figure for the European rejections was recorded: 390 'no' (as against 5,634 in favour) in the oral evidence, and 1,400 'no' (as against 93,000 in favour) in the written evidence. Consequently, the commissioners could readily report that they were satisfied that the proposals were acceptable to an overwhelming majority of Europeans.

Intimidation

In spite of this conclusion from the Europeans, it would have no effect on the final verdict unless the Africans, as the majority of the Rhodesian people, also said 'yes', and this they obviously were not doing. The only way in which the Smith regime could turn an African 'no' into an African 'yes' was by claiming that a 'no' response really meant 'yes', because those who had said 'no' were victims of intimidation. Although the commissioners had already obtained sufficient evidence to satisfy themselves that intimidation by the Rhodesian authorities was for the purpose of silencing opposition to the settlement, what they had yet to establish was that the Africans who were rejecting the settlement were genuinely and freely doing so and not, as Mr Smith had alleged, saying 'no' when they really meant 'yes'. Since a number of allegations of intimidation, obstruction and pressure involving the regime and organisations opposed to the proposals had been received, the Commission was provided with two additional members from Britain to evaluate the charges coming from both sides.

The Commission's conclusions on the subject of intimidation demolished the Rhodesian Front's last remaining hope of discrediting the results of the test of acceptability. They not only failed to convince the Commission of the invalidity of the negative responses on the ground of intimidation but, by charging their opponents with intimidation, they initiated the exposure of the tactics they themselves had employed for the purpose of obtaining a favourable result. The most obvious infringement, which had already been condemned by the Commission the previous January, was the continuing use of the thirty-day detention to prevent ANC supporters from registering their own objections or leading others to reject the proposals. As a result, the number of detentions (on the basis of the regime's own figures) had risen to over 1,700 by 11 March, at the conclusion of the enquiry. The commissioners also found that even before they had arrived in Rhodesia, the thirty-day detention of opponents had been in operation. Other tactics employed by the regime included the denial of public meetings by opponents, pressure on the Chiefs, Headmen and Councillors by the authorities and also pressure by the District Commissioners and the police at Commission meetings. What pressure had been exerted by European employers of Africans had singularly little effect on the results, although the Commission did find that the small number of acceptances that were recorded came from African servants and African farm workers in the European areas. All the more surprising, with all the means of coercion readily at hand, was that the regime still failed to obtain a convincing number of acceptances.

From the African side, the ANC claimed that it was only after the police had acted against the demonstrators in the January disturbances that the people became violent. The violence in Shabani, however, arose from a purely industrial dispute, and the Commission rejected the regime's contention that any local grievance was seized upon and escalated into violence for political motives. The Commission also found no real evidence that the ANC national executive organised violence. Instead, the upsurge of political activity – so long banned – coinciding with the arrival of the Commission, led to situations in which 'agitators' urged people to take part in violent demonstrations against authority. As for the effect of these events on the results of the enquiry, the Commission found it improbable that, with such a tight security system as that which had existed in Rhodesia for several years, a minority could dominate a majority by intimidation in a few weeks. Nor did the Commission think that the ANC would have obtained so great and so swift a response had it not met a potential desire among a majority of the people for leadership in a rejection of the terms and in a protest against the policies of the previous years. The Commission disposed of the intimidation charges by concluding that had there been no intimidation there would still have been a substantial majority against the proposals and that, in spite of the incidents that did occur, the Africans' overwhelming rejection was a genuine, deeply felt expression of opinion. In dismissing the suggestion (put forward by the Rhodesian Front) that the answer should be construed as 'yes', the Commission would not accept that there was ever a moment when a majority on reflection and with some understanding of the proposals would have answered 'yes', and any attempt to try to turn the large majority which rejected the settlement into a 'yes' vote would simply be 'perverse'. With the intimidation issue disposed of as a factor determining the results, the Commission could report to the Foreign and Commonwealth Secretary that the people of Rhodesia as a whole did not regard the proposals as acceptable as a basis for independence.

A Cry of Defiance

Even before the official announcement of the results of the enquiry on 23 May 1972, it was a foregone conclusion that the answer would be a rejection of the settlement. Nothing but a complete distortion of the opinions expressed could have produced any other answer, however much it might have been desired by both the British and the Rhodesian Governments. As *The Times* confirmed, it was hard to imagine a full-scale referendum producing a very different conclusion.[12] Nevertheless, the publication of the report had a tremendous effect on the parties involved both in Rhodesia and in Britain. The Africans were, of course, elated that for the first time in Rhodesian history their opinions had been solicited, recorded and respected. The ANC, with growing confidence, had already established a formal organisation on 10 March 1972, the day before the departure of the Pearce Commission, and the verdict came as a tribute to their efforts in mobilising African opinion.

The Opposition parties in Britain also welcomed the results as vindicating the condemnations of the proposals they had made from the outset. The National Executive Committee of the Labour party, in a resolution on 24 May accepting the main conclusions of the report, congratulated the Pearce Commission on the thoroughness and impartiality of its enquiry. The party had finally come to the conclusion that no further negotiations between the British Government and the Rhodesian Front could produce a settlement acceptable to the African majority and that any further attempt to negotiate an independence constitution would have to include the representative leaders of the African people. It was still convinced, however, that any agreement would need to conform to the Five Principles and, in particular, to the Fifth, which the Conservative Government as well as the Rhodesian Front had no intention of implementing in a similar way after their experience with the Pearce Commission. As a measure of their disapproval of the Government's Parliamentary Motion merely 'taking note of' the Report, the Opposition put down an amendment on 15 June incorporating the demands made in the NEC resolution of 24 May for African representation in any future negotiations and for the intensification and strengthening of the existing sanctions programme.[13]

The defeat of the settlement was a severe blow to the Conservative Government and to the prestige of their chief negotiators, Sir Alec Douglas-Home and Lord Goodman, particularly after the latter's confident prediction of approval. However, rather than admit their miscalculation of African opinion and recognise, as the Report so clearly demonstrated, that the settlement really was unacceptable to the African majority, they chose to blame their failure not on the proposals as such but on African mistrust of the Rhodesian Front. As Sir Alec said, in his statement to Parliament on 23 May,[14] some Africans, but by no means all, were opposed to the settlement proposals; and a great many of them said 'no' because they thought there was no guarantee that the terms would be carried out by the regime. While the Tories could find ample confirmation in the Report of African distrust of the regime, it was sheer distortion of its conclusions to imply that the Africans would have supported the proposals if they had been assured of their implementation. Even after the African veto, the Conservative Government chose to leave the proposals on the table, since Mr Smith had not withdrawn or modified them. Their view, as Lord Goodman stated, was that no great revision of the terms would be necessary to achieve a settlement with a large number of 'moderate' Africans. Although confessing (yet again) that he was not a Rhodesian expert and that he had never really met an African on any terms of intimacy, except 'the very agreeable waiters at the Meikels Hotel', whom he rated as 'yes to a man', he remained convinced that the solution in Rhodesia would have been achieved by the adoption of the proposals, that Mr Smith would have carried them out, and that the Africans might well have been wrong in arriving at the conclusion they did. However much he deplored the answer, he preferred to regard it as 'a cry of defiance' against the regime rather than a condemnation of the scheme he had negotiated, and, for that reason, he suspected that it could not have brought more devastating disappointment to any person than it did to Mr Smith, who had maintained the belief that he was regarded by the Africans as 'father of his people'.[15]

The Report was, of course, deeply resented and bitterly condemned by Mr Smith and his regime.[16] In a broadcast on the day it was issued, he described it as irresponsible, unrealistic, naive and inept. He claimed that the Commission had had 'the wool pulled over their eyes', had bungled the test on which the British had insisted against Rhodesian advice and had spurned the help of Rhodesian authorities in planning and preparing the exercise. Regarding the future of the proposals which had been left on the table by the British Government, the Rhodesians were fully prepared to carry out the agreement if Britain would do so also, but there would be no question of any part of them being implemented unilaterally and there would be no negotiations with a view to changing any of the terms. As for the sanctions measures still in operation against Rhodesia, Mr Smith's view was that the British Government would not wish to punish the Africans for rejecting the proposals by continuing sanctions against them.[17]

The reply to Mr Smith's offer could only have been a negative one. The British Government were in no position to violate the Fifth Principle by enforcing a settlement which had just been rejected by the overwhelming majority of the Rhodesian people and, in the absence of any acceptable agreement, they could produce no justification for abandoning the sanctions programme, which the Africans regarded not as a punishment for them but as a means of forcing better terms from the Europeans. But the pretext that Rhodesia could return to the *status quo*, as Mr Smith had maintained, was merely wishful thinking. The country would never be the same again, as the Labour Peer, Lord Shepherd, had pointed out during the debate on the Pearce Commission's Report.[18] The Africans had been given a voice in the political future of their country and their rejection of the terms was a clear 'no' to the prevailing constitutional system on which they were based. If any lesson emerged from the enquiry of the Pearce Commission, it was that the Africans would need to be consulted in advance on any future constitutional proposals offered to the Rhodesian people for approval. Otherwise, an independence settlement would never be possible.

Notes

See E. Mlambo, *No Future Without Us: The Story of the ANC in Zimbabwe*, 1972.

2. *Rhodesia Herald*, 17 December 1971.

3. Sir Frederick Pedlar, of the United Africa Company, resigned for personal reasons almost immediately after his appointment as a deputy chairman.

4. *Report of the Commission on Rhodesian Opinion*, Cmnd. 4964, 1972.

5. See *Rhodesia: The White Judges' Burden*, a report compiled by a team of lawyers sent to Rhodesia by the International Defence and Aid Fund, May 1972.

6. The Labour party spokesman, Mr Healey, had proposed that the Commission include other than colonial service officials in its membership, such as representatives of African interests, the church and the European opposition. See 829 *HC Deb.*, 29 January 1972, cols. 1406-7.

7. *Rhodesia Herald*, 28 January 1972.

8. 829 *HC Deb.*, 19 January 1972, col. 472.

9. *Rhodesia Herald*, 22 January 1972.

10. Broadcast of 21 January 1972.

11. See 830 *HC Deb.*, 31 January 1972, cols. 45-6.

12. 24 May 1972.

13. 838 *HC Deb.*, 15 June 1972, col. 1769.

14. 837 *HC Deb.*, 23 May 1972, cols. 1225-6.

15. 332 *HL Deb.*, 21 June 1972, cols. 264-7.

16. *Where Did Pearce Go Wrong? A Brief Appreciation of the Pearce Report*, 'Ministry' of Information, June 1972.

17. Interview, Rhodesian Broadcasting Corporation, 28 June 1972.

18. 332 *HL Deb.*, 21 June 1972, col. 228.

11 A TIME FOR REFLECTION

> 'There is only one way to settle our Rhodesian problems —
> we Rhodesians have got to get together and do it amongst
> ourselves.'
>
> Ian Smith, 29 June 1973.

For the Rhodesian Front, a return to the *status quo* may have meant the retention of the constitution they preferred, but it also meant the end of any immediate hope of achieving their 'best first prize' — a settlement with Britain, and with it the recognition of their illegal independence and the end of sanctions. Without reciprocal co-operation from the British, the implementation of the proposals would be a meaningless gesture, from which they would derive no benefit within the country, where the majority had rejected them, or in the world outside, where they had been universally condemned. Nevertheless, something had to be salvaged from the disastrous defeat of their independence proposals by the verdict of the Pearce Commission. The strategy adopted by the Rhodesian Front was to try to convince the British Government, against all evidence to the contrary, that the Africans really did approve of the proposals but had been prevented from saying so by means of intimidation. If Britain could accept this interpretation of the test of acceptability, there would be no further justification for refusing to implement the settlement. The main problem, however, was that the overwhelming majority of the people continued to support the ANC in opposition to the proposals, in spite of the regime's harassment of the organisation by banning its membership cards and detaining or restricting its leaders. Rather than recognise the real spokesmen of African opinion, the Rhodesian Front chose to support and encourage a number of small and unrepresentative pro-settlement organisations claiming to represent the authentic voice of the African people. Mr Smith's refusal to consult with the ANC leaders, announced immediately after the Pearce Commission's report and reaffirmed in the House of Assembly on 21 July, was based on the allegation that the ANC had resorted to intimidation to defeat the settlement. His conviction that 'no useful purpose would be served by meeting these people' survived only until it became obvious that there were no other relevant people to meet.

Failing to convince the British Government of the representative character of the pro-settlement groups, the regime were left with the alternative of suppressing the ANC or making contact with its leaders. The choice was, however, an unreal one. The massive support achieved by the ANC could only be destroyed by means beyond their capacity to maintain, and to attempt to do so would make a mockery of their claim of African support for their proposals. Talking to the ANC was also a calculated risk, since it was likely to arouse the hostility of the Rhodesian Front rank and file, suspicious of any contact with an African movement independent of European control and fearful of a surrender of party principles for the purpose of a settlement with the British. Aware of this dilemma when he met the party congress on 21 September 1972, Mr Smith, while assuring his supporters that there would be no yielding of principle in the direction of multi-racialism, maintained that it would be wrong deliberately to create conditions of 'petty apartheid', which gave the Africans (especially those who were allegedly sorry they had said 'no') no option but to become their enemies. So far as further negotiations with Britain were concerned, he was convinced that it would be a mistake to burn a bridge which they might wish to use some time in the future.[1]

For the Conservative Government, a return to the *status quo* in Rhodesia necessarily involved a continuation of the sanctions programme, at least until a way out of the constitutional dilemma could be found. What that way would be remained an unknown factor, since the settlement proposals, which were still available, were unacceptable to the majority of Rhodesians. In the absence of any other solution, the Tories could only await future developments within Rhodesia. As Sir Alec Douglas-Home had said on the day the Pearce Report was issued, there had to be 'a time for reflection', for the problems of that country could only be solved by Rhodesians themselves. While the 'processes of consultation' proceeded, the Government would maintain the *status quo*, including sanctions, until a satisfactory settlement was reached.[2]

Once the Conservative Government had conceded, however reluctantly, that the verdict of the Pearce Commission would be respected and that the sanctions programme would be continued, there was a general consensus in Britain on the need for 'a time for reflection' in Rhodesia. What differences remained between the Government and the Opposition were more apparent than real. The argument about observing the Five Principles in any future negotiations continued to be a semantic one, although there was some doubt about Tory acceptance of the Fifth, in view of Sir Alec's advocacy of 'the wisdom of reserving judgement in any future test of acceptability'. Even the Labour party's concern about African representation in any new discussions was not all that different from the Conservative Government's vision of 'processes of consultation', and would have carried more conviction as an attack upon Tory methods of negotiation if Labour had not operated in a similar manner while in office. Where they differed in substance, however, was over the Government's insistence that their proposals still provided the basis for a way forward, if only the Africans would appreciate the advantages and measure them against an indefinite continuation of the *status quo* rather than against an ideal solution. As the Labour party spokesman, Mr Callaghan, had said during the debate on the Pearce Report, however long the Foreign Secretary waited, he would not get a different answer or a change of mind from the Africans.[3] Nevertheless, the Conservative Government's proposals were to remain available, just as the Labour Government's *Fearless* proposals had been left on offer to the Rhodesians. The distinction, however, was that the Tory settlement had been put to the test of Rhodesian opinion and overwhelmingly defeated, a fate from which *Fearless* had been mercifully spared by the Rhodesian Front's rejection. Mr Wilson could therefore afford to denounce the Salisbury settlement of 1971 in terms of the Fifth Principle and to condemn the Tory policy of leaving it on the table until it was acceptable as really meaning 'until every articulate leader of African opinion was behind bars'.[4]

The Conservative Government also preferred to retain the proposals for party political reasons, especially as a useful bargaining counter for the annual renewal of the sanctions Order. If there were to be time for reflection in Rhodesia while the *status quo* was being maintained, there had to be something to reflect about. Ever since the return of a Conservative Government there had been growing dissatisfaction among the Tory rank and file about the continuation of sanctions, particularly after their leadership had repeatedly condemned the mandatory sanctions introduced by the Labour Government. The whole subject had been skilfully avoided at the party conference in October 1972, just as it had the preceding year, despite some thirty-seven motions on Rhodesia submitted for discussion. Although Sir Alec had twice won a reprieve from his party critics on the sanctions renewal Order, with the promises, respectively, of negotiations under way or negotiations near completion, after the defeat of the settlement there was little left to offer in the way of compensation. He could revert to his statement the previous June (during the debate on the Pearce Report) that if the Government decided that sanctions had failed in their purpose or evasions were so widespread they were intolerable, they would appeal to the United

Nations for a change of policy. But apparently that stage had not yet been reached, in spite of his complaint that sanctions had become less effective since the agreement had been signed (with exports from Rhodesia recovering to 97 per cent of their 1965 level), and that only four cases of breaches of sanctions had been prosecuted after Britain had submitted some 170 recommendations regarding violations.[5]

So the existing sanctions were to be continued, according to Sir Alec, in order that there would be 'minimum disruption during this period of reflection'. However, as a concession to the critics, who now included over eighty Tory Peers and a number of backbench Tory MPs conducting an anti-sanctions campaign in the correspondence columns of *The Times*, the Government made a few minor changes regarding the restrictions (mainly monetary, travel, educational and medical) for the so-called hardship cases arising from the application of sanctions. While this move may have saved a few votes for the Government, a considerable number of Conservative MPs must have chosen to abstain as a gesture of their disapproval, because the total vote in favour of the continuation Order was only 266, with 29 Tory rebels opposed. Nevertheless, Sir Alec had managed for the third time to retain both the sanctions measures and the unity of his party. He was to survive the same challenge the following year and prove *The Times* wrong in its prediction that 1972 would be the last time for Rhodesian sanctions.[6]

The only relevant issue about sanctions was not whether they should be continued, since Britain could not opt out of an international obligation it had initiated, but how they could be tightened up and made more effective. The Labour party, now in Opposition, could afford to take a bolder line on the question than it had when in government. The party spokesman, Mr Callaghan, had suggested during the debate on the renewal Order that the naval patrol operating off the coast of Beira should be extended, with the association of other countries, to close up the obvious gap at Lourenço Marques. That supplies, including oil, had been reaching Rhodesia through this port was common knowledge, but no action had ever been taken by the Labour Government to prevent this violation of the sanctions effort. When it had been proposed by other countries, particularly in United Nations resolutions, it had been opposed on the ground that it would lead to a confrontation with South Africa. The Tories were no more likely to accept an extension of the Beira blockade now than the Labour Government were when they had the option of applying such a measure. Nor were they convinced by the Opposition's proposal for additional enforcement machinery in the form of a special United Nations commissioner with responsibility for overseeing the entire sanctions pro-gramme,[7] since there was already a Security Council Committee, estab-lished at Britain's suggestion in pursuance of resolution 253 of 1968, to consider the effect of sanctions and to improve enforcement.

Although the Conservative Government had claimed that they were prepared to support the objective of making that Committee a more effective instrument for the application of sanctions when its Special Report of May 1972 was submitted to the Security Council, they entered a number of important reservations on its recommendations.[8] Nor would they accept the Security Council resolution condemning the refusal of South Africa and Portugal to comply with the sanctions measures and the decision of the American Government to authorise the import of chrome from Rhodesia.[9] Instead, they proposed that the most effective way of closing the loopholes through South Africa and the Portuguese territories was to tackle the problem of where the goods originated and arrived. But it was on the political aspects of the Rhode-sian situation rather than the implementation of the sanctions measures that the Conservative Government were most at odds with the United Nations. On the same day that the sanctions resolution was adopted, a draft resolution and two of its paragraphs which were put to a vote separately were vetoed by the British delegation because they called for NIBMAR and for the application of the principle of one man, one vote in testing the opinion of the Rhodesian people.[10] While these demands had repeatedly been rejected by successive British govern-ments, on this occasion the African States sponsoring the resolution forced the British delegation into the embarrassing position of having to resort to a triple veto to block the individual proposals and the resolution as a whole.

The Conservative Government were particularly on the defensive at the United Nations because they were also having to justify a settle-ment with the rebel regime which had been defeated by the overwhelm-ing majority of the Rhodesian people. Nearly a year after that agree-ment the British representative, Sir Colin Crowe, could still maintain that the 1971 proposals, for all their imperfections, offered a reason-able solution and provided a means of halting the trend towards racial discrimination and apartheid in that country. As in the debate in the British political arena, the Government's position was that a period of calm consideration was required on all sides, during which a settle-ment would continue to be sought on the basis of the 1971 agreement. While this objective was being pursued, they refused to be bound by any obligations concerning the political future of Rhodesia. But in spite of the British veto, there continued to be widespread support for the political recommendations contained in the resolution, especially the call for convening a constitutional conference, and when the proposal was made again, by the General Assembly on 7 December 1972, it was adopted by the overwhelming majority of 111-4. Britain once more opposed the measure, this time in the company of South Africa, Portugal and the USA, the latter having been recruited to the opposition over the issue of the import of chrome.[11]

Processes of Consultation

In avoiding any political commitments, the Conservative Government were basing their policy on the hope that the 'processes of consultation' would result in some sort of compromise arrangement being worked out among the Rhodesians themselves. Contacts with the rebel regime had continued after the departure of the Pearce Commission, although the Foreign and Commonwealth Office was still refusing to confirm or deny it by the end of 1972. Rumours of meetings between members of the Rhodesian Front and the ANC had also begun to circulate soon after the conclusion of the annual congress of the Front in September 1972. On the same day that Britain was casting the triple veto at the Security Council, the *Rhodesia Herald* reported that talks between the 'Minister' of Internal Affairs (Mr Lance Smith) and representatives of the ANC had been arranged at the instigation of a British representative of the Monday Club and the Anglo-Rhodesian Society, a Mr Jacob Hutter. The talks were reported to have been halted in October, but resumed again in November, with the regime alternately denying any talks at all or admitting only to meeting with 'some of the more reasonable members'. The prospects of any progress from these encounters was not improved by the regime's harassment or detention of what they considered less reasonable members. Nor was the ANC likely to be amenable to any agreement so long as Mr Smith was continuing his campaign of trying to convince the British that the Africans really had accepted the settlement proposals. In repeating this claim, at a televised press conference on 4 December 1972, he asserted that the influence of the anti-settlement ANC was receding while that of the pro-settlement groups (the African Settlement Convention, the African Settlement Forum and others) was gaining.[12] If this were indeed the case, the regime should have been negotiating with the latter, since their influence was alleged to be on the rise. Instead, they proceeded to renew contacts with the ANC, with the declared intention of considering 'any constructive suggestions' from 'the more responsible members'. Such a possibility was made exceedingly remote, however, by Mr Smith's simultaneous insistence that there could be no question of a conference or any other meeting to discuss amending the terms of the settlement. The only choice that remained open to the Africans was the settlement or the existing constitutional system, which, since the rejection of the former, had been embellished with a series of additional racially restrictive measures. By continuing to increase such measures, while conducting a dialogue with ANC leaders, the regime were in effect offering the 1971 terms not only as an improvement on the existing system but as an alternative to further retrogression towards full-scale apartheid.

While the talks between the regime and the ANC were continuing in an atmosphere of secrecy, the Conservative Government were being kept informed of the proceedings by the informal contacts established after the departure of the Pearce Commission. The various set-backs that occurred, especially as a result of the continuing detention of ANC officials, left little cause for optimism, however. Nor was the regime's attempt to create an image of reasonableness improved by the detention and trial *in camera* of a correspondent of the British Press, Mr Peter Niesewand, for revealing some of the more depressing aspects of what the Rhodesians faced in their war against the guerrillas.[13] Even the usually less vociferous Tory backbenchers were sufficiently shaken by this affront to a white British subject to support a Motion, signed by sixty MPs, deploring the trial without charge and recognising the obligation to maintain sanctions until a just settlement was reached. An even more irate response came from the progressive Tory pressure group, PEST, whose chairman, Mr Keith Raffan, said in a letter issued to the Press on 10 April that Sir Alec's protest should be followed by a much stronger statement declaring the Government's intention of having no further communications with the regime. Communications were continued, however, in spite of the unsolicited advice to break them off, and the tension was somewhat eased by the regime's decision to quash the conviction of Mr Niesewand and deport him (a Rhodesian citizen) to Britain.

Within the same month, a party of Rhodesian officials was in London to continue the consultations. This was followed by the visit to Rhodesia of the Permanent Under Secretary at the Foreign and Commonwealth Office, Sir Denis Greenhill, a secret one until it was leaked from Rhodesian sources at the conclusion of the talks on 25 June 1973. After the meeting had been revealed, the Foreign Secretary was obliged to dispel any false hopes, or doubts, which had arisen regarding its outcome. In a statement to Parliament on 27 June, Sir Alec insisted that the sole purpose of the mission had been to provide the Government with an assessment of the situation in Rhodesia, including the views of the two main protagonists in the talks — the Rhodesian Front and the ANC. The British emissary had not been authorised to take any new proposals to Salisbury, nor to attempt to bring any back.[14] In view of the limited objectives of the visit, the secrecy with which it was conducted seemed an exaggerated precaution on the British side. But with the approaching Commonwealth Prime Ministers' conference in August, the Government could not afford to leave themselves vulnerable to the charge of once more initiating negotiations with the rebel regime.

It was Mr Smith who first broke the silence surrounding the consultations. Almost immediately after the visit from the British emissary, he launched an attack on the British Government for refusing to reach a settlement and preventing the Rhodesians from agreeing on one of their own. 'As long as the ghost of Britain was hovering in the background,' he told the House of Assembly, 'acting as a decoy to the inexperienced and the gullible', they would continue to be plagued by useless, sterile discussions. The only way out for them was for the British to 'get off their backs' and let them get on with their own affairs, because as long as Britain maintained the fiction that it could influence events in Rhodesia, the Africans would continue to believe that a better deal would come from that direction, instead of coming to terms with reality in Rhodesia. But the reality for Mr Smith was that the British would not implement a settlement unacceptable to the majority of the Rhodesian people and that the spokesmen for that majority, the ANC, would not alter their rejection of the proposals. No amount of signatures collected on petitions produced by pro-settlement fringe groups would convince the British of anything different and no minor alterations of the 1971 proposals would gain the acceptance of the ANC. In recounting the contacts with ANC leaders over the preceding months, Mr Smith accused them of wanting to enter into formal negotiations for the purpose of drawing up a completely new settlement. The demands which he alleged they had made (which they in turn denied) — lowering the franchise qualifications, increasing African representation, repealing discriminatory legislation, releasing the detainees — were rejected as 'totally and absolutely unacceptable, individually and as a whole'. For those who thought that a few minor concessions and amendments to the 1971 proposals would win the support of the majority (Lord Goodman's position), Mr Smith held out no hope. The Rhodesian Front would continue to insist that those proposals were not negotiable and that there was no alternative but to retain the 'Constitution'.[15]

Other Interests

Mr Smith's statement on 29 June 1973 marked a turning point in Anglo-Rhodesian relations. Here, at last, was an official admission from the Rhodesian side that a settlement on their terms was no longer within the realm of the possible. The British required proof of African acquiescence; the Rhodesian Front were unable to produce it. But his advice to the British to 'get off their backs' was not merely an outburst of frustration over the failure to get a settlement. It also amounted to a belated recognition that an independence agreement would not come about at the expense of Britain's other interests. As he had warned the business community the previous month, the British decision on whether to implement the settlement would be determined by their concern for their trading partners rather than for the issue on its merits.[16] Although he would still continue, rather nostalgically, to refer to the need for a settlement with Britain, often in response to the mounting economic pressures, his appeals carried increasingly less conviction, particularly as the interests of the European community began to shift to the south[17] and those of the British Government to the north.

Although less forthright than Mr Smith in admitting it, the Conservative Government were also beginning to realise that British interests north of the Zambezi, particularly in Commonwealth Africa, were of far greater significance than any financial or trade benefits to be gained in Rhodesia if a settlement were reached and sanctions accordingly dismantled. Black Africa constituted an important market for British exports and the largest State, Nigeria, had become a vital source for the import of oil. These were the 'other interests' which could not be sacrificed, either for the sake of appeasing the Monday Club critics, who continued to adopt resolutions deploring the failure of a Conservative Government to get a settlement and end sanctions,[18] or for the doubtful prospect of recapturing a stake in the Rhodesian market. At that stage, there was not much left to regain, since the Rhodesian economy had been diversified to meet the requirements of its internal market, its southern neighbours and other countries engaged in 'sanctions busting'. The Tories had apparently learned some hard economic facts, particularly from the Nigerians, whom the Foreign Secretary had consulted during his visit to West Africa in February 1973 and during General Gowon's state visit to Britain the following June. They had also to consider their 'other interests' in the rest of the Commonwealth, and the need to preserve these far outweighed any possible advantages that might accrue from abandoning their international obligations to continue the sanctions measures until a settlement acceptable to the Africans was achieved.

It was perhaps for this reason that the Conservative Government fared rather better at the Commonwealth meeting in Ottawa in August 1973 than at the previous conference in Singapore in 1971. There was also the fact that the Conservatives had been in office for over three years and had yet to show any results from their efforts to reach a settlement in Rhodesia. Like their Labour predecessors, they had tried and also failed, and in the course of doing so had discovered that there was no easy way out of the dilemma of placating the various and conflicting interests, both internal and external, involved in the dispute. The responsibilities of office had also taught them that appeasement of the white regimes in southern Africa was a dubious policy option, which could only result in the loss of other and more vital interests elsewhere. At the Ottawa meeting, Mr Heath therefore refrained from indulging in aggressive statements, characteristic of his performance in Singapore, concerning Britain's unfettered right to do a deal with the Rhodesian rebels, provide the South Africans with arms or support the Portuguese in preserving the remnants of imperial rule. The new departure in southern Africa, so boldly asserted in 1971, was nowhere in evidence in Ottawa. Admittedly, a Conservative Government would retain the right to continue to seek a settlement with the Rhodesian regime and to sell arms to South Africa, the latter allegedly for the purpose of external defence in accordance with the Simonstown Agreement. But they would also join their Commonwealth partners in opposing apartheid and minority rule in southern Africa and in recognising the legitimacy of the struggle of the people of that area 'to win full human rights and self-determination'.

Even in the sensitive area of Anglo-Portuguese relations, the British went along with their colleagues in agreeing to try to use their influence 'to persuade Portugal to grant a negotiated independence to its African colonies'. On this issue, they could hardly have done less, after the revelation in the British Press the previous month of the widespread massacres committed in Mozambique by the Portuguese forces, some of them in collaboration with their Rhodesian allies.[19] The British Government were particularly vulnerable to criticism on this score, having proceeded with the state visit to Britain of the Portuguese Prime

Minister, Dr Caetano, in the face of a storm of protest arising from the simultaneous revelation of the massacres. Although the Government had denied that British arms had been or were being used in Portuguese Africa, no official recognition of the participation of Rhodesian troops in the massacres was forthcoming.[20]

On Rhodesia, the usual differences of approach were in evidence, with the African States, particularly Tanzania, insisting upon a commitment to aid the freedom fighters in southern Africa, and with some of the Caribbean States supporting a plan for a Commonwealth presence in Rhodesia to help bring about a peaceful settlement. Obviously, both proposals were unacceptable to the British, the former because it implied the possibility of using force and the latter because it would be impossible to implement without the consent of Mr Smith. The result was that the suggestion for a Commonwelath peace effort failed to appear in the final communiqué at all, leaving only a vague reference to the British Government's 'welcome' for constructive suggestions, which would be taken into account as the situation developed. Although a recognition of the need to give 'humanitarian' assistance to those in southern Africa engaged in the struggle to achieve self-determination and independence did appear in the communiqué, the British attached a rider reserving their position 'in circumstances in which assistance might be converted into military purposes'. They could hardly have rejected the appeal for humanitarian assistance outright, since they were already committed to supporting the special Commonwealth programme of aid for the education of Rhodesian Africans. They did, however, make a significant concession in agreeing to the inclusion in the communiqué of a subject hitherto regarded as within the domestic jurisdiction of Rhodesia. However oblique the reference, the matter of concern was the detention of ANC officials, which was taking place in Rhodesia throughout the period of the Commonwealth meeting. To express this concern, the Commonwealth members associated themselves with the British Government's 'wish' for the discussions between Mr Smith and Bishop Muzorewa to be broadened and 'the necessary steps taken to remove restrictions so as to enable all groups representative of Rhodesian opinion to take part'. While the processes of consultation continued in Rhodesia, further efforts would be made 'to render sanctions more effective pending an acceptable settlement'. The Commonwealth Sanctions Committee would continue in business and Britain, along with other Commonwealth countries, would be obliged to support those efforts.[21]

The Conservative Government emerged from the Ottawa conference without sacrificing their other interests or incurring any new commitments in order to retain them. With regard to Rhodesia, the *status quo* would be maintained: it was still considered a British responsibility, the use of force remained out of the question and no outside interference from any quarter would be permitted. However, there had been agreement that in Rhodesia the objective was majority rule (however long that might take) and that in southern Africa as a whole apartheid and minority rule were to be opposed and the legitimacy of the struggle to win full human rights and self-determination recognised. In accepting these principles, the Conservative Government were in effect coming to terms with their 'other interests'.

The decision to retain the *status quo* was also in evidence at both the Rhodesian Front congress and the Conservative party conference, although for different reasons and with rather more optimism about it at the latter than the former. For the Rhodesian Front, the *status quo* meant the retention of the constitutional system they had established in 1969 and the abandonment of any further independence negotiations with the British Government. While Mr Smith assured his supporters that he had no intention of trying to reopen talks with Britain, he had also to account for the contacts with the ANC, including his meetings with Bishop Muzorewa since the previous July. The fact that the regime had been talking to the ANC at all was an indication that they still had hopes of talking to the British, who had been holding off from such encounters until the 'processes of consultation' within Rhodesia had produced some results. But this they had not yet done: mainly because what the Rhodesian Front could afford to offer in the way of political advance for the African, without offending the European electorate, was too little to appease even the 'moderate' element in the ANC. Under these circumstances, Mr Smith's prediction of 'no talks for the time being' had become a reality. In any case, the priorities of the Rhodesian Front had already begun to alter: now that an independence settlement with the British appeared to be unobtainable, Rhodesia's prime objective, as Mr Smith told the party congress, was to destroy the 'terrorists'. To secure this end, the Law and Order (Maintenance) Act would be amended to provide the death penalty for anyone convicted of aiding the 'terrorists'. At the same time, the policy of 'separate development' would be advanced by the establishment of regional authorities for Matabeleland and Mashonaland. Thus, with the intensification of racially discriminatory measures, enforced by increasingly repressive legislation, the Rhodesian Front were planning their future for living under the 1969 'Constitution'.[22]

For the Conservative Government, maintaining the *status quo*, as the Foreign Secretary told the party conference on 11 October 1973, meant that Rhodesians should be left in a calm climate to work things out for themselves, with Britain waiting to put the stamp of legality on a settlement. Sir Alec's optimism at this time was influenced by the meetings taking place between Mr Smith and Bishop Muzorewa and also those between the ANC and a small European opposition group, the Rhodesia party,[23] the latter allegedly resulting in an agreement on principles for a multi-racial society. Consequently, he warned the Tory rank and file that to drop sanctions before a settlement would 'pull the rug from under the feet of all those working hardest in Rhodesia for non-racialism or multi-racialism to gain the day'. The motion proposing this course of action, which was invariably submitted, but not always debated, at every Tory conference since the UDI, was this time disposed of by an overwhelming majority on a show of hands. Although Sir Alec had paid lip-service to all the Tory shibboleths regarding sanctions – the costs, the violations and the failures – this year he had also drawn attention to Britain's 'other interests'. Britain as a signatory to a Security Council resolution binding on all members was obliged to keep its word, and the failure to do so would have the effect of arousing that very turmoil in the international community which the Government were attempting to avoid. It would also have an adverse effect upon Britain's economic stake in Africa, including a growing trade with black Africa worth about £885 million a year, compared with the pre-UDI trade with Rhodesia of only £60 million.[24] If his appeal to morality had not sufficed – Conservatives were 'in the habit of keeping Britain's word' – Sir Alec could attribute his victory to acquainting his supporters with the facts about where Britain's real interests lay.[25]

The Conservative Government deployed virtually the same arguments in support of getting the sanctions Order renewed in November 1973, with the materialist aspects of the case left to the Minister of State, Lord Balniel. Their success on this occasion was also due to the Labour Opposition's equally keen support for the cause of Britain's 'other interests', a rather ironic priority for an allegedly 'socialist' party. Their spokesman, Mr Ivor Richard, maintained that the primary economic argument for Britain to maintain sanctions was to safeguard its investments in sub-Sahara Africa. These amounted to £141 million in Nigeria alone (excluding oil) and a total of £457 million in black Africa. To risk a loss of this investment in order to safeguard a doubtful £98 million in Rhodesia was scarcely a sound economic proposition.

It could even be argued that British investment should be deliberately moved away from what was already in Rhodesia and put into 'the lusher pastures' of the rest of Africa,[26] a measure which would also have the effect of intensifying sanctions.

While the Conservative Government were at one with the Opposition in their appreciation of Britain's economic priorities, they remained far more optimistic about the outcome of the consultations then proceeding in Rhodesia. Otherwise, no major policy differences emerged over the sanctions issue, at least not between the two front benches. Only the Rhodesia Lobby MPs were out of line, repeating their performance at the Tory party conference the previous month. If anything, the eighth debate on the renewal of sanctions was marked by indifference: the vote on the Order amounted to a total of only 159 votes from all parties combined, with the Tory rebels casting some 26 of them against.[27]

Nevertheless, the Labour party, since returning to Opposition, had taken a more militant line on the issues involved in southern Africa in general and Rhodesia in particular. Less was heard of the generalities of the Five Principles, which had become, at least in the view of most of the Africans, as dead as the Tory Government's 1971 settlement. The party was also beginning to recognise the growing significance of the liberation movements in southern Africa. Although the financial support which had been provided, in particular the Rhodesia Fund, had been designated for 'humanitarian' purposes, other types of assistance were also being considered. The most difficult decision for a party which had ruled out the use of force while in government was the attitude it ought to take towards those who were resorting to force to obtain the ends which the Labour Government had failed to achieve for them. However commendable the party's aid for humanitarian purposes might be, it would not help to rid the Africans of the oppression endured under white minority rule. At least some acknowledgement of this dilemma appeared in the draft programme on Labour's foreign policy, published in 1973,[28] which recognised that, since violence was already being used by the minority regimes in southern Africa to preserve their positions of power, the force to which the liberation movements had resorted had been provoked by the refusal of those regimes to allow peaceful and democratic change. On this ground, a future Labour Government would support that struggle and be prepared to have high-level governmental contacts with representatives of the liberation movements, provide assistance via governmental and international organisations and promote their participation in the relevant committees and specialised agencies of the United Nations.

In pursuance of the recommendations contained in the foreign policy paper, the National Executive Committee, at the party conference in October 1973, accepted 'unanimously and wholeheartedly' a resolution recommending financial and diplomatic support for the liberation movements struggling against the white minority regimes in southern Africa. The NEC spokesman, Mr Callaghan, raised no objections to the commitment, assuring the delegates that a Labour Government would oppose apartheid and racial inequality wherever they might prevail. Nor did Mr Wilson, who told the conference that not only the moral future of Britain but its real interests were bound up with the support of freedom movements in southern Africa.[29] What this commitment involved was not specified, but the Rhodesian Front took it seriously enough to protest that the Labour party's support for 'terrorism' showed a 'callous and cynical disregard for the lives and welfare of Rhodesian blacks'.[30] Mr Smith even went so far as to rule out any future negotiations with Mr Wilson because he was deemed to be guilty of 'siding with the terrorists'.[31]

Zambia and the Liberation Movement

Along with the 'consultative processes', which continued intermittently throughout 1973 and into the early months of 1974, the Rhodesians were also concerned with the threat of guerrilla incursions, which had escalated since the offensive launched in December 1972, and the effect of the increasing conflict on their relations with Zambia. Although Mr Smith had admitted, in his New Year address in 1973, that there had been 'a few incidents' on the north-eastern border (around Centenary and Mt Darwin), which presented 'a new problem on a new front', he had passed this off with the claim that the security forces had meted out to the invaders 'salutary retribution'. But some indication of the seriousness of the situation caused by the incursions was the call-up of more Territorial units to strengthen the forces in the north-eastern border area and the enactment in January 1973 of the Emergency Powers (Collective Fine) Regulations, imposing collective punishment on tribal villages and communities for harbouring 'terrorist enemies of the State'.

Mr Smith's reaction to the new threat, including a series of landmine explosions in the north-western area near the Zambezi, was to panic. In retaliation for the guerrilla attacks, which he claimed had been mounted from Zambian territory, he announced on 9 January 1973 that the border between the two countries would be closed, and all rail and road transport into and out of Zambia (except for copper exports) would be prohibited. Although the ban would have a serious effect on Zambian imports, more than half of which continued to come through Rhodesia from South Africa and the Mozambique ports, it would also be a considerable blow to Rhodesia Railways, in terms of the loss of freight revenue, which it could ill afford at this stage of the sanctions war. Zambia had already diversified a considerable amount of its external trade, and alternative routes of transport, both road and rail, were being utilised and prepared, including the new rail link being constructed by the Chinese to Dar es Salaam. While Zambia would be hard pressed to get all of the copper out, or the essential imports in, without the use of Rhodesia Railways, President Kaunda nevertheless banned further copper exports through Rhodesia and, the following month, confirmed that the border would remain closed permanently, irrespective of a Rhodesian decision to reopen it.

Not only Zambia, however, would be the loser as a result of Mr Smith's action, since the permanent closure of the border would achieve what the sanctions measures had thus far failed to accomplish — the elimination of one of Rhodesia's largest sources of foreign exchange earnings. Ironically, the South Africans, who had not been consulted before Mr Smith took the decision, would also be adversely affected, since they were, next to Britain, Zambia's largest source of imports (an estimated £40 million in 1970), and would be obliged to resort to alternative and more costly routes to maintain the level of their trade. Thus Mr Smith, by his precipitous action, had succeeded in antagonising all of the parties concerned — the Zambians, the British, the South Africans and the Portuguese — without even obtaining the compensation of an admission from the Zambian Government that guerrillas were operating from their territory or an assurance that they would be deterred from doing so in the future.

Nevertheless, Mr Smith proceeded to justify the border closure, telling a press conference on 31 January that, while history might prove that it was a wrong decision, no one was 'infallible', and he still believed that the decision was a right one. On his failure to consult South Africa or Portugal, he was on less sure ground, saying that if they had been consulted, those countries would have been blamed for forcing Rhodesia into taking the action. He even accepted, as 'a very realistic, practical statement', Mr Vorster's implied rebuke that it was not South Africa's policy to impose sanctions on other countries. As for the British reaction, he continued to operate under the delusion that the border closure would have no effect whatsoever on the chances of an independence settlement, although Sir Alec Douglas-Home had stated in Parliament only two days before that it was 'a most regrettable development', which could only make more difficult the search for a settlement and increase the level of tension in the area.[32]

In spite of the Foreign Secretary's condemnation, described by the Zambian President's letter to the Security Council on the same day as 'a loud silence on the aggressive activities of their illegal colony', the Conservative Government were reluctant to allow any outside interference in a dispute which they had hoped could be settled by the good offices of their Minister of Overseas Development, then in Zambia, although President Kaunda had ruled out the possibility of participating in the dialogue with the rebel regime which Mr Richard Wood was seeking to bring about. However, when the issue was brought before the Security Council at the end of January, as a result of an appeal by Zambia and several other African States for an emergency meeting, they were obliged to defend their policy of non-intervention in a dispute provoked by a territory for which they were legally responsible and on whose soil foreign troops were operating against a fellow Commonwealth member. The charge with which they were confronted, in the words of President Kaunda's letter to the Security Council, was that for the previous seven years Zambia had borne the greatest part of the burden to end the rebellion against the British Crown, a struggle in which Britain had been 'an unwilling partner'.[33]

The main decision to emerge from the Security Council meeting was the dispatch of a special mission, consisting of four Council members (Austria, Indonesia, Peru and Sudan) to assess the situation in the border area between Zambia and Rhodesia following the imposition of the blockade, including the special needs of Zambia. As expected, the mission confirmed the existence of tension on the Zambian-Rhodesian border, and reported that, in the course of its visit to London and Lusaka, the British Government had reaffirmed their responsibility for Rhodesia and the Zambian Government had emphasised that the closure of the southern route was permanent, unless there was a political change in Rhodesia in terms of majority rule. Its recommendations on the urgent economic needs of Zambia were embodied in a resolution unanimously adopted by the Security Council on 10 March 1973, appealing to all States, the United Nations and its specialised agencies for immediate technical, financial and material assistance to enable Zambia to achieve its policy of economic independence.[34] Although the British delegation had supported the resolution, with 'the greatest sympathy for Zambia's economic difficulties', they refused to be committed to the Zambian decision to abandon the southern route until majority rule was established in Rhodesia and to the political recommendations which the Council sought to impose, particularly those which would require British intervention.[35]

Having failed to obtain any satisfaction from the British Government in terms of political action, the Security Council turned its efforts towards tightening up the economic pressure. But where the British drew the line was on any proposal that would affect their economic relations with South Africa and Portugal. It was mainly on this ground that they opposed a draft resolution calling for the limitation of imports from South Africa and the Portuguese territories to the quantitative levels in 1965, a measure designed to block the export of Rhodesian products disguised as South African or Portuguese in origin. When the resolution containing this recommendation was put to the vote, the British delegation (joined by the Americans, who were importing chrome above the 1965 level) resorted to the veto — their ninth on the Rhodesian issue. Even on the alternative resolution, which called upon all States merely to 'inform' the Security Council Sanctions Committee of their existing sources of supply of the main products exported by Rhodesia and the quantities of those goods obtained from Rhodesia before the UDI, they chose to abstain.[36]

In rejecting both political intervention and increased economic pressure against the rebel regime,[37] the Conservative Government were reconciled, during their last few months in office, to await the outcome of the talks proceeding within Rhodesia. There was little cause for optimism, however, in spite of the willingness of the ANC to continue discussions with a regime determined to maintain the *status quo* and to remove from the political arena any opponent seriously challenging their right to do so. As one after another of the ANC leaders disappeared into detention (an estimated thirty-three by August 1973), including the acting vice-president, Mr N.K. Ndhlovu, others filled their places, with a new vice-president, Dr E.M. Gabellah, and a secretary-general, Dr Gordon Chavunduka, elected the following October. Although the ANC negotiators continued to stress the moderation of their claims — they were not insisting on immediate majority rule or one man, one vote — they had also to consider the pressures from those of their colleagues in detention, in exile or in the liberation movement, who would have considered anything short of these objectives a virtual sell-out. The fact that they were engaging in talks with the Rhodesian Front was suspect in the view of many African nationalists, who were convinced that no agreement could ever be reached with a party dedicated to the preservation of white supremacy. What the ANC really expected to come out of these talks was never made clear, unless it was the propaganda value they hoped to gain by creating the impression of reasonableness. Their leader, Bishop Muzorewa, had certainly conveyed this impression, particularly in his address to the Rhodesia National Affairs Association on 29 May 1973, which stressed the ANC's belief in the possibility of creating a multi-racial society. The Rhodesian Front, however, had never accepted even the pretence of 'partnership', which had been espoused by their predecessors in office, and therefore had no electoral obligation to implement it. Their motive in continuing to talk with the ANC was to pave the way for talks with the British, who had made the internal dialogue a precondition for any further negotiations for an independence settlement. But this objective had its limitations, since the British, who were the object of the exercise to impress, had no intention of intervening until that dialogue had produced some tangible results. This it never did, however, even after over a year of efforts.

When the Tories left office in February 1974, the two sides were still going through the motions of talking, but it was evident that they were not speaking the same language. Mr Smith had thus failed to get the settlement which he had expected would come as a result of the return of a Conservative Government in 1970. If he retained any hopes for legal recognition of his illegal regime, he would be obliged to seek it from a party and a Prime Minister with whom he had refused to negotiate, on the ground of their support for the liberation movement which was threatening his survival in power.

Notes

1. *Rhodesia Herald*, 22 September 1972.
2. 837 *HC Deb.*, 23 May 1972, col. 1226.
3. 838 *HC Deb.*, 15 June 1972, col. 1774.
4. *Report of the 71st Annual Conference of the Labour Party*, Blackpool, 1972.
5. 838 *HC Deb.*, 12 June 1972, col. 968; 15 June 1972, col. 1764.
6. David Wood, 10 November 1972.
7. 845 *HC Deb.*, 9 November 1972, cols. 1215-21.
8. Resolution 318 (1972) adopted 28 July 1972 by 14–0, with one abstention (USA).
9. Resolution 320 (1972) adopted 29 September 1972 by 13–0, with two abstentions (UK, USA).
10. The draft resolution was defeated 29 September 1972 by 10–1, with four abstentions.

11. Resolution 2945 (XXVII). On the same day, Britain voted against resolution 2946 (XXVII), concerned with sanctions infringements, which was adopted by 93–8, with 23 abstentions.

12. *Rhodesia Herald*, 5 December 1972.

13. See 'What Smith Really Faces in Rhodesia', *Africa Report*, March-April 1973.

14. 858 *HC Deb.*, 27 June 1973, col. 1552.

15. Rhodesia, *Parliamentary Debates*, vol. 84, 29 June 1973, cols. 638-53.

16. Address to the Associated Chambers of Commerce at Victoria Falls, *Rhodesia Herald*, 6 May 1973.

17. The Rhodesian Front chairman, Mr Desmond Frost, called for a 'Southern African Economic Market', with a co-ordinated defence pact, in his address to the party congress. Ibid., 21 September 1973.

18. Meeting of 28 April 1973, *The Times*.

19. See *The Times*, 12 July 1973, for a full report of the massacres.

20. See Mr Heath's account of the meeting with the Portuguese Prime Minister. Ibid., 10 August 1973.

21. *Commonwealth Prime Ministers' Meeting 1973, Final Communiqué*, Ottawa, 10 August 1973, HMSO, *A Year Book of the Commonwealth*, 1974.

22. For the congress proceedings, see *Rhodesia Herald*, 21, 22 September 1973.

23. The Rhodesia party had been formed in November 1972, with membership drawn mainly from the former ruling Establishment.

24. Trade with Rhodesia was put at £40 million by the Tory MPs, Mr Christopher Brocklebank-Fowler and Mr Alan Haselhurst, in a letter to *The Times*, 10 October 1973, supporting sanctions.

25. *Report of the 91st Annual Conservative Party Conference*, Blackpool, 1973.

26. As suggested by Mr Michael Williams and Mr Michael Parsonage in an article in *The World Today*, September 1973.

27. 863 *HC Deb.*, 8 November 1973, cols. 1255, 1317-20.

28. *Labour's Programme, 1973*, Ch. 13.

29. *Report of the 72nd Annual Conference of the Labour Party*, Blackpool, 1973.

30. *Rhodesia Herald*, 4 October 1973.

31. Ibid., 29 October 1973.

32. 849 *HC Deb.*, 29 January 1973, cols. 931-2.

33. Although the British supported resolution 327 (1973), adopted 2 February 1973 by 14-0, with one abstention (USSR), which expressed concern for the economic hardships confronting Zambia, they abstained (with the USA) on resolution 326 (1973), also adopted on 2 February, which included a recommendation for the withdrawal of South African forces from Rhodesian territory.

34. Resolution 329 (1973).

35. Resolution 328 (1973), also adopted on 10 March 1973, by 13-0, with two abstentions (UK, USA), called upon Britain to convene a constitutional conference, secure the release of political prisoners, the repeal of repressive and discriminatory legislation and the removal of restrictions on political activity.

36. The vote on the draft resolution was 11-2, with two abstentions (Austria, France). Security Council resolution 333 (1973) was adopted 22 May 1973 by 12-0, with three abstentions (UK, USA, France). The British also refused to accept some of the recommendations contained in the second Special Report of the Security Council Sanctions Committee, which was also debated on 22 May.

37. As proposed by General Assembly resolutions 3115 and 3116 (XXVIII), adopted 12 December 1973 by 108-4, with 15 abstentions, and 101-5, with 22 abstentions.

12

THE NEW REALITIES

'It's nice to have your friends standing with you when you've got a bit of a problem.'

Ian Smith, 15 March 1974.

In its election manifesto of February 1974, the Labour party's commitments on Rhodesia and southern Africa were much less precise than those contained in the foreign policy statement of the previous year, particularly on NIBMAR, which was not mentioned at all, and on the means by which a settlement would be sought. The only specific pledges on Rhodesia were that the policy of sanctions would be intensified and that the Fifth Principle would be observed; and these were repeated in the Queen's Speech on 12 March. In southern Africa as a whole, all forms of racial discrimination and colonialism would be opposed and the means to this end would include support for the liberation movements in that area and 'a disengagement from Britain's unhealthy involvement with apartheid'. Whether the latter included the sizeable British trade and investments in the Republic of South Africa was not specified,[1] but in view of the record of the previous Labour Government on this issue, it was highly unlikely. It was more likely to include military than economic disengagement, since the party was committed to reimpose the ban on the sale of arms to South Africa (which the Tories had lifted) and to review all defence arrangements, including the Simonstown Agreement for naval co-operation with the South Africans, which had become a political liability without even the compensatory value of a strategic asset since the abandonment of Britain's east of Suez policy.

When the Labour Government took office, there was no immediate cause for turning their attention (which was then primarily focused on the European Economic Community) to the Rhodesian issue, since they, like their predecessors, were resigned to standing aside while the consultations proceeded within Rhodesia. That they were still continuing was all the more remarkable, considering the obstacles and deadlocks that had been encountered over the previous year. But the ANC was determined to carry on the talks and both the Central Committee in January 1974 and the inaugural congress in March had confirmed this decision. However, among the leadership, there were varying degrees of optimism about the whole exercise, ranging from

those who thought an agreement still possible to those who were doubtful of any results ever emerging, other than evidence of their own good
faith. Among the former was the president, Bishop Muzorewa, who was
largely responsible, as head of the party delegation, for the talks having
lasted as long as they did. Although extremely cautious about revealing
the contents of the negotiations, he was still convinced in January 1974
that there was a possibility of success, if only Mr Smith were prepared
to meet them 'half-way' as they were ready to go 'half-way' to meet
him. Whether half-way included parity of representation was not
specified, although this was certainly the least that the Africans would
consider short of majority rule. Some indication of the disagreement
within the ANC leadership emerged from the Bishop's admission that
if agreement were reached, the 'hard-line' resisters among the African
nationalists could be expected to exploit any test of acceptability.[2]
If the Bishop were already looking ahead to means of implementing
the Fifth Principle, he was far in advance of the official party pronouncements on the negotiations. The statement issued by the publicity secretary, Dr Edson Sithole, following the Central Committee
meeting on 13 January, denied that there had been any progress at all
in the talks and reaffirmed that the ANC would only agree to a settlement which would be acceptable to the African people as a whole.[3]
Any differences among the leadership were, however, temporarily sub-
merged in the enthusiasm engendered by the inaugural congress on 2
March, at which the Bishop called for a constitutional conference
representative of all Rhodesian opinion; and the 850 delegates adopted
a resolution asserting majority rule and one man, one vote as the
Council's main goal. Nevertheless, they also agreed that the talks with
the rebel regime would continue,[4] and from these it was most unlikely
that majority rule would emerge.

In spite of the militant line taken at the ANC congress, the Rhodesian Front still had hopes of buying off those members who were
willing to go along with their president's advice of meeting Mr Smith
'half-way'. They were also concerned with assuring the European
electorate that they, unlike their rivals in the Rhodesia party, who were
claiming to have reached agreement with the ANC, would not sacrifice
their essential principles for the purpose of gaining an independence
settlement from the British. Although they had managed to hold the
two seats contested in the by-elections at the end of February 1974,
there was a considerable protest vote (about 45 per cent) for the
opposition candidates of the Rhodesia party and the right-wing Rhodesia National party. While the former campaigned for renewed negotia-

tions for a settlement, the party of the right regarded any negotiations as a sell-out of white supremacy. Between these two possibilities, the Rhodesian Front chose the middle way: negotiations would continue but no concessions would be made. Much of the support which they lost to the extreme right could be attributed to the panic and fear arising from the recent killing of European civilians in the north-eastern region near Centenary, which brought the guerrilla war very near to the centre of European settlement. The loss of votes to the Rhodesia party was a warning from a different constituency: those who were becoming impatient with the regime's inability or unwillingness to produce any results from the long months of negotiations with the ANC. Had it not been for the disarray among the Rhodesia party leadership, which was to culminate in the resignation of the party leader, Mr Allan Savory, the Rhodesian Front might have lost the Sinoia by-election. Instead, Mr Smith made capital out of the differences among his opponents by calling a general election for the following July, which would catch the European opposition with a new and untried leader.

The Hand of Friendship

During the interval between the ANC congress in March and the Central Committee meeting in June, the whole situation in southern Africa was transformed by the overthrow of the fascist regime in Portugal, on 25 April, and the decision of their military successors to bring about the independence of the Portuguese territories in Africa. The ANC could now afford to wait for a better offer, since time was on their side, and the rebel regime would be under extreme pressure to defend yet another front, once Mozambique, with the vital supply ports of Beira and Lourenço Marques, came under the rule of the African liberation movement, FRELIMO. Although the regime took the outwardly correct line that it was not their intention to concern themselves with the internal affairs of their neighbouring territories, they were sufficiently worried about the turn of events for Mr Smith to make a call upon the South African Prime Minister, Mr Vorster, at the end of May to confer on a joint approach to the new situation arising from the collapse of the Portuguese empire in southern Africa.

It was against this background that the Central Committee of the ANC met on 2 June to decide upon the constitutional proposals considered by the two sides for the past year. Whether these proposals were actually an 'agreement', as Mr Smith claimed, was extremely doubtful, because when they were put to the vote of the 25-member

Central Committee, which included the ANC's negotiators, they were unanimously rejected.[5] If any ANC members had agreed to such terms, which they vigorously denied, they were certainly not accepting them at that time. From the statement of Dr Edson Sithole at the end of the meeting, it was not surprising that the ANC had said 'no', since the offer was virtually the same as the 1971 proposals which they had also rejected. The only improvement, if it could be regarded as that, was provision for an extra six African seats, but these would have to be 'earned', because Africans would not qualify for any additional seats (they already had sixteen, of which only half were directly elected) until there had been a 24 per cent increase in the number of Africans on the voters' roll. At this rate, the achievement of parity was modestly calculated at between 40 and 60 years. Other aspects of the so-called 'agreement' recalled the 1971 proposals on such matters as racially discriminatory legislation and the review of cases of the detainees by a special tribunal. Apparently no provision for safeguards had been made, at least while the Africans lacked a blocking third against retrogressive amendments, but then there was nothing in the terms worth safeguarding so far as the Africans were concerned as long as the Europeans continued to control the means of access to political power. It was mainly on this ground that the ANC rejected the offer, but there was no finality in a rejection accompanied by a call for further negotiations on the African franchise and representation in Parliament.

The outcome of the talks was not unexpected; only the length of time taken to produce the result required some explaining, but then neither side wanted responsibility for the breakdown. The moderation of the ANC produced some accolades from the European Establishment, with the Centre party condemning the proposals as falling far short of what was necessary for 'planned progress.towards a sharing of power'. In addition, Sir Roy Welensky emerged from his retirement to say that he was not surprised at the rejection either, since even parity was an estimated 40-60 years off. He appealed to Mr Smith to make some significant concessions, including giving the Africans some executive responsibility, because 'time was running strongly against Rhodesians of all colours'.[6] But the Rhodesian Front were in no position to respond to any advice about concessions, with an election coming up the following month. At the same time, however, they could not afford to be vulnerable to the criticism that they had once more failed to produce an independence settlement. Their way out of this dilemma was to place the responsibility for the breakdown of the negotiations squarely upon the ANC and to blame the European Establishment for encouraging the Africans to believe that they could get more concessions by holding out against the Rhodesian Front offer. The party chairman, Mr Desmond Frost, put the case the day after the rejection had been announced by accusing the ANC of stopping progress towards a settlement, as it had done at the time of the Pearce Commission. By so doing, he claimed, they showed that they did not want the hand of friendship; they wanted the whole body.

If, as Mr Frost had suggested, the ANC was against the settlement terms, then it had not always been so, according to Mr Smith's version of the negotiations. As a means of shifting the blame for the failure and also of causing dissension within the ANC, he claimed that there had been a definite agreement between himself and Bishop Muzorewa but that the militant ANC members had overriden the decision with a veto.[7] The controversy over whether the ANC rejection had been a unanimous one had already been raised, and supposedly settled, in the Rhodesian Press the week before Mr Smith's revisionist interpretation. The rumour put out by the *Rhodesia Herald* on 5 June was that the vote on the proposals in the Central Committee had been 14-9, that the more moderate members had been shouted down by the hard-liners demanding nothing less than parity and that severe pressure had been exerted on the committee by nationalist elements in Lusaka and London. On the same day, Bishop Muzorewa, in support of Dr Edson Sithole's statement that the decision had been unanimous, dismissed the rumour as 'absolutely evil and false' and the alleged voting figures as 'utter nonsense'. If it had been true that only the hard-liners in the ANC Central Committee would accept nothing less than parity, then Bishop Muzorewa was, or had become, a hard-liner too, for he also told the BBC on 11 June that nothing short of parity would now be acceptable to the ANC.

The question of whether further talks would serve any useful purpose was decided not on its merits but as a result of the Rhodesian Front taking one step too many in a series of repressive acts against the African opposition. This time they ordered the detention of Dr Edson Sithole, one of the ANC's chief negotiators and most able officials. His detention on 20 June resulted in the suspension of the talks by Bishop Muzorewa, who claimed that the appointment of Dr Sithole to the ANC negotiating team had been approved by Mr Smith. The official reason given for the arrest by the 'Minister' of Law and Order, Mr Lardner-Burke, was a violation of the conditions under which Dr Sithole had been released from detention, which included restriction of movement to within a ten-mile radius of Salisbury.[8] Presumably an official reason for detention could always have been found, but the timing of the arrest could not have been worse, so far as the resumption of negotiations was concerned, unless the regime actually intended to provoke the breakdown and thereby lay the blame on the ANC for refusing to continue the talks. There was also the possibility that the regime had been planning to remove Dr Sithole in any case,[9] particularly since he had been responsible for revealing that no progress had been made in the negotiations and for insisting that the rejection of the regime's offers had been a unanimous one. Having been a detainee until 1970, Dr Sithole was already suspect by the regime, and Mr Smith told the Assembly the day before the arrest that he had uncovered evidence of links between certain ANC officials and the banned African nationalist groups outside Rhodesia. Although there was nothing new about this 'evidence', the timing of its revelation could have been designed to coincide with the arrest of Dr Sithole or any of the other ANC officials.

Whatever the link between the arrest and the halting of the negotiations, Mr Smith had already produced an alternative to the bilateral talks with the ANC, from which the Rhodesian Front could expect no further gains, even on the propaganda level. Instead, he proposed to hold a 'round table conference', on the lines of the *indaba* he had always preferred, in which all groups of African opinion would be invited to participate. But the Bishop was having none of this either, and on the same day that he broke off the negotiations over the Sithole arrest he also rejected the new scheme as 'meaningless', because all responsible African groups were already represented in the ANC. What he suspected as the basis for the offer was Mr Smith's design to strengthen the insignificant pro-settlement groups by bringing them into the constitutional discussions. Since Mr Smith had told the Assembly of his proposal for the round table conference the day before the Sithole arrest, it was evident that he had already planned an alternative form of consultation with African opinion, irrespective of the reaction he might provoke from the ANC over the Sithole detention.

A State of Uncertainty

In his statement to the Assembly on 19 June, Mr Smith had also announced that a general election would be held on 30 July, again for the alleged purpose of ending 'the state of uncertainty' in the country resulting from internal and international developments. This would supposedly result from giving the people of Rhodesia (at least the white ones) another opportunity of deciding 'which way they wished to go' and 'which way they would like to be governed'. There was no doubt about their choice, however, since Mr Smith had purposely timed the election to coincide with the disarray of the European opposition. The Rhodesia party was still in the throes of a leadership crisis, having just elected Mr Timothy Gibbs, son of the former Governor, to succeed Mr Allan Savory as leader. The party had already suffered from the resignation of two of its most prominent members, Mr Roy Ashburner and Dr Morris Hirsh, because of Mr Savory's leadership; and its image as a European party wasn't improved by the latter's decision to stand as an Independent and to proclaim that if he had been a black African he would be a 'terrorist' too, because even the ANC's moderate demand for parity had been rejected outright. In contrast, by pledging that there would be no sell-out to the Africans, Mr Smith could also expect to benefit from the gratitude of a European electorate apprehensive about maintaining the privileged position which their counterparts in the neighbouring Portuguese territory had so recently and so rapidly lost. In such a time of crisis, the white laager mentality would be bound to prevail and the tendency, as in the past, would be to trust the known and leave it all to 'good old Smithy', who had got them through all the difficulties of the previous decade.

For the ANC, the election, like the proposal for a round table conference, was also 'meaningless'. To participate in a contest in which only eight directly elected seats were allotted to Africans would be to condone a political system which they had already condemned and the changing of which had been the objective of their long and abortive negotiations. Although the official ANC line was to boycott the elections, by refusing to put up candidates for the African seats, some of their supporters defied the ban by standing as Independents in the contests for the eight African seats. Nor was the ANC agreed, as their African nationalist party predecessors had been, on whether the boycott should apply to the casting of votes as well, at least by some 7,000 Africans qualified to exercise the franchise. It was hardly surprising that over two-thirds of them chose to do so, after they had been advised by the ANC president, Bishop Muzorewa, on 1 July, to use their vote 'wisely' by eliminating the 'Government stooges' campaigning for the regime's scheme for settlement by a round table conference. As a result, all of the pro-settlement candidates, including those of the African Progressive party, led by Mr Chad Chipunza, a former champion of Federation, were annihilated (most of them losing their deposits) and six of the seven supporters of the ANC won their seats. For the latter, however, it was somewhat of a pyrrhic victory, since they were ordered to resign from the ANC, at a subsequent meeting of the Executive Council, and the Bishop was obliged to make a public statement after the meeting denying a party split.[10] His intervention against the Rhodesian Front, far less effective in terms of influencing any votes, was also, in a sense, a deviation from the official boycott of the election. In an eve-of-poll statement, he came out with a warning to the European electorate that a vote for the Rhodesian Front would be a vote for confrontation, because the regime were to blame for the repression of the African people and the racial discrimination which they suffered. By endorsing the Front and the policies for which they stood, the Europeans would prevent the achievement of a settlement and thereby ensure a future conflict between the races.

For the Rhodesian Front, the Africans were so remote from the reality of what was virtually an all-European contest that Mr Smith did not even think it necessary to rebuke the ANC president or to reply to any of his charges. In fact, he even exonerated the Bishop from responsibility for the rejection of the agreement by placing the whole blame on 'ANC factions led by Dr Sithole' and 'factions of the Rhodesia party working against the interests of Bishop Muzorewa'. The all-white Rhodesia party, whom he castigated as 'the old liberal Establishment' resurrected as 'the new left', was charged with having provoked the election by 'conniving behind the Government's back' in holding its own constitutional negotiations with the ANC. To explain away his party's failure to reach an agreement with the ANC, Mr Smith accused the Rhodesia party of having advised the Africans that they would get better terms if they waited until that party came to power. Obviously, the Africans could not have fared worse, but what the Rhodesia party had to offer them — a blocking third in Parliament, a common voters' roll with a highly qualified franchise, and a commission to consider lessening racial discrimination — fell far short of the ANC's demands.[11] Nevertheless, it was the European vote, not the African, that concerned Mr Smith, and his strategy was to convince the European electorate that the Rhodesia party stood for appeasement, for the abandonment of the white man's position and for a sell-out to African nationalism. Following this onslaught on his fellow Europeans, he appealed to the country, in an eve-of-poll broadcast, for 'national unity above all else'. At the same time, he warned that Rhodesia's enemies were hoping for a defeat or at least a serious set-back for the Rhodesian Front and, for that reason, every seat which the party lost would 'give great joy and satisfaction to the Organisation of African Unity, to their protégée in the House of Commons, Miss Joan Lestor

[Parliamentary Under Secretary at the Foreign and Commonwealth Office], to ZAPU and ZANU in Lusaka and Dar es Salaam, to terrorism and to international communism'. Whatever the effect of this dire warning, the end result was that the Rhodesian Front held all of the fifty European seats. What Mr Smith hailed as a victory for unity, Bishop Muzorewa described as a product of fear and a panic vote for white supremacy.

Since the results of the election were a foregone conclusion, the Africans could expect no further progress towards a negotiated agreement, so long as the Rhodesian Front refused to make any meaningful concessions and Mr Smith held out for his round table conference. Their only remaining hope of breaking the deadlock was to appeal to the British, even though, from past experience, this approach had not yielded any positive results. Nevertheless, as the Pearce Commission had so clearly revealed, the Africans retained a basic faith in the ability of the British to influence events in Rhodesia, a belief that was shared by a large part of the international community, although with considerably less toleration for the British failure to exercise it. However, African expectations from a Labour Government in 1974 were not what they had been in 1964, when the election of a party pledged to NIBMAR had been heralded with anticipation of the long-awaited liberation from white minority rule. Not much was left in the way of illusions after *Tiger,* and even less after *Fearless*, and it had been a Labour Government which had rejected the use of force to prevent the UDI or revoke it after it had occurred. Nevertheless, in Opposition, the Labour party had supported the Africans in their rejection of the 1971 proposals, insisting upon African approval for any negotiated agreement, recognised the legitimacy of the liberation movement and pressed for more effective sanctions. Moreover, the Africans could still count upon support from various groups within the Labour movement, which had always been committed to the liberation of southern Africa.

There was some doubt about the initiative for the talks between the ANC and the Labour Government, which were held on 1 July 1974, but according to the secretary-general, Dr Chavunduka, the British Prime Minister had asked for a delegation to come to London to discuss the breakdown of the constitutional talks in Rhodesia. There was also the possibility that the Labour Government had first been approached by former ANC officials in London on their own initiative, since a spokesman for Bishop Muzorewa in London knew nothing about such a meeting a week before it was to take place.[12] However the talks may have originated, it was unlikely that Bishop Muzorewa

would have been able to participate, since his passport had been con-
fiscated by the regime. Instead, the delegation comprised the secretary-
general, the vice-president, Dr Gabellah, and his predecessor in that
office, Rev. Canaan Banana, then in exile in London. For the ANC, the
main purpose of the meeting was to convince the British that they were
the only genuine spokesmen for African opinion in Rhodesia and, as
such, they had rejected the Rhodesian Front's proposals for a settlement and Mr Smith's scheme for a round table conference. What
they proposed instead was a constitutional conference in which all
groups of opinion in the country would be represented, but how this
was to be brought about without the agreement of the Rhodesian
Front was not indicated. Nor was there any evidence of what the
Labour Government intended to do about ending the deadlock resulting from the breakdown of the talks between the ANC and the regime.
The Foreign Secretary, Mr Callaghan, could only offer what he had
already said in Parliament on 20 March, namely, that no solution would
be acceptable to Britain unless it had the support of the African people.
Nevertheless, the ANC delegation expressed satisfaction with the
mission, and at their press conference on 2 July they claimed that one
of the main achievements of their meetings had been the British Government's recognition of the ANC as the voice of the African people of
Rhodesia. Also a gain for the Africans was Mr Wilson's announcement
in Parliament at the end of the talks that the 1971 proposals no longer
remained on the table and that there would be no consideration of any
deal with the Rhodesian regime until the proposals put forward were
approved by the majority of the population.[13]

If the object of the general election in Rhodesia had been to end the
state of uncertainty resulting from internal and international developments, as Mr Smith had alleged, then it failed in its purpose. The
Rhodesian Front had sought a mandate for the *status quo* and had
been returned to power to maintain it. Although the victory was also
a personal vote of confidence in Mr Smith's leadership, the limitations
on his choice of policy came less from the European voter, from whom
he had obtained another term of office, than from his party leadership,
from whom he could expect dismissal if he were to make any meaningful concessions to the Africans. Whether his popular support among
Europeans was sufficient to override the objections from his party
colleagues was never tested, either because he was unwilling to take the
risk of doing so or else because he genuinely did not believe in any fundamental departure from Rhodesian Front principles. The alternative
was more of the same, but the same was no longer relevant in a situa-

tion which had indeed been transformed by internal and international events.

After the election Mr Smith returned to his scheme for a round table conference as though nothing had happened in the interval. Since he first proposed it in June, the ANC had rejected the plan as 'meaningless', the British Government had endorsed the ANC's decision at the meetings in London and the African pro-settlement groups who favoured it had been repudiated by the African electorate. Even the Asian community, which had hitherto been considered as a safe European ally (at least until the Rhodesian Front devised discriminatory property and residential legislation directed against them), had come out against the 1971 proposals, which they had initially accepted, and supported the ANC demand for a constitutional conference.[14] Nevertheless, Mr Smith had a ready explanation for these events. As he told a group of Rhodesian journalists in a post-election interview on 2 August 1974, he had received reports of 'quite a lot of intimidation', which accounted for the ANC rejection of the Rhodesian Front proposals as well as the defeat of the pro-settlement groups in the election. Although he was unable to announce a firm date for the round table conference, which was not surprising in view of the likelihood that no one except the pro-settlement Africans would attend, he intended to invite the ANC even though he did not accept that it was the most representative group of African opinion. On a wave of euphoria carried over from the electoral landslide, Mr Smith was optimistic about his 'confidential communications' with the British Government concerning the procedure by which they would recognise a settlement reached with the Africans at the round table conference. Even on the external threat, arising from the FRELIMO take-over in Mozambique, he was 'hoping for the best but preparing for the worst'. Alternative trade and transport routes were being constructed, a new rail link with South Africa was nearly completed and the defences of the eastern border were being strengthened. In all of these preparations to meet the new situation, he was confident of the whole-hearted co-operation of the South African Government.

Things Fall Apart

Within a matter of weeks, Mr Smith's glowing post-electoral forecast began to ring hollow. The hopes he held out failed to be fulfilled and the grim reality of Rhodesia's situation became increasingly apparent, although not yet to most of the European electorate. All of the possibilities of disaster, which had been present ever since the UDI, seemed to materialise at the same time, although in varying degrees of intensity. The Africans were refusing to continue 'meaningless' consultations, the British Government were intervening on their side, sanctions were having a more serious effect, the war against the guerrillas was becoming an increasingly heavy burden on finance and manpower, the outflow of the European population was accelerating and even the South African Government were beginning to question the cost of propping up a regime whose continuing existence was a doubtful proposition.

One of the first cracks came, unexpectedly, on the South African front, where the continued maintenance of armed forces in Rhodesia had become a financial burden and a detriment to relations with black Africa. It had also become a source of dissatisfaction among the forces themselves, operating for the previous seven years on Rhodesia's borders, ostensibly for the purpose of preventing the passage of South African guerrillas *en route* to their homeland. Since they had not been sent there to fight Rhodesia's war, the loss of South African lives in this cause was increasingly resented. One indication of this dissatisfaction appeared on the day that Mr Smith was indulging in his post-electoral forecast of continued co-operation from South Africa, with the announcement that the South African Government were offering bonuses to policemen who would volunteer for service on Rhodesian territory. Nor were relations improved by Mr Smith's reaffirmation of his unwillingness to compromise on a settlement, which he announced during his visit to the Pretoria Trade Show on 24 August. In dismissing the advice of his critics in the South African Press (including *Die Transvaler* and *Die Vaderland*), he retaliated by attacking them for trying to force him into appeasement.[15] In return, he got a sharp warning from another powerful sector of South African opinion, the all-white Trades Union Congress, whose general secretary, Mr Albert Grobbelaar, on a fraternal visit to Rhodesia at the end of August, said that Rhodesians could not count indefinitely upon South African support continuing while they were refusing to settle their own internal problems at South Africa's expense.[16]

While Mr Smith was attributing South African allegations that Rhodesia had become an embarrassment to 'certain left-wing elements' in that country, he was also encountering similar criticism at home. Although pressure for a settlement had always come from the Establishment parties and their supporters in the business community, it was now beginning to emerge from within the ruling party itself. Mr Smith had usually coped with such attacks in the past by crediting his party with having procured increasingly better terms with each round of negotiations with the British — from pre-UDI through *Tiger* and *Fearless* to the 1971 proposals. He had made this claim during the recent election and his party chairman had castigated the business community for backing the opposition campaign for a compromise solution. But now, far from being able to hold out any promises of better terms, he did not even have the 1971 proposals to offer, since Mr Wilson had announced in July that they were no longer on the table. Nor could he any longer count upon the success of his round table conference scheme, which had been formally rejected by the ANC on 8 August and by other African groups who followed the ANC example.[17]

Consequently, Mr Smith had little encouragement left to offer his party supporters when he was urged by the Rhodesian Front congress on 19 September to 'expedite' settlement negotiations — the first time in three years that such a request had appeared on the agenda. While continuing to maintain that a settlement was 'desirable but not essential', he nevertheless agreed to renew his efforts to obtain official recognition for Rhodesia. However, he warned that even if it took one, two or ten years, his regime were prepared to 'ride this one out' rather than give way on their principles or sacrifice their standards. Since he was not 'over-optimistic' about the prospects of a round table conference nor willing to consider anything but 'quiet and constructive' talks with black leaders, it looked as though there was no alternative to 'riding it out'.[18] In any case, he was awaiting developments in Mozambique and in the British general election a fortnight later, although both events had been predetermined, as far as Rhodesia was concerned, by Portugal's decision to hand over to FRELIMO and by the determination of both parties in Britain to leave the final decision with the African population. Whether the Rhodesian Front would, however, have another ten years to 'ride it out' had become an extremely doubtful proposition.

The Rhodesian Front's renewed interest in seeking a settlement was a reflection of their growing concern about the deteriorating security situation and the price they were being required to pay for it. The regime's initial efforts to suppress any information about the guerrilla offensive begun in December 1972, the revelation of which had led to Mr Niesewand's detention, could no longer be maintained while the casualty figures continued to mount, the call-up was extended for military service and reserve duties and a massive resettlement of Africans in 'protected villages' was being instituted. Although most of the casualties were in fact blacks, Europeans were also being killed, including civilians as well as the security forces, of which twelve were South African police.[19] The cost to the European taxpayer was also revealed (conveniently after the election) in the budget introduced on 29 August, which provided for a 10 per cent surcharge on all individual and company tax for the previous year, to meet at least a portion of the mounting budget deficit. Defence expenditure was increased by about 17 per cent and about half as much again was being allocated to sectors directly concerned with the guerrilla war, such as road communications and internal affairs, the latter including the cost of constructing the resettlement villages for tribal Africans. Since many Europeans had settled in Rhodesia as an escape from higher taxation, and also conscription, in other countries, the introduction of both measures was bound to have an adverse effect upon keeping the Europeans already there and attracting others to come in. European immigration in 1973 had been the lowest since the UDI, with a net white gain of 1,680 and a 50 per cent rise in European emigration. In spite of the Rhodesian Front's intensive immigration campaign – 'Settlers 74' – to reverse this tide, an outflow of over 1,000 had been recorded for April 1974. Unrecorded was the loss of a considerable number of Europeans who voted with their feet by leaving the country permanently 'on holiday'. For prospective white immigrants, the state of uncertainty prevailing in Rhodesia in 1974 was scarcely an attractive proposition.

Notes

1. By 1974, British exports to South Africa had risen to £525 million and investment to nearly £2,000 million.

2. *The Observer*, 20 January 1974.

3. *Rhodesia Herald*, 14 January 1974.

4. Ibid., 3 March 1974.

5. See Gordon Chavunduka, *The ANC*, Occasional Paper No. 1, 1975, for the terms and the unanimous vote to reject them.

6. *The Times*, 4 June 1974.

7. In an interview with the BBC on 11 June and in the House of Assembly the following week. See Rhodesia, *Parliamentary Debates*, vol. 87, 19 June 1974, cols. 10-20.

8. Ibid., cols. 209-10.

9. Dr Sithole subsequently disappeared, allegedly kidnapped by Rhodesian security forces.

10. *Rhodesia Herald*, 8 August 1974.

11. The terms were revealed by Mr Allan Savory in Rhodesia, *Parliamentary Debates*, vol. 88, 19 June 1974, cols. 46-9. He claimed that agreement was reached on a 'Constitutional Formula for Rhodesia in Principle' on 21 April 1974.

12. *Sunday Times*, 23 June 1974.

13. 875 *HC Deb.*, 4 July 1974, cols. 597-8.

14. *Rhodesia Herald*, 20 September 1974.
15. Ibid., 26 August 1974.
16. The *Guardian*, 2 September 1974.
17. Mr Smith also alleged that Bishop Muzorewa had first accepted and then rejected the scheme for a round table conference. See Rhodesia, *Parliamentary Debates*, vol. 88, 25 September 1974, cols. 1311-16.
18. *Rhodesia Herald*, 20 September 1974.
19. According to the official communiqué for October 1974, the deaths included 400 guerrillas, 150 African civilians, 14 European civilians and 49 members of the security forces.

13 RESOLVING THE CONFLICT

'How any politician who has been through the mill can
remotely believe that a constitutional conference will lead to
majority rule is beyond any cerebral conception.'

Ahrn Palley, 13 January 1975.

However much the Rhodesians needed a settlement as a way out of
their predicament, in spite of Mr Smith's bravado that it was 'desirable
but not essential', they were not likely to get one unless they were
prepared to meet the conditions laid down by the Labour Government
after their return to office in October 1974. Just before the general
election, the Foreign Secretary, Mr Callaghan, had told the UN General
Assembly that a new approach was being considered as a result of
Portugal's decision to grant independence to its African colonies, particularly Mozambique, where developments in that territory had introduced 'new realities' into the Rhodesian situation.[1] In preparation for a
reassessment of policy the Foreign Secretary had held consultations
with heads of British Missions in Africa to obtain the views of a number
of African Governments on possible courses of action. The main issue
on which they were all agreed was the need for a constitutional conference, but how this could be brought about was still unresolved. The
ANC had pressed this demand on the Labour Government at their
meeting the previous June, as had the other nationalist groups in exile.[2]
The United Nations had also called for such action in nearly every resolution on Rhodesia over the previous decade, and most of the Commonwealth leaders had done the same at successive Prime Ministers' meetings. But they had all met with opposition from British Governments,
Labour and Conservative, unwilling to incur the hostility of a regime
with whom they were seeking a settlement by means of bilateral negotiations.

Perhaps the most striking departure from the Labour Government's
previous policy was the recognition that the Rhodesian problem could
not be settled through negotiations between Britain and the illegal
regime. As the Foreign Secretary conceded, during the debate on the
renewal of the sanctions Order, it was not for Britain to tell Africans
what sort of settlement they should or should not support; it was for
them to decide and work out for themselves. The emergence of a new
African government in Mozambique had rendered totally futile 'the

236

juggling with parliamentary seats for Africans and the offering of majority rule in the some time, never-never land future'. Any settlement would therefore have to recognise that Africans would play the major part in government, although the interests of the white minority would be reflected. As Mr Callaghan envisaged the inevitability of change, Mr Smith had a problem that would not go away: it would get worse year by year until the illegal regime either made their peace with Britain and the world community or were replaced by others who had the confidence of the majority of the Rhodesian population. Although there was no indication of how the Labour Government would hasten that change, other than by tightening up existing sanctions,[3] the Foreign Secretary would be visiting the black African States at the end of 1974 to obtain their views on a Rhodesian settlement.

By the time the Foreign Secretary announced the Labour Government's new approach, the initiative had already been taken up by the African States themselves.[4] Although Britain had become reconciled to standing aside until the Rhodesians produced sufficient evidence of agreement to merit its intervention, the countries most directly threatened by an extension of the conflict had concluded that no solution would be likely to emerge within Rhodesia unless pressure were exerted upon the contestants from their respective supporters outside. The opening of the diplomatic offensive was prompted by the removal of the Portuguese colonial presence and the resulting vulnerability of the Rhodesian regime to guerrilla invasions from a considerably extended front. In this transformed situation, Zambia and South Africa had become the main protagonists, with South African military forces operating on Rhodesia's borders and guerrillas based in Zambia confronting those forces. For South Africa, the alternative had become increasing involvement in a war which the Rhodesians could not sustain without massive outside support or a complete military disengagement. To achieve the latter, however, a cease-fire, and also a political settlement, were essential.

Britain's role, in this new alignment of forces, had become a largely irrelevant one. The Zambians, having long since abandoned any hope of British intervention, had decided that the only available means of effecting a change in the military conflict was an approach to the source of the regime's power. They therefore began, at first tentatively, to reopen diplomatic contacts with South Africa, previously attempted in 1971, but aborted by Mr Vorster's premature revelation. However, before President Kaunda's special emissary, Mr Mark Chona, began his series of secret meetings with the South Africans in October 1974, the

Zambian Government informed Britain of their intentions. At a meeting between their Foreign Minister, Mr Vernon Mwaanga, and Mr Callaghan on 10 August in Geneva (where Britain was engaged in the Cyprus negotiations), agreement was reached on the project, and on the establishment of a committee, representing Tanzania and Botswana as well as Zambia and Britain, to review the situation in Rhodesia as a result of the diplomatic contacts.

The South African response to the Zambian initiative was welcomed by President Kaunda as 'the voice of reason'.[5] In reply to Mr Vorster's offer of détente,[6] the Zambian President put forward his disengagement scheme, calling for the withdrawal of South African forces from Rhodesian territory as an essential precondition for peace in the area. What Zambia could offer in return was control of the guerrilla forces operating from its own and from neighbouring territories, with the compliance of Tanzania, Botswana and Mozambique. Although the South African Prime Minister held out no promise of an immediate withdrawal, maintaining that their forces were protecting South Africa against 'terrorism', he conceded that changes could be expected within the next six months.[7]

For the rebel regime, the time limit envisaged for the duration of South African support was a clear warning: the alternative had become a negotiated settlement with the Africans or a continuation of guerrilla warfare without South African assistance. Whether Mr Smith would draw the obvious conclusions remained uncertain from his usual contradictory pronouncements. Although he had paid lip-service to 'any efforts to foster peaceful co-existence',[8] in his UDI anniversary address he did not conceal his contempt for 'those who advocated appeasement and compromise on principle, even before they have reached the stage of negotiating'. As for the reluctance of South Africa to remain in 'the same boat', he told the Johannesburg *Financial Mail* on 15 November that, while he welcomed South African material support and the presence of their police units, if the Rhodesians had to do the task themselves, they would not hesitate to do so.

Mr Smith's declaration of confidence in Rhodesia's ability to 'go it alone' left him in the position of being the only obstacle to what was developing into an atmosphere of détente. This posture did not go unnoticed by the European Establishment, particularly the leader of the Rhodesia party, Mr Timothy Gibbs, and the former Federal Prime Minister, Sir Roy Welensky, the latter now convinced that a settlement was possible as a result of the peace initiative undertaken by what he regarded as 'the most important white man in the sub-continent' and 'the most important black leader south of Nigeria'.[9] Mr Smith, however, was also under pressure from the intransigent right — the Rhodesia National party and the new United Conservative party formed by the supporters of the former 'Minister' Mr William Harper — and it was to this constituency that his strictures against appeasement of 'terrorists', lowering of standards or departing from principles were directed.[10]

While Mr Smith was engaged in publicly disclaiming any intention of doing so, he had, in fact, already yielded to South African pressure. On 3 December 1974, it was officially announced in Salisbury that a number of African leaders of the banned ZAPU and ZANU parties, including Mr Nkomo, Mr Mugabe and Rev. Sithole, had been released from detention to attend talks in Lusaka with the African Presidents (of Zambia, Tanzania and Botswana) involved in the preliminary negotiations. The British, notably absent from the proceedings, claimed that they had been kept informed about the plans during their meetings in London with representatives of the African States, presumably begun after the Zambian Foreign Minister had first approached Mr Callaghan on the intended initiative the previous August.[11] For Mr Smith to have consented to the release of the nationalist leaders to enable them to participate in talks in an African country from which guerrilla invasions were being mounted was a concession of such magnitude that it could only have been procured by severe pressure from the South Africans. Although Mr Smith had been talking with the ANC leaders for well over a year, he had firmly ruled out the possibility of recognising the claims of the detainees to be spokesmen of the African people, because of his equation of the forces of political opposition with those of 'terrorism'. However, the prospect of a cease-fire on the part of the guerrillas, arranged through the intervention of Zambia, undermined the regime's case for continued detention as a deterrent against 'terrorism', and the weight of South African pressure in support of the Zambian initiative proved to be the decisive factor in opening the way for the meeting in Lusaka.

Although the South Africans succeeded in getting the Smith regime into negotiations with the African nationalists and the black Presidents, in Lusaka on 6 December,[12] they could not have got any advance commitment on what the Rhodesians were prepared to accept in the way of a settlement. If they had, the Rhodesians subsequently changed their minds. While the exact cause or causes of the breakdown of the Lusaka talks remained obscure, the official version put out by the Smith regime raised the question of their motive in going into the talks at all, other than to show a willingness to their South African protectors. According to the statement issued by the office of the 'Prime Minister', after a 'Cabinet' meeting on 7 December, the regime had agreed 'to mount a constitutional conference on certain conditions', namely, that there would be 'a cessation of terrorism' and that there would be 'no lowering of standards'. Claiming to have entered the negotiations under these conditions, the regime then maintained that they had been informed by the African Presidents that there would be no halting of 'terrorism' unless it were agreed that a precondition of the constitutional conference was that it would be on the basis of 'immediate majority rule'. Although the source of the alleged ultimatum was not specified in the official statement, Mr Smith claimed, in an Independent Television News interview two days later, that the Tanzanian President and 'extremist elements' from Rhodesia had started 'ruling the roost'. While proposals from these sources were not acceptable to the regime, they would nevertheless continue to pursue their stated objective of 'promoting peaceful co-existence' in southern Africa.[13]

In spite of the credibility gap established by the official Rhodesian explanation, since it was inconceivable that South Africa would have been a sponsor of a conference to impose immediate majority rule or that Zambia would have entertained a conference to perpetuate the principle of 'no lowering of standards', the South African Prime Minister exonerated them (and also the Zambians) from the blame, preferring to regard the whole episode as a temporary set-back to their long-range peace plans for the area. According to Mr Vorster's version, the discussions foundered as a result of 'the new demand' at the end of the proceedings, a demand in total conflict with the spirit, intent and result of the agreement up to that point. Whether he intended to confirm the Rhodesian claim of being given an ultimatum of immediate majority rule was not specified, but he did maintain that Rhodesia had throughout 'fulfilled its obligations in terms of its commitments'. Having exonerated Rhodesia, Zambia and all of the other parties at Lusaka who had made 'an honest attempt to find a solution' (but not those who had made 'the new demand), he attributed the failure to 'influences exerted by certain circles' militating against the attempt to reach a settlement. On the credit side, however, he noted the useful contacts established and the favourable climate created, which were sufficient to encourage South Africa to continue its efforts to bring the parties together again around a conference table. The alternative, as Mr Vorster envisaged it, was 'too ghastly to contemplate'.[14]

Within three days of the South African warning, Mr Smith had announced, in a televised broadcast, that, as a result of the exchanges which had continued after the breakdown of the Lusaka talks, the difficulties had been resolved. In particular, he had received assurances that 'terrorist' activities would cease immediately and that the proposed constitutional conference would take place without any preconditions. To create the right atmosphere for the holding of a constitutional conference, he had accordingly agreed to release the African leaders from detention and restriction and to permit them to engage in 'normal activity in terms of the laws applicable to all Rhodesians'. For the Europeans who would feel concerned at the implications of these developments, he offered the reassurance, first, that it was the regime's firm intention to maintain law and order and, secondly (as at Lusaka), that they were not prepared to deviate from their standards of civilisation. And for those who might have seen the parallel with the situation in neighbouring Mozambique, he insisted that there was no possibility whatever of a similar train of events occurring in Rhodesia. While Rhodesians were called upon to accept the new situation, to put behind them the differences and recriminations of the past and to look to the future, they were nevertheless warned to take appropriate precautions against continuing acts of 'terrorism' and carefully safeguard the security of commercial information.

If Mr Smith's reversal of policy on 11 December 1974 had been influenced by the South African peace offensive, it could also be attributed to the fact that he was now confronted for the first time in a decade with a united African nationalist movement. Although the Lusaka talks had ended in deadlock, a major *coup* for the African Presidents was their success in getting a unity agreement among the African parties represented there. At a meeting on 7 December, the two main groups, ZAPU and ZANU, which had maintained separate organisations throughout the years of their banning and exile, together with a splinter group, FROLIZI, led by Mr James Chikerema, agreed to consolidate their forces under a reconstituted African National Council, then the only legal African nationalist organisation surviving inside Rhodesia. Whether the ANC could continue to operate as such, after incorporating the membership of the banned parties, was dependent upon the regime's response to an organisation dedicated, in the terms of its unity agreement, to 'the inevitability of continued armed struggle and all other forms of struggle until the total liberation of Zimbabwe'. The revision of the ANC constitution and the enlargement of its executive to include the new members was to be effected at a congress the following March, provided that it could reconcile the internal differences existing among its component parts, particularly on the issues of a cease-fire and the timing of majority rule. The unity of an organisation that embraced such a diversity of views as those of the more 'moderate' members of the ANC and those of the militant ZANU wing was bound to be fragile. Nevertheless, there was no doubt about the party's commitment to majority rule as the only basis for independence, and a statement to this effect was made to the Press by Bishop Muzorewa on 12 December, in reply to Mr Smith's offer the previous day of a constitutional conference without preconditions. As the Bishop said, the ANC was ready for talks with the regime, but the venue, the chairmanship and the agenda for those talks had first to be settled between the two sides before a discussion of the constitutional issues could even begin.[15]

Retreat from Lusaka

During the months following the Lusaka talks, the prospects of a constitutional conference, 'without preconditions', as Mr Smith had pledged, gradually receded. The differences between the two sides were not limited to the procedural questions of how such a conference should be arranged, with the Africans committed to a British presence, preferably in the chair, and to London (or at least another African country) as the venue, and the regime holding out for an all-Rhodesian membership meeting inside the country under the chairmanship of Mr Smith. While these issues might have been subject to compromise, the substantive divisions were so fundamental as to cast doubt upon the possibility of a successful outcome of a conference, even if one could be staged. Most of the differences arose over what had been agreed at Lusaka, particularly on the subjects of a cease-fire and the release of political prisoners. But the most crucial division was over the issue of majority rule, on which no compromise appeared to be possible after the Rhodesian regime had rejected the Lusaka proposals on the basis of their refusal to recognise this principle. Even though Mr Smith had subsequently conceded, in his broadcast of 11 December, that a constitutional conference would take place without preconditions, he was obviously excluding the condition of majority rule, which remained, so far as the rebel regime were concerned, non-negotiable. This was evident from his remarks in a BBC interview only a few days later (15 December), in which he admitted that the thought of African majority rule had never entered his head, he doubted that it ever would, and he still believed that there would be no black rule in Rhodesia in his lifetime. As a self-confessed 'right-winger' and the leader of 'the right-wing party in Rhodesia', he firmly believed in a qualified franchise and was opposed to the counting of heads 'like the counting of sheep'. His only concession towards sharing power was a recognition that the Africans must be brought along and that if he found any of ability or merit he would be prepared to give them a chance, provided that they were willing to co-operate in the face of extremist pressures against their doing so.

Mr Smith's determination, even by the end of 1974, to cling to the same outworn clichés and positions that had been responsible for both the origin and the prolongation of the conflict, notwithstanding the precarious condition of the country and the outside pressures for a settlement, was an indication of the depth of his concern with retaining the support of the European electorate. Party political pressures were certainly responsible for keeping him in line with previous Rhodesian Front commitments, as the chairman, Mr Desmond Frost, revealed in a statement two days after the BBC interview, relegating the decision to attempt negotiations to 'something that the South Africans started' as a means of getting international recognition for Rhodesia. Dismissing the prospect of majority rule as unrealistic and as something that the Africans and the Press were attempting to foster, Mr Frost warned that unless the Press indicated to the Africans that their demands were unrealistic, it could lead to a right-wing backlash[16] – as Mr Smith had been aware when he assumed the role of 'a right-wing leader' of 'the right-wing party'.

Also in dispute between the two sides was the regime's good faith in carrying out their part of the agreement to release those still detained and restricted and to implement the cease-fire as agreed. The two issues became inextricably linked because the Africans would not attend a constitutional conference until the detainees were released and the informal cease-fire would not become a formal one until a date for the conference had been set and meaningful discussions begun. On the other side, the rebel regime would not continue to release the detainees until a complete cease-fire had been observed by the guerrilla fighters. The cease-fire issue was further complicated by the manner in which the regime attempted to implement it, with the Rhodesian Air Force dropping leaflets over the fighting areas calling upon the guerrillas to abandon their arms and surrender or withdraw to their bases outside Rhodesia. That some fighting would continue was inevitable, not only as a result of the difficulty of getting the cease-fire message across to the guerrilla forces as emanating from their own leaders and not the enemy, but also as a result of the determination of certain ZANU forces to continue the war of liberation as the only certain means of assuring the victory of the African majority. Consequently, the regime, well aware of the differences that had arisen within the nationalist camp over the implementation of the cease-fire, were able to take advantage of the violations which had occurred as a means of both dividing the nationalist movement and delaying the implementation of any constitutional commitments to the Africans which would have the effect of alienating the regime's European supporters.

Further evidence of the regime's retreat from the Lusaka agreement came with the announcement by the 'Minister' of Law and Order, Mr Lardner-Burke, on 10 January 1975, one month after Mr Smith had announced the decision to release the detainees, that no more were being released because the guerrilla forces were not observing the cease-fire. In an interview in the *Rhodesia Herald*, he claimed that not only had 'terrorists' failed to obey explicit instructions from their alleged leaders to cease hostilities, they had increased their activities in some areas and, since the cease-fire was announced, more 'terrorists' had actually crossed the border into Rhodesia. Furthermore, he had evidence of pamphlets with a 'violent and racialistic content', presumably printed in Zambia, being circulated in the operational areas urging guerrillas to continue fighting and accelerate the war. Although he would reveal no figures on the number of detainees still being held, it was evident from the numbers being cited by the ANC and by former detainees who had themselves been released that considerably less than one-third of those down for release by the regime had managed to achieve their freedom before the halt was called. According to Mr Mugabe's statement to the Press on 15 December, up to 300 of his ZANU members were still being held at that time; and Mr Chikerema, at an OAU meeting in Dar es Salaam on 14 January, the week after the Lardner-Burke announcement, claimed that only about 100 of some 600 detainees had been released by then. The dispute concerned not only the number of detainees still held but also the grounds on which they were being detained. While the ANC claimed that all political prisoners were equally entitled to be freed, the regime were maintaining that those captured as guerrilla fighters or those arrested for aiding 'terrorism' were special categories excluded from the agreement on release.

The British Approach

While the Rhodesians were engaged in charges and counter-charges over the implementation of the Lusaka agreement, the British Foreign Secretary was pursuing his meetings with African leaders, proposed the previous November as the Labour Government's new initiative towards a Rhodesian settlement.[17] There was an air of unreality about the whole exercise, since the real decisions were being taken elsewhere – not only in Rhodesia itself but also in Lusaka and Pretoria. But the visit had been announced before it was known what effect, if any, the initial efforts of the African States towards a détente would produce. By the time Mr Callaghan arrived in Africa at the end of 1974, his presence there was no longer a significant factor so far as enhancing the prospects of a settlement in Rhodesia was concerned. If there was anything to be gained from the effort, it was the improvement of relations with the Commonwealth leaders in Africa, not an achievement to be underrated in view of the strains imposed by the differences of approach over Rhodesia during the years since the UDI. The fact that a British Foreign Secretary thought it necessary to consult African opinion on the conditions for a settlement was no more than a belated recognition that it was now the African leaders themselves who were actually determining the conditions that would be acceptable as a settlement. Britain had no immediate contribution to make to the dialogue that had already begun before the Foreign Secretary's visit; its responsibility was limited to conferring legality upon the end product. For the first time since the UDI, the initiative for a settlement had shifted to the African continent and Britain's role at this stage of the proceedings was to be kept informed of the new developments.

This was evident from the Foreign Secretary's report to Parliament that the main purpose of his visit had been to obtain a clear idea of the views of the six Commonwealth countries he visited and to work out a common policy with them in order to take advantage of the recent initiatives of the African Presidents as well as the South African Prime Minister. What he found, as a result, was that there was now a greater degree of understanding between Britain and the African Governments than at any time since the UDI: in President Nyerere's words, their policies were now 'converging'. What accounted for this new relationship was not an alteration of African opinion, which had remained constant, but a reversal of British policy, particularly its belated recognition of majority rule as the only basis for an independence settlement. Once this principle had been accepted by the British, the only remaining differences with the African Governments were the methods of achieving it. Although Mr Callaghan had conceded to the African leaders that the Rhodesian problem could only be finally settled by a constitutional conference, there was no indication of what Britain would do to bring this about. To the two requirements which he regarded as essential — observance of the provisions of the Lusaka agreement and direct exploratory talks between the ANC and the Smith regime — Britain had no contribution to make. As before, the British Government would be ready to do anything that would contribute to a settlement, but only after the people of Rhodesia themselves had got down to working out what sort of constitutional solution would be acceptable to them.[18]

Although the Foreign Secretary had originally planned to visit only the Commonwealth countries of Zambia, Botswana, Malawi, Tanzania, Kenya and Nigeria, his statement on arrival in Lusaka that he would be willing to meet anyone if he thought it would further the objectives of securing a constitutional settlement immediately raised the question of a possible meeting with the Rhodesians and also the South Africans. In any case, Mr Callaghan had expected to meet the Rhodesian African leaders while he was in Lusaka, irrespective of whether the Europeans took up his open invitation to meet 'anyone' while he was there. However, the six-member ANC delegation which was to fly to Lusaka for the meeting was prohibited by the regime from leaving the country. The official reason for refusing permission for the visit was that 'no request had been received by the Rhodesian Government from either the Zambian or British Governments for ex-detainees to visit Lusaka'. Since the ex-detainees had been permitted to attend meetings in Lusaka with other African leaders since the previous November, the regime's action to prevent this particular meeting was an obvious snub to the British Foreign Secretary. It also amounted to a clear indication by Mr Smith that neither he nor any member of his regime had any intention of conferring with a Labour Foreign Secretary whose Government were now committed to African majority rule as the only basis of an independence settlement. If the Rhodesians were, as Mr Callaghan had suggested in Lusaka on 31 December, like 'men stranded in the middle of an ice-field', they certainly had no intention of taking up the British offer 'to help save them from themselves'.[19]

Instead, Mr Callaghan managed to arrange a 'surprise visit' to South Africa, as he put it, 'to explore Mr Vorster's mind'. The visit to South Africa had not originally been included in the itinerary, partly because of the offence which it might have caused to a large section of the Labour party and also to several African leaders whose opinions were being sought on the policy to be adopted towards Rhodesia in the context of the transformed situation in southern Africa. There was the additional question of how South Africa would respond to a proposed meeting with a representative of a Government which had reimposed the arms embargo, threatened to terminate the Simonstown agreement on the naval base and supported United Nations policy on the occupation of Namibia. However, despite these strains in their relationship, South Africa was indebted to Britain (and also to the USA and France) for the veto cast on 30 October 1974 to prevent its expulsion from the United Nations. As for African reactions, having first cleared the visit with the Zambians, who themselves had by this time experienced some fifteen official meetings with the South Africans, Mr Callaghan was assured that no offence would be caused to the leaders of the African States still to be visited. On this aspect of the visit, the British and the Africans, especially the Zambians, were agreed: the future course of the rebel regime would be determined in Pretoria.

Although Mr Callaghan had denied, while announcing the intended visit, that its purpose was to urge Mr Vorster to exert pressure on Mr Smith to get a settlement, this was the obvious objective, and one which the Zambians had pursued in their own diplomatic efforts of the preceding months. For the British, there was also the question of South African military forces on the territory of what was still, in law, a British colony. The presence of those forces had been a continuing source of friction between Britain and South Africa, with the latter refusing to remove them at the request of successive British Governments and with Britain having to answer for its inability to affect the situation before the world community at the United Nations. Although Mr Vorster had already indicated, in his series of exchanges with the African leaders, that South Africa would be prepared to withdraw its forces as soon as there was a halt to 'terrorist' activities, the delay in implementing the pledge had been attributed to the failure of the African nationalists to control their forces in the field. Since South Africa had already lost the lives of some half-dozen of its police in incidents occurring during the few weeks following the announcement of the cease-fire, it could claim that the conditions for its withdrawal had not yet been established. Mr Callaghan could therefore expect no immediate reversal of South African policy on this subject. However, since the support which South African forces were providing for the Rhodesians remained one of the main weapons of coercion which Mr Vorster had at his disposal to exert pressure on the regime, the mere threat of their withdrawal could be invoked as a means of influencing Rhodesian attitudes towards a settlement, whatever Mr Smith might say to the contrary. Furthermore, the South Africans had to consider the fact that the retention of their forces on Rhodesian soil was a major obstacle to realising the détente they were seeking to promote with black Africa. If South African military units were to be withdrawn, it would not be as a result of British pressure to do so; it would be because it was no longer in South Africa's interest to keep them there.

On the other main issue raised in the course of the talks – a constitutional conference – there was also no indication of agreement. While Mr Callaghan had encountered from all of the black African leaders he had consulted a demand for Britain to stage a constitutional conference, the South Africans were noticeably unenthusiastic about such a proposal. Having opened their own dialogue with black Africa, they apparently expected Mr Smith to do the same with the Rhodesian Africans. Although they might be prepared to exert the necessary pressure to get Mr Smith to recognise the principle of majority rule, which they had come around to accepting as an inevitable result of Rhodesia's constitutional development, they were less inclined to exert that influence for the purpose of ensuring a British presence in the proceedings. Their main concern was to have a stable and peaceful neighbouring country across the Limpopo, even if that objective could only be realised by the implementation of majority rule. For them, a black government in Rhodesia would mean an end to the guerrilla war which threatened their own security and to the sanctions which inhibited the expansion of their economic relations with black Africa. As Mr Callaghan summed up the position after the meeting in Port Elizabeth on 5 January, he and Mr Vorster were looking at the situation from different perspectives. While Rhodesia was a national security matter of some magnitude for South Africa, for Britain it was a matter of 'honour' – of redeeming its pledge to ensure a transition to African majority rule.[20]

Détente or Confrontation?

With a complete deadlock between the ANC and the rebel regime, not only on the fundamental issue of majority rule but also on the procedural means of staging a constitutional conference, President Nyerere's assessment of a protracted armed struggle was probably a more accurate one than Mr Callaghan's vision of a settlement with 'justice and honour'.[21] Even the precarious détente established by the African Presidents was beginning to show signs of strain, with the South African failure to produce any change in the Rhodesian situation other than a withdrawal of their forces from forward positions on the Zambezi, officially announced in Salisbury on 11 February. The African Presidents were also under fire from the Organisation of African Unity for engaging in diplomatic contacts with South Africa without prior reference to that organisation. Regarding the whole exercise as a South African manoeuvre to split the black African camp, the Council of Ministers' meeting in Addis Ababa on 22 February recalled that OAU policy on the issue of 'dialogue', established in 1971 in response to the efforts of the Ivory Coast, was that only liberation movements should speak to South Africa. Since OAU support would be required for the liberation struggle, it was essential to establish a consensus on the objectives of the détente being pursued by the African Presidents. The result of the effort to reconcile the differences in approach was a compromise agreement – the Dar es Salaam Declaration – adopted by the Foreign Ministers on 10 April 1975, and endorsed by the OAU summit the following July. In effect, it provided that, while the African States would support 'genuine negotiations' in order to facilitate the transfer of power to the African majority, they would also 'undertake the necessary preparations for the intensification of the armed struggle should peaceful solution to the Rhodesian crisis be blocked'. Although there would be no change in the OAU policy of 'total isolation of the apartheid regime' in South Africa,[22] the diplomacy of détente would nevertheless continue, since this remained the only effective means of exerting sufficient pressure on the rebel regime to achieve the 'genuine negotiations' called for in the Declaration. The African Presidents had thus gained a reprieve to continue their diplomatic efforts. And South Africa had been rewarded for withdrawing its forces in Rhodesia to their camps[23] and for intervening with the Smith regime to secure the release of Rev. Sithole, detained on an unsubstantiated charge of an assassination plot against his rivals for the ANC leadership and convicted instead for supporting a continuation of guerrilla warfare.[24]

The alternative of 'genuine negotiations' or armed struggle was also the subject of a heated debate at the Commonwealth Prime Ministers' conference, which opened in Jamaica at the end of the same month. On this occasion, as before, the African States had to take into account the continued reluctance of the British to be committed to any policy that envisaged the use of force, however conditonal. Nor would they be moved from this position by the strong appeals for material assistance for the liberation movement's 'freedom fighters' made by the African States and by the ANC representatives at the conference, Bishop Muzorewa, Rev. Sithole and Mr Nkomo. This was evident from the communiqué issued at the conclusion of the meeting on 6 May,[25] which merely 'took note of' the determination of the liberation forces and the African States supporting them to achieve their objective by peaceful means if possible, and their recognition of 'the inevitability of intensified armed struggle should peaceful avenues be blocked by the racist and illegal regime'. It was also confirmed by Mr Wilson himself, in a statement to Parliament after returning from the conference. According to his account, when he and the Foreign Secretary were asked whether they were prepared to provide either arms or money for guerrilla activities, they gave 'a flat rejection', saying that they would 'in no circumstances be involved in such activities'.[26]

If there were divisions over support for armed struggle, there was virtual unanimity on the objective of NIBMAR, no small achievement after a decade of wrangling over its meaning and application. On this subject no British, or any other, reservations were recorded in the communiqué; the commitment was unconditional. The Heads of Government clearly reaffirmed their 'total support for the struggle of the people of Zimbabwe for independence on the basis of majority rule and pledged to concert their efforts for the speedy attainment of this objective'. What these efforts would be, however, was less clear. The British were contemplating a meeting with the Smith regime, at Ministerial level, to consider the prospects for a constitutional conference and for the resumption of talks between the ANC and the regime, broken off after the arrest of Rev. Sithole on 4 March. But such a proposition was not likely to impress those Commonwealth leaders who had already witnessed the results of a decade of visits by British Ministers to Rhodesia.[27] If a constitutional conference were to be brought about, it would be as a result of the pressures exerted upon the Rhodesian contenders by their external supporters, and Britain, having renounced intervention in the conflict, did not have that pressure to exert.

As at former Commonwealth meetings, the British preferred to rely on sanctions as a method of bringing about the removal of the rebel regime. Although previous efforts in that direction had not produced the desired effect, by 1975 the situation had been transformed as a result of the control of Rhodesia's transit facilities through Mozambique by the new FRELIMO Government. Since the bulk of Rhodesia's exports and imports was dependent on access to these facilities, their removal would be a severe blow to its economic survival. At the same time, however, Mozambique would suffer a considerable loss to its own economy if it closed its borders to the Rhodesians, and for that sacrifice it was entitled (as were Zambia and Botswana) to compensation by the international community. The British Government therefore proposed, as a new departure in the sanctions campaign, to make a substantial contribution to an international programme of financial assistance to enable the Mozambique Government to apply sanctions against Rhodesia. On this proposal, the Commonwealth leaders recorded their unanimous approval and endorsed the recommendation that an initiative should be taken by their Governments at the United Nations to establish a programme of assistance for Mozambique, in terms of Articles 49 and 50 of the Charter. In addition to the financial contribution to Mozambique, Britain was also prepared, according to Mr Wilson's report to Parliament, to consider assistance in relation to the needs of Zambia and Botswana, a matter which he claimed to have discussed with the Zambian President. Whether President Kaunda had also been a party to the request for money for 'guerrilla activities', he did not say, but if he had been, he could only have got Mr Wilson's 'flat rejection' as a reply. Nevertheless, Mr Wilson was convinced that, as a result of the transformed situation in southern Africa, this had been 'by far the best Commonwealth conference' that any of them could remember.

Although the rebel regime had condemned the 'arrogant demands' of the African nationalists at the Commonwealth conference,[28] and the ANC leader, Mr Nkomo, had maintained that a constitutional conference could only be held with Britain,[29] negotiations between the ANC and the regime were resumed on 22 May, and with Mr Nkomo in attendance. But there had been no change in the positions of the two sides during the months following the suspension of the talks over the arrest of Rev. Sithole. Each was still insisting that the other had not fulfilled the terms of the Lusaka agreement, and Mr Smith was again denying the possibility of handing over power to Africans in his lifetime[30] and threatening to talk to 'other groups of Africans' because the ANC lacked leaders of the necessary calibre and status to present adequately a reasoned and logical case.[31] Even when the two sides had come around to agreeing (on 12 June) that a constitutional conference should take place, once more a deadlock arose over the venue, since a conference inside Rhodesia would exclude the ANC leaders in exile, particularly Rev. Sithole and his supporters.

Under these circumstances, it was most unlikely that any further progress would be forthcoming without the intervention of the African States supporting the respective sides, particularly since the British Ministerial visit at the end of June had not had any noticeable effect on the deadlock. While the African Presidents supported the ANC's stand on a venue outside Rhodesia, they were even more concerned with the growing threat of a split in the ANC ranks, which would have the effect of weakening their position in the negotiations with the regime. It was already evident, particularly after the stormy meeting of the ANC Executive Committee in Highfield on 1 June 1975, during which some thirteen Africans involved in intra-party rioting outside the meeting hall were killed by security forces, that the rivalry between former ZAPU and ZANU supporters had not been reconciled by their incorporation into the ANC. The movement was already physically divided, with an external wing, including Rev. Sithole, Mr Chikerema and (later) Bishop Muzorewa in Lusaka. Within Rhodesia a struggle for the leadership of the ANC was also proceeding, with the ZAPU wing determined to get Mr Nkomo elected as president in place of Bishop Muzorewa, and the ZANU wing equally determined to retain the leadership of the Bishop, at least until a full ANC congress to include the exiled members could meet to elect a new leadership. Differences had also arisen over the alternative of negotiations or armed struggle, with some of the ZANU supporters committed to force as the only acceptable means of liberation.[32]

So long as these intra-party manoeuvres persisted, the ANC was in no position to present a united front in any negotiations with the regime, particularly with Mr Smith intervening with his stated preference for Mr Nkomo.[33] It was for this reason, along with the continuing deadlock over the constitutional conference issue, that the African Presidents decided to intervene. Accordingly, a twelve-member ANC delegation was summoned to Lusaka to join the exiled leaders there in talks with President Kaunda, and a meeting of the ANC and the African Presidents was to follow in Dar es Salaam on 5 July. The result of the discussions was a resolution of the factional differences (although a temporary one), with the leadership of Bishop Muzorewa confirmed, and an agreement to work together for 'an intensification of the armed struggle'. Whether a negotiated settlement, which the African Presidents had been attempting to bring about, was still possible would depend upon the response of the regime to the ANC demand for holding the conference outside Rhodesia.

While the African Presidents were intervening with the ANC, the South Africans were exerting pressure to get Mr Smith to the conference table. The impetus for his doing so came with the announcement (on 1 August) of the withdrawal of South African forces in Rhodesia, coinciding with the decision of the OAU summit to endorse the Dar es Salaam Declaration on the necessity of armed struggle should peaceful means be blocked. The result of the South African intervention was an agreement signed in Pretoria on 9 August by Mr Smith, Mr Vorster and the Zambian representative (Mr Mark Chona), which provided for a meeting between representatives of the Smith regime and the ANC with a neutral venue, namely, in South African railway carriages on the Victoria Falls bridge between Rhodesia and Zambia. The formal meeting, which was to enable the parties to express their 'genuine desire to negotiate an acceptable settlement', was to be followed by committee discussions *within* Rhodesia; thereafter the parties would meet again in formal conference anywhere agreed, in order to ratify the committee proposals. The implementation of the agreement by the two parties involved was to be ensured by the African States participating in the détente.[34]

If the Lusaka agreement broke down because of conflicting interpretations of unwritten commitments, the Pretoria agreement, which was written, signed and guaranteed, contained the seeds of its own destruction. Although the formal opening meeting at Victoria Falls would be taking place on neutral territory, the real discussions, on substantive issues, would be held inside Rhodesia, as Mr Smith had always intended. Consequently, the banned ANC members, who would be able to (and did) attend what Mr Smith envisaged as 'a half-hour ceremony' at Victoria Falls,[35] would be excluded from the subsequent negotiations because of the regime's refusal to grant them immunity to attend. In these circumstances, it was inevitable that the Victoria Falls meeting, which lasted for only twenty-four hours, would collapse in complete disarray. The only gain recorded, according to Mr Vorster, was his opportunity for 'long and penetrating discussions with President Kaunda', with whom he intended to continue his efforts to find a solution.[36]

The Message of the Sixties

The Declaration of Intent to negotiate a settlement, which was to have been adopted at the abortive Victoria Falls conference, was finally agreed on 1 December 1975 by the Smith regime and the ANC wing led by Mr Nkomo. Mr Smith had given way on the immunity guarantee and Mr Nkomo had accepted that the meetings would be held inside Rhodesia. By this time, however, the issue of immunity for the external members of the ANC (including the newly established Zimbabwe Liberation Council, based in Lusaka) was no longer a relevant one, as a result of the split in the ANC which had occurred in September. Although the faction inside Rhodesia still loyal to Bishop Muzorewa had attempted to preserve his leadership of the movement while he was abroad on a fund raising tour, the faction of former ZAPU supporters had succeeded in staging a rival ANC congress (on 28 September) to elect Mr Nkomo president, a decision denounced by the Muzorewa supporters.[37]

In the atmosphere of extreme bitterness and enmity following the party split, it was not likely that Mr Nkomo, after having won from Mr Smith the concession of immunity for ANC members to participate in the conference, would choose as members of his negotiating team any of his rivals for leadership of the ANC. It was perhaps for this reason that Mr Smith could afford to concede the point on immunity, since any decision to exclude the externally based leaders from the conference would be Mr Nkomo's not his. In any case, Mr Smith had made it clear during the period leading up to the negotiations that his preference for the ANC leadership was Mr Nkomo. As for the preference of the African Presidents who had tried, and in vain, to restore the unity of the ANC,[38] their policy had become one of standing aloof until the party had sorted out its own leadership crisis. But, since Mr Nkomo had become the official leader inside Rhodesia and, as such, was seeking their support and recognition, some response was required. It was perhaps best summed up by President Kaunda, following his meeting with Mr Nkomo, in a statement in Lusaka on 22 November: 'If Mr Nkomo clinches an agreement with Mr Smith on the basis of majority rule, then the Zimbabwe Liberation Council led by Bishop Muzorewa would become irrelevant. And if he does not, then he will become irrelevant.'[39]

It was also possible that Mr Smith, too, would become irrelevant if the talks broke down, although, unlike Mr Nkomo, he had no rivals available to take over. His dilemma, as before, was that if talks were to succeed, as the South Africans, and also the British, were insisting that they must, the concessions he would have to make to the Africans would be unacceptable to his European supporters. In attempting to reassure both, he only succeeded in antagonising the forces exerting pressure upon him. For his admission to Associated Press on 19 September 1975, that the sharing of power between Rhodesia's black and white population was 'absolutely logical', and that an African had as much right as any other Rhodesian, of whatever colour, to any position in the country,[40] he was severely censured by the party chairman, Mr Desmond Frost, at the Rhodesian Front Congress the following week. Although he succeeded in preventing the congress from adopting resolutions calling for the abandonment of the policy of détente and the implementation of the party's commitment to separate development,[41] there remained among the Rhodesian Front membership a considerable resentment about South African intervention in their affairs to promote a multi-racial solution, subsequently expressed in the resignation of a key 'Minister', Mr Wickus de Kock.

These internal contradictions within the Rhodesian Front were undoubtedly connected with Mr Smith's outburst against the South Africans, in an interview with London Weekened Television on 12 October, in which he accused Mr Vorster of having wrecked the chances for a settlement between himself and Bishop Muzorewa by embarking upon the détente negotiations. If the purpose of the onslaught, which was totally without foundation, had been to bolster the morale of the white Rhodesians, its effect was both short-lived and counter-productive. The following week Mr Smith was in South Africa assuring Mr Vorster that he had been a 'willing party' to his laudable efforts to achieve peace in southern Africa.[42] And as evidence of his willingness to continue to be one, after his return to Salisbury he embarked upon the preliminary talks with Mr Nkomo, without preconditions, that were to culminate in the signing of the Declaration of Intent on 1 December 1975.

When the first formal session of negotiations opened on 15 December, Mr Nkomo was leading the ANC delegation, although only his own wing was represented, and among his 22-member team was his former legal adviser, Mr Leo Baron (now Zambia's deputy Chief Justice), who had been detained by the Rhodesian authorities for his activities on behalf of the African nationalists. In negotiating again with a European minority regime, Mr Nkomo was once more obliged to consider what he had recognised, belatedly, in 1961, namely, that 'no sane leader could disregard the voice of his people and his supporters'.[43] This time, however, he had to satisfy not only the African population in Rhodesia, and the external wing of the ANC, which had condemned the negotiations in advance, but also the African Presidents, who would accept majority rule as the only basis for a settlement.

But even a transitional stage leading to majority rule, which was what the ANC delegation envisaged when they went into the talks, had yet to be accepted by the Smith regime, which continued to maintain that they would never be a party to any agreement that did not retain government in 'civilised and responsible hands for all time'.[44] As Dr Ahrn Palley had predicted at the beginning of that year, it was inconceivable that a constitutional conference would lead to majority rule, so long as the Rhodesian Front refused to accept that principle and the British remained unwilling to intervene to enforce it. The breakdown was, in fact, inevitable, and when it occurred, on 19 March 1976, Mr Nkomo was obliged to admit that they had come to the end of the road: any further talks with Mr Smith would be irrelevant. After months of evasiveness and prevarication by the regime, it had become clear to him, as it had much earlier to Mr Wilson, that he and Mr Smith were living in different worlds and, indeed, speaking different languages.[45] Although Mr Smith confirmed Mr Nkomo's conclusions, with a statement to the Press that he did not believe in black majority rule, 'not in a thousand years', he did not abandon the possibility of further negotiations. While blaming the British Government for having 'bedevilled the local scene' by advising the ANC on what they should or should not accept, he nevertheless appealed to them to exercise the responsibility they still claimed to retain by actively assisting in a resolution of the constitutional impasse.[46]

Notes

1. General Assembly, *Official Records*, 29th Session, 2240th Meeting, 24 September 1974.
2. The Parliamentary Under Secretary, Miss Lestor, had conferred with ZAPU and ZANU representatives in Lusaka, following the meeting between the ANC and the Government in London.
3. 880 *HC Deb.*, 8 November 1974, cols. 1398-409. The sanctions Order was carried by a vote of only 124-23, the Rhodesia Lobby voting against. The Government abstained on a United Nations resolution calling for a widening of sanctions. See General Assembly resolution 3298 (XXIX), adopted 13 December 1974 by 112-0, with 18 abstentions.
4. Some of the material in this section first appeared in my article 'Rhodesia: the Challenge of Detente', *The World Today*, September 1975.
5. *Sunday Times* (Johannesburg), 27 October 1974.
6. Speech to South African Senate, *Senate Debates*, no. 9, 23 October 1974, col. 3340.
7. Speech in Nigel, 5 November 1974, *The Star* (Johannesburg), 6 November 1974. The reference was also interpreted as changes in South Africa's internal situation.
8. *Rhodesia Herald*, 2 November 1974.
9. Ibid., 29 October 1974.
10. Interview in *Sunday Mail* (Salisbury), 1 December 1974.
11. Foreign Office Press statement, 5 December 1974.
12. The regime was represented by the Secretary to the 'Cabinet', Mr J. Gaylard, and the 'Attorney-General', Mr E.A.T. Smith. The main African nationalist leaders attending were Bishop Muzorewa, Mr Nkomo, Rev. Sithole, Mr Robert Mugabe and Mr James Chikerema.
13. *Rhodesia Herald*, 8 December 1974.
14. *The Star* (Johannesburg), 9 December 1974.
15. *Rhodesia Herald*, 13 December 1974.
16. *The Times*, 18 December 1974.
17. See my article 'Resolving the Rhodesian Conflict', *Ufahamu*, vol. 5, no. 3, June 1975.
18. 884 *HC Deb.*, 14 January 1975, cols. 189-200.
19. *The Times*, 1 January 1975.
20. Press conference, *Rand Daily Mail*, 6 January 1975.
21. *The Nationalist* (Tanzania), 9 January 1975. President Nyerere told the

OAU Liberation Committee on 8 January that if the proposed constitutional conference failed, the guerrilla war would be intensified.

22. *Daily News* (Tanzania), 11 April 1975.

23. The withdrawal was announced on 10 March, following the arrest of Rev. Sithole on 4 March. Although the Zambian Foreign Minster had told the OAU meeting that a complete withdrawal would take place at the end of May, Vorster refused to confirm the report, in *House of Assembly Debates*, 21 April 1975, col. 4502.

24. The release was announced in a televised broadcast by Mr Smith on 4 April, the day after a visit from the South African Foreign Minister and two days after the special court had upheld the detention.

25. *Commonwealth Prime Ministers' Meeting, Final Communiqué*, Kingston, 6 May 1975, *The Times*, 7 May 1975.

26. 892 *HC Deb.*, 13 May 1975, cols. 244-6.

27. A visit of the Minister of State took place on 29 June, but no progress was indicated.

28. Mr Edward Sutton-Pryce in the 'Prime Minister's' Office, *Daily Telegraph*, 5 May 1975.

29. Press conference in Salisbury, 21 May 1975, *Rhodesia Herald*, 22 May 1975.

30. Interview on BBC television (Panorama), 12 May 1975.

31. Speech at Inyanga, 26 May 1975, *Rhodesia Herald*, 27 May 1975.

32. Even within the ZANU ranks in Lusaka divisions over this issue, as well as tribal and leadership rivalry, had resulted in widespread violence and killings, in the course of which the ZANU leader, Mr Herbert Chitepo, had been murdered.

33. In an interview with British television on 26 June 1975.

34. An official announcement of the details was made in Salisbury on 12 August. A statement from the Foreign and Commonwealth Office, welcoming the agreement, claimed that the British Government had been trying to promote such discussions and had been in close touch with the authorities concerned. (*The Times*, 13 August 1975.)

35. *Rhodesia, Parliamentary Debates*, vol. 91, 13 August 1975, col. 478.

36. *The Times of Zambia*, 28 August 1975, claimed that agreement had been reached on all the points on the agenda, including 'a declaration of intent' to negotiate a settlement, before the breakdown over the ANC demand for immunity for its members.

37. *Rhodesia Herald*, 29 September 1975. Bishop Muzorewa had expelled Mr Nkomo on 11 September, for allegedly causing the split by attempting to seize the leadership and negotiate with Mr Smith, after Mr Nkomo had denounced the formation of the Zimbabwe Liberation Council.

38. The African Presidents, in Lusaka from 13-15 September, had urged the ANC 'to resolve urgently the problems of unity to facilitate the liberation of their country'. (*The Times*, 16 September 1975.)

39. *Observer*, 23 November 1975.

40. *The Times of Zambia*, 21 September 1975, interpreted the statement as a recognition of the possibility of a black Prime Minister.

41. *Rhodesia Herald*, 26 September 1975.

42. Ibid., 21 October 1975. South African Press criticism of Mr Smith's attack came from both the English and Afrikaner newspapers.

43. Press statement, 17 February 1961, on rejection of 1961 Constitution.

44. Mr Smith's New Year broadcast.

45. *The Times*, 20 March 1976.

46. *Rhodesia Herald*, 22 March 1976.

REDRESSING THE BALANCE

'Our determination to bring democratic majority rule to Rhodesia has at times been seen to be at best equivocal.'

David Owen, 9 October 1977.

The British Government's role, as the various stages of the negotiations proceeded, had been that of an interested, but detached, party.[1] Although committed by pledges to the African States, the Commonwealth and the United Nations to convene a constitutional conference, they had not done so because the conditions which they regarded as essential for a settlement, namely, agreement among the Rhodesians themselves, had not yet been established.[2] While there was certainly no evidence, at the conclusion of the ANC's abortive negotiations with the Smith regime in March 1976, that those conditions existed, they nevertheless responded to Mr Smith's appeal to assist in resolving the conflict. But the solution which they proposed — a transition to African majority rule over a period of eighteen months to two years and the negotiation of an independence constitution implementing majority rule — was basically what the ANC had advocated and the Smith regime rejected during the preceding three months of negotiations. In announcing the offer in Parliament on 22 March, Mr Callaghan showed an awareness of this dilemma by conceding that the British Government were in no position to impose such a solution. Instead, they were aiming to fulfil their legal and moral responsibility by putting forward proposals for others to consider, those who had more power in the area than they did. If those proposals were taken up by the parties concerned, then they would be willing to contribute financial and other assistance to ensure a background in which both racial communities could live and work together in an independent Zimbabwe. In a settlement achieved along those lines, they were confident that agreement would follow on a cessation of guerrilla activities and the lifting of sanctions.[3]

The timing of the British Government's proposals was directly related to the diplomatic exchanges which had been proceeding among the Americans, the Zambians and the South Africans in the aftermath of the Angolan civil war[4] and also to the developments which had been taking place in southern Africa itself. The front-line African States had already begun to prepare for an intensification of the armed struggle, since it had become evident long before the actual breakdown of the negotiations that they were not likely to yield any results acceptable to the Africans. One of those States, Mozambique, had taken the decision, on 3 March 1976, to close its borders to all traffic with Rhodesia, thus cutting off that country's access to the Indian Ocean ports of Beira and Maputo. Although the Rhodesians had begun to divert their traffic to South African ports after the FRELIMO take-over, an estimated 25-30 per cent of their trade was still dependent on the routes through Mozambique, and the capacity of the South African ports to handle the additional amount was in doubt. In compensation for Mozambique's economic loss, resulting from the full implementation of sanctions, financial assistance would be forthcoming from a United Nations fund set up for that purpose. Britain was already pledged, by the decision of the Commonwealth Prime Ministers' conference of the previous year, to make a substantial contribution to that fund. Although Mozambique had not declared a state of war, the border closure was decided, after a meeting of the front-line Presidents, in retaliation for raids by Rhodesian forces in 'hot pursuit' of guerrillas operating from bases in Mozambique. An intensification of the war from those bases could therefore be expected, particularly after the formation in Mozambique of a unified high command of the Zimbabwe People's Army (ZIPA) to lead the offensive.[5]

Another factor influencing the British Government's proposals for a settlement was the continuing presence of Cuban forces in Angola, and the possibility of their being deployed for a similar purpose in Rhodesia. In the same week that Mr Callaghan had announced the terms for majority rule, he and Mr Wilson had summoned the Soviet ambassador in London to express Britain's concern about the danger of a war in southern Africa arising from the presence of foreign troops in that area, a warning repeated to the Foreign Minister, Mr Gromyko, when he arrived for an official visit the following week. Although there was no evidence of foreign soldiers engaged in the Rhodesian conflict (except for the mercenaries recruited by the Smith regime), the main source of arms and training for the guerrillas remained the Soviet Union, Cuba and, to a lesser extent, China. This had been the case for over a decade, since no military assistance was available from the West. However, the large-scale intrusion of foreign troops in the Angolan civil war had set a precedent, and one which could be repeated to turn the tide in Rhodesia.

American Intervention

A revival of the diplomatic efforts initiated by Zambia and South Africa in 1974, but abandoned after the abortive Victoria Falls conference and the South African invasion of Angola, was the immediate outcome of the threat of an Angolan solution in Rhodesia.[6] This time, however, the leading participant in the exercise was the United States, which had previously stood aside from the Rhodesian conflict (other than to import chrome from the rebel regime) but had been brought in, after backing the losing side in Angola, by the prospect of increasing Soviet influence in the area of southern Africa. The main object of the diplomatic offensive, the Rhodesians, now faced the possibility of an invasion from foreign forces which they could not contain without outside assistance. Although South Africa remained their only source of support since the closure of the border with Mozambique, it was not likely that that country would risk another military confrontation with the Cubans after the disastrous intervention in Angola and the ensuing set-back to its policy of détente with black Africa. In these conditions of virtual isolation, the only choice for the regime was to concede to the growing international demand for African majority rule or face the consequences of an unwinnable war. Although these alternatives had been clearly set out in the British proposals, they had been rejected by Mr Smith as 'no less extreme than those of the ANC'.[7] However, while the British might make use of the threat of a Cuban invasion to bring about a Rhodesian surrender to the inevitability of black rule,[8] the Smith regime remained convinced that if that threat became a reality, the Western Powers would intervene to defend them against 'communism'.[9]

Any remaining illusions that the regime might have retained about Western intentions regarding their survival ought to have been dispelled by the unqualified commitment to African majority rule announced by the American Secretary of State, Dr Kissinger, in Lusaka on 27 April 1976. While pledging support for the British initiative, he also took the opportunity to warn all outside Powers against interfering in Africa's internal affairs. How the American Government intended to implement their new policy over the objections of the rebel regime was not revealed, but a firm endorsement of the Lusaka Manifesto of 1969 on the liberation of southern Africa and a pledge to consult closely with the front-line Presidents were indications that they were committed to obtaining a settlement that would preclude the possibility of outside military intervention. While Dr Kissinger offered the Europeans an assurance of financial assistance and the protection of minority rights in an independent Zimbabwe, he also made it clear that the regime could not expect any American support, either in diplomacy or in material help, at any stage in their conflict with African States or African liberation movements. On the contrary, they would face America's unrelenting opposition until a negotiated settlement was achieved. In the meantime, his Administration intended to support the UN Security Council resolution to compensate Mozambique, by providing $12.5 million of assistance, and to urge the US Congress to repeal the Byrd Amendment allowing the import of Rhodesian chrome.[10]

With Dr Kissinger's own intervention in the dispute, 'shuttle diplomacy' rapidly replaced the more conventional methods of the previous détente exercise. Having first consulted the black African States, particularly Zambia and Tanzania, the way was cleared for talks with the other main party concerned, South Africa, which were held first in Bavaria on 23 June and then in Zurich on 4 September, both against a background of violent racial clashes in Mr Vorster's own country. Again, as in the case of the earlier détente effort, South Africa was the main source of influence with the Smith regime, since it remained their vital life-line with the world outside. What South Africa could look for in exchange for its co-operation towards a settlement were an American commitment of defence against Soviet expansion in the area, the prestige attached to association with the Western Powers and a respite from United Nations pressure for the extension of sanctions to South Africa itself, particularly if concessions were not forthcoming on the independence of Namibia and reforms of the apartheid system prevailing within the country.

Although the Kissinger-Vorster talks were conducted in secrecy, South African acceptance of majority rule as the basis for Rhodesian independence had been announced by the Foreign Minister, Dr Muller, prior to the Zurich meeting.[11] What was less certain, however, was whether Mr Vorster would be prepared to exert sufficient pressure on Mr Smith to bring him around to accept majority rule. Thus far, he had taken the diplomatically correct line that South Africa did not engage in boycotts of other countries nor intervene in their internal affairs. As he put it, they could point out alternatives, they could point out realities, they could advise; but that was as far as they had gone in the past and that was as far as they were prepared to go in the future.[12] Whatever he may have told Dr Kissinger at the Zurich talks regarding his influence with Mr Smith, it was sufficiently encouraging for the American Secretary of State to return to Africa the following week to continue the series of meetings he had begun the previous April. Before setting out, however, he first conferred with Mr Callaghan, now Prime Minister, and the new Foreign Secretary, Mr Anthony Crosland; and his deputy in the State Department, Mr William Schaufele, consulted the African Presidents, who had been meeting in Dar es Salaam, on the prospects for a round of shuttle diplomacy.

The Kissinger peace mission to southern Africa began, on his own initiative, on 14 September 1976, with a meeting in Tanzania with President Nyerere. It ended some ten days later with the announcement of agreement by Mr Smith, who had been brought into the talks in Pretoria between Dr Kissinger and Mr Vorster. Although the Rhodesian leader's consent to a two-year transition to majority rule, after he had declared repeatedly that it would never come in his life-time,[13] appeared to be a breakthrough towards a settlement, Mr Smith had specified, in his broadcast speech of acceptance, that he agreed to majority rule provided that it was 'responsible' rule. As he later clarified this position, at a press conference in Salisbury on 5 November, he did not 'find anything about majority rule in the five principles' of the Kissinger package. 'Responsible' rule, according to his definition, meant rule by a majority of the whites (whom he claimed were 'Africans') together with the 'moderate' Africans who were prepared to go along with them.[14]

In addition to the uncertainty regarding Mr Smith's acceptance of majority rule, it was revealed, by the US Under Secretary of State, Mr William Rogers, that the proposals Dr Kissinger offered Mr Smith had not been specifically cleared with the African Presidents whom he first consulted in the round of shuttle diplomacy.[15] It was their understanding, and this was confirmed by President Nyerere at a press conference on 21 September, that he would put to Mr Smith the conditions laid down by Mr Callaghan the previous March.[16] But Dr Kissinger was obviously aware of the fate of the original British plan when he offered a variation that would be acceptable to Mr Smith. Although the proposals were subsequently regarded as 'Anglo-American', there was no indication of what contribution, if any, Britain had made to their revision. Mr Smith had certainly made it clear, two days before he met Dr Kissinger, that if the Americans were not prepared to go outside the British offer there would be no chance for a settlement. And Dr Kissinger, by agreeing to meet Mr Smith in these circumstances, had abandoned his initial stand that he would not talk to the Rhodesian leader unless the British terms were accepted in advance.[17] By the time they met in Pretoria on 19 September, an official American spokesman had announced that the USA might ask the British to alter their plan; and a correspondent in South Africa had reported that Dr Kissinger was confident that the British Prime Minister would agree to 'a softer line on the Rhodesian issue'.[18] At the conclusion of the talks, Dr Kissinger claimed that, while Mr Smith had accepted certain proposals made by himself, they had been made with the agreement of the American and British Governments.

What those proposals contained, however, was not revealed by either Dr Kissinger or the British Government. Instead, it was left to Mr Smith to announce to the world the agreement he had accepted. As his party chairman, Mr Desmond Frost, put it, he 'clarified certain garbled versions of Dr Kissinger's package'.[19] From this clarification, it was evident that the most significant addition to the original British offer was the provision of a framework for the transition government leading to majority rule. That government, according to Mr Smith's interpretation, would be dominated by the white minority, which would hold the key posts of chairman of the 'supreme' Council of State and the ministries of defence and law and order. Although the Council of Ministers (appointed by the Council of State) would have an African majority and an African 'First Minister', its decisions would be taken by a two-thirds majority, which would enable the white membership to obstruct the transition to black rule. In effect, the whites would have a double veto, since the Council of State, which was entrusted with the vital task of directing the procedure for establishing an independence constitution, would operate on the same basis.[20]

Not unexpectedly, the terms of the agreement, as set out by Mr Smith on 24 September, were denounced by the African Presidents, in a joint statement in Lusaka two days later, as 'tantamount to legalising the colonialist and racial structures of power'. In their view, and also that of the African nationalists, any details relating to the functions and powers of the transition government should be decided by a conference of 'the authentic and legitimate representatives of the people of Zimbabwe'. Although the Africans had rejected these conditions, there was no finality in a statement which also called upon the British Government to convene a conference which would establish a transition government reflecting majority rule and prepare for a full constitutional conference to work out the independence constitution.[21] So far as they were concerned, Mr Smith was still committed to the principle of majority rule in two years, whatever his interpretation of the means of achieving it, and they intended to hold him to a pledge underwritten by his South African protectors as well as by Britain and the USA.

The British Government, which had remained understandably sceptical about a settlement emerging from the shuttle diplomacy concerning their colony, were now faced with the dilemma of either responding to the African appeal to convene a conference or allowing what progress had been recorded on the principle of majority rule to go by default. To intervene at this stage, however, was not a policy they would have initiated. Their position all along had been that a conference should be convened only after a firm agreement on majority rule had been reached; and they had ample grounds for suspecting that it had not. In view of Mr Smith's negotiating record, it was possible that he had agreed this time because he was convinced that the Africans would never consent to a scheme that permitted the white minority to control the transition government leading to majority rule. By accepting the plan, however, he could use their rejection as an excuse for abandoning his commitment to implement majority rule. Thus, with Mr Smith maintaining that the Kissinger package was 'non-negotiable'[22] and the Africans insisting on altering it, negotiations on the basis of those proposals were not likely to yield an agreement.

Britain's reluctance to become involved in a dispute which it had neither brought about nor had the power to affect was evident from the compromise solution it sought. While a conference was convened, in Geneva on 28 October 1976, it was presided over not by the responsible Cabinet Minister, Mr Crosland, but by the permanent representative at the United Nations, Mr Ivor Richard. Although Mr Richard (a former MP) was elevated to Cabinet rank to convey the importance Britain attached to the occasion, his function at the conference was limited to that of a moderator between the competing delegations. In that role, however, he was left with virtually nothing to negotiate about, since the Smith delegation would not even consider either sacrificing their control of the transition government which the Kissinger plan gave them or permitting a British presence in Rhodesia during the transition. In addition, Mr Richard was confronted with the claims of four rival African delegations, which were led, respectively, by Bishop Muzorewa, Rev. Sithole, Mr Nkomo and Mr Mugabe, the latter two having combined their forces in a Patriotic Front representing most of the former ZAPU and ZANU members and their guerrilla supporters, and with the backing of the front-line Presidents. While there were no significant policy differences among the rival African delegations, with all committed to independence within a year, a transition government reflecting majority rule and a British presence to ensure that it would be achieved, they remained divided by their rivalry for the leadership of an independent Zimbabwe. However, since elections to determine their respective support among the African population (the Muzorewa proposal) were a non-starter in a police State, the claims of the rival contenders remained unresolved.

In these circumstances, the British Government's position that the Rhodesian conflict could only be settled by the Rhodesians themselves left little hope for a peaceful solution.[23] At the end of seven weeks of fruitless negotiations, the only point on which all parties concurred was that no agreement had been possible. Although a declaration of intent to continue the talks was accepted, it was unlikely that there would be a second round in view of the results of the first. After the recess, however, the shuttle diplomacy would be resumed, this time with Mr Richard following in the path of his predecessor, Dr Kissinger.

When the Richard mission began at the end of 1976, its purpose was envisaged as assuring the Africans that majority rule would be achieved without obstruction and the Europeans that the process would be peaceful and orderly. However, since the Smith regime's acceptance of majority rule had yet to be established, there was no basis for negotiations towards that objective. The British initiative was therefore subject to the same limitations as their proposals of the previous March. Unless the regime agreed to a British presence in Rhodesia during the transition period, and Mr Smith confirmed their rejection in his broadcast of 24 January 1977, the British Government were in no position to impose such a solution. Again, they had put forward proposals for others to consider, those who had more power in the area than they did. However, the main source of that power, South Africa, having also rejected any deviation from the Kissinger package, was unlikely to exert its influence for the purpose of altering it. Nor would the front-line Presidents call a halt to the guerrilla war, which South Africa was also demanding as a condition for supporting majority rule, unless they were satisfied that a British presence in the colony would, in fact, ensure black rule. Since that presence would have amounted to only a resident commissioner (and deputy), who would have presided over a council entrusted with security matters, the result of such a limited commitment would be unpredictable. In any case, the British scheme, because it reflected the reality of African majority rule in the transition government,[24] would remain unacceptable to the Smith regime so long as they had the assurance of South African support in rejecting it.

Anglo-American Initiatives

Although the British Government were not prepared to impose a solution unacceptable to the white minority regimes of southern Africa, they were equally unable to allow their diplomatic efforts to go by default solely on the basis of Mr Smith's rejection. The lesson to be derived from yet another failure to get a settlement was that any further attempt would require the support of the international community, and in particular of the USA, to supplement Britain's limited power. In spite of the fact that the latest effort had been initiated by the US Secretary of State, the extent of American backing for the British proposals remained uncertain while the new Carter Administration was preparing to take office. But one indication of continuing American concern was the immediate decision to send their representative at the United Nations, Mr Andrew Young, on a diplomatic mission to meet with the African Presidents in Tanzania. In addition, the new Secretary of State, Mr Cyrus Vance, opened his first press conference in Washington with a warning to the Rhodesian regime that under no circumstances could they count on any form of American assistance in their efforts to prevent majority rule or to impose an internal settlement excluding leaders of the black nationalist movements. So far as the Carter Administration were concerned, the British proposals remained 'a valid basis for negotiation' and they intended to support the British Government in implementing them.[25] However, what the Americans intended to do about the Rhodesian rejection of those proposals was not revealed. Since Mr Smith was proceeding with his plan for an internal settlement with 'moderate' Africans and predicting that 'in ten years' time things would be very much the same',[26] the prospects for a negotiated settlement were not encouraging.

Not deterred by the Rhodesian threat to introduce their own version of 'responsible' rule, with some minor modifications of racially discriminatory legislation such as the Land Tenure Act,[27] a new joint Anglo-American effort was devised to get the contending parties back into negotiations. The leading participants this time were the new Foreign Secretary, Dr David Owen, former Minister of State who had replaced the late Mr Crosland, and Mr Andrew Young. Although Dr Owen undertook a brief 'fact-finding' tour of southern Africa in April, which included meetings with the front-line Presidents (who had just been visited by the Cuban and Soviet Presidents) and also with the South African Prime Minister and Mr Smith, negotiations were subsequently continued at the official level, by a 'consultative group' led by Mr John Graham, a deputy under secretary at the Foreign and Commonwealth Office, and including the US ambassador to Zambia, Mr Steven Low. While these preliminary soundings proceeded in Lusaka, Salisbury,

Dar es Salaam and Maputo, Dr Owen resumed his consultations with Mr Vance and Mr Young on the provisions to be included in a constitutional settlement.

There was no indication of any progress in the Anglo-American initiative to achieve majority rule by negotiation when the Commonwealth Prime Ministers assembled in London in June 1977. On the contrary, Mr Smith had once more reverted to his contention that he had never accepted African majority rule[28] and his regime's counter-insurgency campaign had been stepped up to include frequent raids on the front-line States of Zambia,[29] Botswana[30] and Mozambique.[31] Under these circumstances, the African States represented at the conference were understandably sceptical about the prospects of yet another British diplomatic initiative, even one that carried the support of the USA. Although there was a general consensus on the objective of an independent Zimbabwe by 1978, delegates were, as Mr Callaghan admitted, resigned to war as 'the only way in which Mr Smith and the white population can be brought to the point where majority rule is secured'.[32] Nevertheless, the renewed attempt to reach a settlement was not ruled out as a complement to that struggle, provided that it entailed 'not only the removal of the Smith regime but also the dismantling of its apparatus of repression, in order to pave the way for the creation of police and armed forces which would be responsive to the needs of the people of Zimbabwe and ensure the orderly and effective transfer of power'.[33] Thus the war would continue, as the British Prime Minister had been obliged to recognise (while condemning the supply of Soviet arms with which to conduct it), but a negotiated settlement would also be pursued as a means of achieving independence on the basis of majority rule.

Having obtained Commonwealth support, although a qualified one, for pursuing the peace initiative, the British Government's intention was that Dr Owen would return to southern Africa for consultations on the terms of the constitutional settlement. However, the report which Mr Graham's consultative group brought back to London on 11 July indicated that Mr Smith was 'disappointed and dissatisfied' with the proposals, which he claimed were 'completely outside the parameters which had been agreed with Dr Owen at the commencement of the settlement initiative'.[34] Nor had the Graham group fared all that much better in Lusaka, where they met with the leaders of the Patriotic Front, immediately after Mr Nkomo and Mr Mugabe had obtained the endorsement of their alliance by the OAU summit conference. Although agreement had been achieved on the necessity of establishing a Bill of Rights, an independent judiciary and free elections on the basis of one man, one vote, the Patriotic Front could not accept the proposal to hold a constitutional conference until Britain had first succeeded in 'removing the causes of war'.[35] As their allies in the front-line States had also insisted at the Commonwealth conference, a genuine settlement must involve agreement not only on constitutional change but also on the dismantling of the Smith regime's 'apparatus of repression'.

Any remaining hope that the negotiations might yet proceed was, however, dashed by Mr Smith's decision to hold a general election on 31 August, allegedly for the purpose of renewing his mandate for a settlement and also of convincing the British that they were not dealing with 'a weak and divided Rhodesia'.[36] Although the British response was to dismiss the election as 'largely irrelevant', as the Prime Minister put it,[37] the fact that it was taking place at that particular time and under a highly restrictive electoral system which was to be dismantled by the settlement, was both a snub to the British initiative and an indication of the Smith regime's response to the proposal for one man, one vote. Nor could there be any remaining illusion on that score after Mr Smith assured his white supporters that he had rejected the terms put to him by the consultative group because 'there was no hope of anything other than one man, one vote'.[38] It was on the basis of these assurances that Mr Smith obtained his mandate for a settlement from an overwhelming majority (some 84 per cent) of the white electorate, and in the process succeeded in destroying the rebels who had threatened the unity of his party. However, since Mr Smith differed from his rebels not in essence but only in degree, his retention of all fifty white seats carried no particular mandate, other than a personal vote of confidence, so far as obtaining a settlement was concerned. What that settlement would entail remained equally unclear, since any hopes that Mr Smith might have cherished of an internal one had been destroyed by the unqualified rejection by the nationalist leaders within Rhodesia, Bishop Muzorewa and Rev. Sithole (who had returned on 10 July with the regime's permission), of any plan that was not based on the principle of one man, one vote. Whether any 'moderate' Africans could have been recruited for such a scheme was not established, however, because Mr Smith's electoral promise of 'the establishment of a broad-based government including black Rhodesians, to promote a climate of trust and confidence', was quietly buried in the euphoria of the electoral landslide.[39]

While the Rhodesians were engaged in electioneering, with the Rhodesian Front candidates vying with their former colleagues, now in the

Rhodesian Action party, to convince the electorate that only they could ensure the preservation of government in 'civilised' hands, the details of the settlement plan were being worked out by Dr Owen and Mr Vance.[40] Support for the plan was also being sought from the front-line States, whose chairman, President Nyerere, was consulted on the subject by President Carter during his official visit to the USA on 4 August, and also by Dr Owen when the Tanzanian leader stopped over in London on his return. Although the contents of the package remained secret, it was evident that the stumbling block would remain the means by which majority rule would be implemented. Since the previous efforts, first by Dr Kissinger and then by Mr Richard, had broken down over the issue of control of the transition government and, in particular, the security apparatus, any new scheme would require the presence of an external force to ensure that the goal of majority rule would be achieved peacefully, democratically and without obstruction. Although the proposals put by Mr Richard included a token British presence, which had been unacceptable to the Rhodesian Front, no provision had been made for dismantling the security forces of the white regime, which the African nationalists and also the front-line President were now demanding as part of any constitutional settlement. What would replace those forces, however, had yet to be agreed. The possibility of a Commonwealth peace-keeping force, frequently considered at the Prime Ministers' meetings, was no longer in favour by any of the members who might be called upon to participate; and in the view of the African Presidents the forces of the Patriotic Front should assume the responsibility for policing the transition to an independent Zimbabwe. Since the Smith regime and also their South African allies had ruled out any participation by the guerrilla forces, such an arrangement would be unacceptable to them, as it would be to the rival nationalist factions led by Bishop Muzorewa and Rev. Sithole, which had no forces of their own in the field.

Although the final details of the settlement were approved by Dr Owen and Mr Vance in London on 13 August, following their consultations with the South African Foreign Minister, Mr R. F. Botha, the plan was not published until 1 September, the day after the Rhodesian general election. Whether the delay was designed for the purpose of avoiding an outright rejection by Mr Smith, since he could scarcely be expected to accept a plan for his abdication while he was appealing for another term in office, was not revealed. In any case, the leaks which had emanated from the American delegation to the UN conference on apartheid in Lagos, particularly regarding the future of the regime's security forces, had obliged Mr Smith to reject the plan before it had been officially proposed.[41] An additional factor accounting for the delay was the insistence of President Nyerere, on behalf of the front-line States, on a clarification of the terms for dismantling the security forces so that they would accord with the Commonwealth communiqué. According to his version, after obtaining President Carter's commitment to this view, he had found 'some confusion' in London when he returned to consult with Dr Owen.[42] However, he claimed that he had subsequently obtained the assurance that both Britain and the USA agreed to the removal of the Rhodesian armed forces before independence and that the new army of an independent Zimbabwe would be built up from ZIPA.[43] Although no confirmation of his claim was made in either London or Washington, the fact that he had made it was sufficient to arouse the opposition of Mr Smith, as well as Rev. Sithole,[44] and also the Conservative party leader in Britain, Mrs Margaret Thatcher.[45]

If the clarification of terms by President Nyerere contributed to a favourable reception from the front-line States when Dr Owen and Mr Young brought their proposals to Lusaka on 27 August, it had the opposite effect on the South Africans, with whom the Anglo-American team met in Pretoria two days later. The response was not entirely unexpected, since Mr Smith had already expressed confidence, after meeting with Mr Vorster on the 27th, that the South African Government would support him in whatever decision he made regarding the settlement proposals. An additional factor contributing to the coolness of the South African response was the growing hostility of the white regime to the Carter Administration, and to Mr Young in particular, for the strong line they had taken in condemning apartheid as a violation of human rights, a hostility which Mr Vorster had directed against President Carter earlier that month for 'promoting chaos and anarchy' in southern Africa as a 'repayment' to American blacks who had contributed to his electoral victory.[46] There was also the allegation, from 'diplomatic sources' quoted in the South African Press, that Mr Vorster's hard-line attitude' after his meeting with Dr Owen and Mr Young was largely the result of what he regarded as 'a fatal breach of trust by the British and the Americans'. Although Mr Botha refused to disclose why he had initially supported the plan, at least as 'deserving serious consideration',[47] when he met with Dr Owen and Mr Vance in London, it was alleged that the plan shown to the South African Foreign Minister did not include provisions for 'the terrorist take-over of the Rhodesian security forces', but that these provisions were later inserted as a result of President Nyerere's 'persuasion' of

President Carter.[48] However, it was inconceivable that Mr Vorster could have remained unaware of such provisions until he received them from the Owen-Young team, and Dr Owen had already conceded after the talks with Mr Botha that the South Africans 'will want to see the final Anglo-American proposals before they form a judgement'.[49]

Although the South Africans showed remarkably little enthusiasm for the settlement plan, and even less for exerting pressure on the Rhodesians to accept it, they did not reject it outright as a basis for discussion. Nor did Mr Smith, when it was presented to him by Dr Owen and Mr Young (and published as a White Paper) on 1 September.[50] However, at a Press conference the following day, he characterised some of the key provisions, such as the formation of a new Zimbabwe national army based on the guerrilla forces and the presence of a United Nations peace-keeping force during the transition period, as 'crazy' and 'insane'. He could not conceive of destroying his 'wonderful' security forces — 'probably some of the best that this world has ever seen for the kind of task that they have to do'[51] — although he was prepared to consider some other 'reputable' forces coming into Rhodesia, as he put it, 'to assist in containing the situation against terrorism'. Nor could he accept the provision on which the whole plan was based, namely, that he should surrender power to a British resident commissioner (Field Marshal Lord Carver), whose functions would be to administer the country during the transition, conduct the elections leading to independence and take command of all armed forces in Rhodesia, apart from the UN force. Again, it seemed to him a crazy suggestion that a government should be asked to dissolve themselves without even knowing what their replacement was going to be. But he was in no doubt that if they accepted the proposals a British resident commissioner installed in Rhodesia would be a 'complete dictator', under the instructions of the British Government. Nevertheless, since Mr Smith was not 'rejecting anything out of hand', he would form a special subcommittee to consider the details. They had had 'crazy proposals' before, he concluded, and had always managed 'to shrug them off and go on'.[52]

In spite of Mr Smith's rejection of the essential features of the plan, there was no indication that the Anglo-American initiative would be abandoned, as it had been the previous January, solely on the basis of Mr Smith's objections. On the contrary, Dr Owen went ahead with plans to approach the United Nations, and Mr Young confirmed America's commitment to seeing the process through to the end. The time schedule was not being made by Mr Smith, he warned, and no one, least of all Mr Smith, should be under any impression that US pressure would cease if the proposals were rejected.[53] The decision to move ahead with the plan was given some encouragement by the agreement of the front-line Presidents, at a meeting in Maputo on 23 September, that the proposals formed 'a sufficient basis for further negotiations between the parties concerned'. Although the chairman, President Nyerere, noted that the plan still had 'many negative elements' and left 'many questions unanswered', there was general agreement that a breakthrough had been made in that, for the first time, Britain proposed the removal of Mr Smith, the integration of the guerrillas into a Zimbabwe army and the introduction of a United Nations peace-keeping force.[54] However, the security forces were not to be totally disbanded, as the Presidents and also the Patriotic Front had urged, since the Rhodesian police and certain elements of the army would be placed under the command of the resident commissioner during the transition period. While the Patriotic Front continued to advocate that their own forces should be in control after the removal of the rebel regime,[55] with the endorsement of the plan by the front-line Presidents they were obliged not to press their claims when the co-operation of the United Nations was being sought.

The British Government's approach to the United Nations was indeed a new departure, as the Presidents had noted, since all previous Governments had maintained that Rhodesia was the sole responsibility of the United Kingdom. Although the UN had been resorted to for the imposition of sanctions, every attempt by other member-States to go beyond that limited programme had been blocked by British delegations, frequently by the use of the veto in the Security Council. That there was still considerable opposition within Britain to further UN involvement was evident from the Conservative party conference decision 'deprecating' the Labour Government's encouragement of interference in Rhodesia by outside Powers and maintaining that a lasting solution could be found only 'in an agreement reached between Rhodesians of all races'[56] – in effect, Mr Smith's internal solution. Nevertheless, the Government were convinced that their initiative at the UN would for the first time evoke the co-operation rather than the hostility of those States which, over the years since the UDI, had been critical of Britain's abdication of its responsibilities as the administering Power. Although there was always the possibility of a Soviet veto at any stage of the negotiations,[57] the support of the front-line States, and also of the Patriotic Front leader, Mr Nkomo, who participated in the Security Council debate on 28 September, ensured endorsement of the initial step, namely, the appointment of a UN representative (General Prem Chand of India) to enter into discussions with all parties in Rhodesia concerning the military and 'associated arrangements' necessary to achieve the transition to majority rule.[58] Although Dr Owen, in introducing the resolution, had given the assurance that a favourable vote would not commit any member-State to the plan, since further UN approval would be sought for the establishment of the peacekeeping force and also for the plan as a whole, he was already anticipating the opposition that would arise in the future should their peaceful efforts to obtain majority rule be blocked by the white minority regimes of southern Africa. As he had warned, in an address to the General Assembly the previous day, if the negotiations produced a settlement which the Security Council could endorse, 'the world would not allow South Africa to continue in the face of such a settlement to sustain an obdurate, illegal regime in Rhodesia were it to refuse to give up power'.[59]

In spite of Dr Owen's warning, there was singularly little encouragement to be derived from the Rhodesian response to the efforts of Field Marshal Lord Carver and General Prem Chand to negotiate the transitional arrangements. Although Mr Smith had been urging Lord Carver to come to Rhodesia since the previous September, he made no effort to see him until the fifth and final day of his visit (allegedly because he was watching a cricket match in Bulawayo) and after the meeting he confirmed that there had been no agreement on either the implementation of the cease-fire or the disposition of the security forces.[60] Nor did the British diplomatic team led by Mr Graham fare any better from their talks with Rhodesian officials, which continued after the departure of the Carver mission. In addition to the objections contained in the 5,000-word memorandum prepared by Mr Smith's sub-committee, Rhodesian officials were also insisting that the independence constitution had to be agreed before the details of the transitional arrangements could be considered. A further setback to the Anglo-American initiative was Mr Smith's agreement on 24 November with the ANC factions led by Bishop Muzorewa and Rev. Sithole to negotiate an internal settlement, allegedly based on majority rule and universal suffrage but qualified by provision for the retention of 'white confidence' and 'standards'.[61]

While Dr Owen, and also Mr Young, maintained that the Anglo-American proposals were still 'on course' and 'very much alive', the momentum of their diplomatic efforts could not be sustained with some of the Rhodesian parties otherwise engaged. Although prospects for an internal settlement, in view of previous abortive attempts, appeared remote, the fact that the black participants were willing to allow the whites far more power than the Anglo-American terms allotted them was a considerable incentive for compromise on the part of the whites. But whatever the outcome of those negotiations, the exclusion of the Patriotic Front limited the possibility of an agreement that would obtain international acceptance. So far as the front-line States were concerned, the transfer of power in Rhodesia remained a British responsibility; and if they did not pursue the initiative, President Kaunda warned, 'even this one will go into the limbo where all other initiatives have gone'.[62] Their ability to do so, however, would be determined by the support which others, and in particular the USA, were prepared to contribute to ensure a solution to the Rhodesian conflict. As Dr Owen conceded, 'on her own Britain cannot bring peace to Rhodesia'.[63]

Notes

1. The Government had welcomed the agreement on the Declaration of Intent signed on 1 December 1975, wishing Mr Nkomo well in his efforts to negotiate a settlement but stressing that Britain took no side in the ANC split. (*The Times*, 2 December 1975.)

2. According to Mr Callaghan's statement during the debate on the renewal of the sanctions Order. The vote was only 83-13, with the Conservatives abstaining and the Rhodesia Lobby voting against. (898 *HC Deb.*, 31 October 1975, cols. 1949-55).

3. 908 *HC Deb.*, 22 March 1976, cols. 29-44.

4. A Foreign and Commonwealth Office representative, Sir Anthony Duff, had been sent to South Africa on 8 February, and from there to brief officials in Washington. The Zambian diplomat, Mr Chona, had conferred with Mr Callaghan on his return from Washington on 13 February. Lord Greenhill had been sent to Rhodesia for talks with Mr Smith on 26 February, but no progress was recorded. See 905 *HC Deb.*, 18 February 1976, cols. 1271-4; vol. 906, 2 March 1976, cols. 1097-102.

5. *Observer*, 15 February 1976. The front-line Presidents met in Kilimani, Mozambique on 7 February to plan the military strategy to follow the breakdown of the negotiations.

6. Some of the material in this section first appeared in my article 'Rhodesia: The Road from Luanda to Geneva', in *The World Today* (March 1977); and in *Europa Archiv* (10 March 1977).

7. *Rhodesia Herald*, 24 March 1976.

8. Mr Callaghan issued the warning in an address to his constituency in Cardiff on 13 February 1976.

9. Broadcast of 6 February 1976. A similar statement was made by the Defence 'Minister', Mr van der Byl. (*Rhodesia Herald*, 17 February 1976.)

10. Full text, *Department of State Bulletin*, LXXIV, 1927, 31 May 1976.

11. In an address to the National party congress in Natal on 13 August. (*The Star* (Johannesburg), 14 August 1976.) However, the preamble containing

the acceptance of majority rule was released by the South African mission at the United Nations.

12. Statement to the Press at the Zurich meeting. (*The Times*, 6 September 1976.)

13. Mr Smith had also assured his party congress, meeting in Umtali the previous week, that the control of government would be retained in 'responsible' hands. (*Rhodesia Herald*, 17 September 1976.)

14. *The Times*, 6 November 1976.

15. *New York Times*, 28 September 1976.

16. *Daily News* (Tanzania), 21 September 1976.

17. Press conference, 17 September 1976; *Observer*, 19 September 1977.

18. Quoted by Radio Salisbury and Radio Johannesburg, 19 September 1976.

19. Statement to the Executive Committee of the Rhodesian Front, 29 September 1976.

20. *Rhodesia and the Anglo-American Proposals* (Salisbury: 'Ministry' of Information, February 1977).

21. *The Times of Zambia*, 27 September 1976.

22. *Rhodesia Herald*, 7 October 1976.

23. See Mr Crosland's address to the UN General Assembly, *Official Records*, 31st Session, Plenary Meeting, 5 October 1976.

24. The Africans would have held twenty of the thirty places in the Council of Ministers; and four of the five places in the inner cabinet or advisory council. See *Rhodesia and the Anglo-American Proposals*.

25. *New York Times*, 1 February 1977. The new Vice-President, Mr Walter Mondale, who was subsequently made responsible for African policy, conferred with British Ministers in London during his tour of Western Europe in January 1977.

26. Televised press conference, 4 February 1977.

27. The Smith regime's proposal to amend the Land Tenure Act to allow all races to purchase land in white areas, although subject to rigid restrictions, led to a split in the Rhodesian Front culminating in the resignation of twelve MPs, the party secretary and other officials. The amendment was enacted on 4 March, with the vote of six Africans to provide the necessary two-thirds majority.

28. Rhodesian 'Policy Statement', *Rhodesia Herald*, 30 March 1977.

29. President Kaunda complained that Britain, in the role of 'Mr Smith's post office box', alerted Zambia to the threat of a 'pre-emptive strike' by Rhodesian forces. (Radio Lusaka, 16 May 1977.)

30. Britain abstained on Security Council resolution 403 (1977), adopted 14 January 1977 by 13-0, which condemned Rhodesian aggression against Botswana, on the ground that it did not want to prejudice the 'delicate negotiations' on the future of Rhodesia. But it supported resolution 406 (1977), unanimously endorsing the recommendations of the economic mission to Botswana, on 25 May 1977.

31. Britain supported Security Council resolution 411 (1977), condemning Rhodesian aggression against Mozambique and pledging material assistance, which was adopted unanimously on 30 June 1977, following a five-day invasion of Mozambique territory by Rhodesian forces.

32. *The Times*, 11 June 1977.

33. *Commonwealth Prime Ministers' Meeting, Final Communiqué*, London, 15 June 1977; ibid., 16 June 1977.

34. *Rhodesia Herald*, 12 July 1977.

35. *Times of Zambia*, 8 July 1977.

36. *Rhodesia Herald*, 19 July 1977.

37. 935 *HC Deb.*, 19 July 1977.

38. *Rhodesia Herald*, 12 July 1977.

39. In an 80 per cent poll, the Rhodesian Front won 44,228 of the 52,342

votes cast. The RAP won 4,904 and the National Unifying Force (a coalition favouring majority rule) won 2,647.

40. Dr Owen also conferred with President Carter on 23 July. The Graham team followed on to Washington for talks with State Department officials.

41. Address at Wankie, *Rhodesia Herald*, 27 August 1977.

42. *Times of Zambia*, 16 August 1977.

43. *Observer*, 21 August 1977.

44. Rev. Sithole proposed instead that the two armies would have to be integrated. (Interview with Reuters, 22 August 1977.) His party support had been bolstered by the defection of about a dozen senior officials from the Muzorewa UANC.

45. Mrs Thatcher wrote to Dr Owen that the proposal to disband the security forces would be 'quite wrong' and could involve 'incalculable risk to the safety and confidence of all the people of Rhodesia, black and white alike'. (*The Times*, 27 August 1977.)

46. Address to Foreign Affairs Department, *The Star* (Johannesburg), 6 August 1977.

47. *Rand Daily Mail*, 15 August 1977.

48. *Sunday Times* (Johannesburg), 18 September 1977.

49. *The Star* (Johannesburg), 13 August 1977.

50. *Rhodesia: Proposals for a Settlement*, Cmnd. 6919, 1977.

51. Allegations of brutalities by the security forces (especially the Selous Scouts) against the civilian population had been made by the International Commission of Jurists, the Catholic Commission for Justice and Peace and other church representatives. See *Racial Discrimination and Repression in Southern Rhodesia* (Geneva: ICJ, 1976).

52. *Rhodesia Herald*, 3 September 1977.

53. Statement to the House of Representatives Sub-Committee on International Relations, quoted in *Daily News* (Tanzania), 9 September 1977.

54. *Times of Zambia*, 24 September 1977.

55. Joint statement by Mr Nkomo and Mr Mugabe, *Daily News* (Tanzania) 15 September 1977.

56. *Report of the 95th Annual Conservative Party Conference*, Blackpool, 1977. The Labour party conference, however, censured the Government for not going far enough by advocating material support for the 'freedom fighters' and sanctions against South Africa. See *Report of the 76th Annual Conference of the Labour Party*, Brighton, 1977.

57. In Moscow on 11 October, Dr Owen obtained Soviet agreement 'on the principle of the earliest establishment of an independent Zimbabwe so that power should be in the hands of the majority of the local population'. (*The Times*, 12 October 1977.)

58. Security Council resolution 415 (1977) adopted 29 September 1977.

59. General Assembly, *Official Records*, 32nd Session, Plenary Meeting, 27 September 1977. A similar warning, including the threat of economic sanctions, especially oil, had allegedly been made by Mr Vance during the negotiations with Mr Botha in London the previous August. (*The Star* (Johannesburg), 15 August 1977.)

60. *Sunday Mail* (Salisbury), 13 November 1977.

61. *Rhodesia Herald*, 25 November 1977. The main issues were the extent of white representation, a 'blocking mechanism', separate voters' rolls and the composition of the security forces.

62. Interview in *The Times*, 1 December 1977. Subsequently, Dr Owen and Mr Young resumed negotiations with the Patriotic Front, at a meeting in Malta on 30 January 1978.

63. 'Challenge to Britain in Africa', *The Observer*, 9 October 1977.

INDEX

277